PLACE NAMES

of Glacier National Park

by Jack Holterman

Including Waterton Lakes National Park

T0127502

Third Edition

RIVERBEND
PUBLISHING

Place Names of Glacier National Park
Third Edition copyright © 2006 by Jack Holterman
Published by Riverbend Publishing, Helena, Montana.
Printed in the United States.

4 5 6 7 8 9 10 MG 20 19 18 17 16 15

ISBN 13: 978-1-931832-68-7
ISBN 10: 1-931832-68-4

Printing History:
Originally published as *Place Names of Glacier/Waterton National Parks,* © 1985 Glacier Natural History Association, and © 1996 Jack Holterman

Second Edition (expanded, corrected, and updated) published as *Let the Mountains Sing: Place Names of the Waterton-Glacier International Peace Park,* © 2003 Jack Holterman

Third Edition (minor corrections and deletions for length) published as *Place Names of Glacier National Park,* © 2006 Jack Holterman.

Cataloging-in-Publication data is on file at the Library of Congress.

RIVERBEND PUBLISHING
P.O. Box 5833
Helena, MT 59604
Toll-free 1-866-787-2363

www.riverbendpublishing.com

CONTENTS

EDITOR'S NOTE

A FEW NOTES ARE IN ORDER ABOUT THE WAY THIS MATERIAL IS PRESENTED.

Some place names are marked by an asterisk (*). This indicates that the name in question is government-approved. However, not all government-approved names are so marked. Commonly known approved names, such as Glacier National Park, Kalispell, etc., are not marked.

You may notice that Jack generally uses the word "Indian" rather than "Native American." I asked him about this, and he explained to me that the original use for the phrase "Native American" was as a name for precursors of the Ku Klux Klan. For this reason many American Indians do not like to use the phrase. The Canadians also do not use it. Attentive readers will also become quite aware that Jack writes about the native peoples of this continent with deep respect; it is clear that he does not use the word "Indian" disrespectfully.

Finally, you will occasionally find in these pages the unusual phrase "U.S. American." I asked Jack about this, since more typically in the United States we simply say "American," and his reply was: "I use 'U.S. American' because people from other countries in the Americas can be confused if we use 'American' or 'America' just for the U.S. So I specify which kind of American I'm talking about." It is my feeling that Jack is avoiding more than just confusion; in personal conversation he also seemed interested in avoiding the arrogance implied in appropriating the general term "American" to refer to people from just one part of the Americas.

Wangden Kelsang

ACKNOWLEDGMENTS

THE NAMERS OF WATERTON/GLACIER PLACES ARE MANY, from the famous to the unknown, the casual one-time visitor to the pioneer. James Willard Schultz and George Bird Grinnell are responsible for the majority of Indian names of features on the east side of the park before 1900.

As more and more names were attached to mountains, passes, rivers, and lakes, Park Superintendent Eivind T. Scoyen, in 1938, directed Park Naturalist George C. Ruhle to inventory the names and to restore many of them back to their Native American origins.

So, we are indebted to Dr. Ruhle for recording many of the names in common use today.

In the 1950s and 1960s, Donald H. Robinson and Francis H. Elmore added more information to the growing card file. Robinson produced the first published listing as an appendix to his *Through the Years in Glacier National Park*. In 1963, this file became a separate publication with editing and new material by Maynard Bowers.

Later, Edwin L. Rothfuss (Chief Naturalist from 1971 to 1979) contracted with the new author, through the Glacier Natural History Association, to produce a current names manuscript.

Special thanks to Sara Bufton, Patricia Hewankorn, and Nancy Joseph of the Kootenai Culture Committee. They were most helpful in translating the difficult spoken sounds to the written work.

Similar thanks to the late Elder, Windy Boy, and Joe Stanley, from the Cree Committee.

Blackfeet Indians that contributed include Francis X. Guardipee, Floyd Middle Rider, and many others too numerous to name.

An archivist from the West Point Military Academy, Kenneth W. Rapp, also provided input and assistance.

Malcolm Campbell, former park employee, volunteered to edit the final manuscript of the first edition and provided some very valuable help.

Dr. Lex Blood, Flathead Valley Community College, Professor of Geology, made sure that the names of rock formations and geological terms were correct.

Glacier National Park employees, past and present that helped with the project include: Jerry DeSanto, Paula Dustin, Dennis Holden, Beth Ladeau, Marilyn Lazo, Clyde Lockwood, Terry Parsons, and Ellen

Seeley. Seasonal Park Archivist Mark Duntemann found, organized, and kept track of the many reference documents.

This second edition was edited by Wangden Kelsang with sponsorship from Sharon DeMeester of Paper Chase Copy Center.

The author would also like to thank the staffs of the Columbia Falls and Kalispell branches of Flathead County Library.

Others that contributed are:
Laura Blasius, technologist, Alberta Environment
Walter A. Denny, Rocky Boy Cree
Fred DesRosier, local resident
Roland Flinsch, son of Flinsch peak explorer
Marge Foot, librarian, *Great Falls Tribune*
Paul Fossler, local resident
Donald G. Frantz, authority on Blackfeet (Canada)
Randolph Freeman, head of Geographical Names, Alberta
Charley Green, local resident
Tony Incashola, Saint Ignatius resident
Mr. & Mrs. Pat Left Hand, Elmo residents
Bea Macomber, local resident
Joe McDonald, head of Salish-Kootenai Community College
Wick R. Miller, University of Utah
Emily Moke, former Glacier Park, Inc. employee
Michael P. Musick, National Archives
Joe Opalka, local resident
Dr. M. J. Orbell, archivist, Baring Brothers, London
D. F. Pearson, Canadian Committee in Geo. Names (British Columbia)
Gordon Pouliot, local resident
Alan Rogers, Waterton Lakes Park
Patricia Scott, secretary, Rocky Boy Reservation
Virgil K. Vogel, helped with Nyack name
Thain White, local resident
Clyde M. Lockwood, Chief of Interpretation, Glacier National Park

INTRODUCTION

ARE YOU A NOUN OR A VERB? A thing or an event—or both? If you have been brought up speaking English, you have been—brainwashed into thinking of yourself as a noun, or a substance, or a square to which motions, conditions, or verbs just happen as accidents. And the names you would apply to nature would suggest a world full of things you could grab hold of, control, and consume. But if you had been raised in a tipi in the precarious buffalo days of nomadic wandering among ever-flowing winds and rivers, herds, and flocks, you might have thought of yourself as a circle, always in flux with process or relationality as the fundament to which everything else is an accident. And the names you would scatter around would suggest a world in which you would adapt and survive.

People of European descent usually live in square or angular beds, houses, lots, blocks, and surveys. Indigenous people tend to live in circular tepees, wigwams, and hogans, pitched in camp circles on a circle of seasons.

The English language uses nouns as its touchstone to reality. The Algonquin languages (Blackfoot and Cree, for example), with their emphasis on flowing movement, find their touchstones in verbs. These are two very different paradigms for the universe: one imperial, the other evolutionary. So our study of place names sets us at the cutting edge of a fundamental theme in the philosophy of science at the turn of the millennium. As one philosopher puts it, we question "which is the prior reality, processes or things?" Is the world we are naming in stasis or in flux?*

Whichever of these cosmologies you settle for, you will have to apply it to the specific chunk of the globe we are concerned with in this book: Glacier Country. I take "Glacier Country" to mean the general areas that include Waterton Lakes National Park, Alberta, a contiguous portion of British Columbia, and a similar area of Glacier National Park, Montana.

Our Glacier Country, you may notice, forms a biological ecosystem (or a society of ecosystems) and an historical, even a cultural, "ecosystem."

Accumulated over a span of two centuries, the names that have been foisted onto Glacier National Park and the surrounding areas appear at first glimpse as a crazy quilt of tiny vignettes, but on closer scrutiny, emerge as a grand mosaic in which the record of the lives of many persons intertwine.

Listed in alphabetical order are the names within the boundaries of Glacier National Park according to the U.S. Geological Survey topographical map of 1968. Also included are the place names of Waterton Lakes National Park in Alberta. Names outside both parks are selected at my discretion for historical, traditional, or geographical association with the parks. Not all the names listed for Glacier National Park are officially approved by the Board on Geographic Names in Washington, D.C., but down through the history of this area, geologists, railroad workers, surveyors and even government mapmakers have given minimal attention to the official approval of names.

Among the Indian names from many tribes, special emphasis falls on Blackfoot and Kootenai names and in the northeastern corner of Glacier Park a number of Cree terms. This arrangement is partly artificial and partly the result of the habitats of these tribal groups. Other occasional visitors to the area of these parks were the Stonies (Stoneys), Sarcees, Salish, Crows, Shoshonis, Gros Ventres, and Nez Perces with perhaps a few Iroquois voyageurs (who initiated the era of fur trapping) and a few Delaware and Shawnee mountain men. But these people have left few names to record their passing. Ironically, some major mountains and waters are named for an occasional tourist or politician or unknown passer-by. Many of the Native American names are of recent origin, but a few are the oldest names of all: Belly River, Chief Mountain, Two Medicine, Kintla, Sacred Dancing.

About 1925 the Great Northern Railway engaged authors J. W. Schultz, Mary Roberts Rinehart, Helen Fitzgerald Sanders, and probably Frank Bird Linderman to give Glacier Park some publicity. Schultz, by that time, was well known for his autobiographical novel *My Life As an Indian*, begun in exile in San Francisco in 1907. But now he came back to the haunts and trails of his younger, wilder days and with the help of old comrades Eli Guardipee, Curly Bear, and others, he composed his study of place names in Glacier National Park and called it *Signposts of Adventure*. It was Schultz's plan to begin at the southeastern corner of the park and work northward on the eastern slopes assigning Blackfeet names. Beginning with names of persons whose portraits were painted by George Catlin in 1832 at Fort Union, he would then add names of persons recorded by Prince Maximilian and Charles Bodmer. He would top off the project with names of persons prominent in more recent times.

In the 1930s the interest in place names re-emerged. Dr. Ruhle of the U.S. National Park Service revived some of Schultz's forgotten names by switching them to other features. This move was in accordance with the expressed wish of the U.S. Board on Geographic Names for more American Indian terms and preferably in the native languages.

9

In fact, switching names around has been a great part of the game in Glacier. In 1933 nineteen of the twenty-four railway stations between Cut Bank and Columbia Falls had their names changed. A lady of influence with railway officials is credited with inspiring a project for applying park place names to railway stations. (*Great Falls Leader*, January 20, 1933.) However, a Great Northern timetable that seems to date from five years earlier lists all but one of the "new" names as already in place. Sometimes both the old and new names survived together. Cadmus became Gunsight, Seville became Sundance (but is still applied to that part of the reservation), Carlow became Fort Piegan, and Browning was glamorized into Fort Browning. Durham was transformed into Triple Divide, Kilroy became Spotted Robe, Talbot was changed to Bison, Lubec to Rising Wolf, Arklow to Cataract, Fielding to Blacktail, Highgate to Singleshot, Java to Nimrod, Essex to Walton, Paola to Pinnacle, Garry to Hidden Lake, Nyack to Red Eagle, Doody to Silvertip, Egan to Grizzly, Coram to Citadel and back to Coram.

Anyone who reads through this book will be struck by the absurdity of some names and yet by the lyrical beauty of others. First, let's look at the theater of the absurd: Names of passing visitors, plus nonsense names perhaps purporting to be authentic Indian terms (e.g. Wahcheechee or Emanon), plus names that are racist, sexist, or political, plus names that disregard ecological significance. Note too the policy of slapping male names onto solid things like mountains and female names onto ephemeral things like lakes and rivers and waterfalls.

You may look in vain for poetry or find it where you least expect. And you must realize that most Indian names in Glacier are not authentic. Brian Reeves cautions us that in the Native concept a mountain may have a persona of its own and does not stand in need of another attributed to it. "Personal place naming is a Western European rather than a Native American tradition." Many American Indian "names" are really not names as much as descriptions of events using a verb as basic: "where we dance," "how the eagle runs." The Blackfoot root for "to name" is also the root for "to sing," *(n)inihki*, and may refer to song, dance, or healing. Your name is your song and may carry a special manitu or spiritual charisma.

One of the Blackfoot elders is supposed to have complained to Schultz somewhat like this: "No one listens to our side of what happened long ago. Let the names on the mountains tell our story."

So we shall. Let the mountains shine and rumble. Let the mountains talk. Yes, let the mountains sing!

---

*See statements by R. Buckminster Fuller in *I Seem to Be a Verb*, and Joseph A. Bracken, S. J. in *The Divine Matrix*, p. 11, and anything by or about Alfred North Whitehead.

LANGUAGE

IF YOU HAVE ASSUMED THAT THE LANGUAGES of native America are simply gibberish, you are in for a shock. They are grammatically and syntactically sophisticated, sometimes more complex than English, sometimes more expressive, sometimes less. English-speakers who despair at subjunctives will panic at the complex subjunctives of Algonquin languages like Cree and Blackfoot. In any case, these languages inevitably reflect a very different paradigm or worldview. Each language portrays a universe of its own, and it will often be difficult to fit the universe of one language into the universe of another. Even languages close to English in origin, such as French, German, and Spanish reveal these problems to speakers of English. You cannot penetrate a "foreign" language without also penetrating the universe it represents.

What is the worldview that English represents? Have you ever thought about it? You should before you venture into the worldviews of other languages, especially those of a culture very different from your own.

Place names in the Waterton/Glacier region are frequently derived from Blackfoot, Kootenai, and Cree.

Kootenai

Here are a few hints about Kootenai: The consonants *h, k, l, m, n, p, s, t, w,* and *y* are approximately as in English. But a dot over *k, p,* and *t* indicates a sound midway between those letters and *g, b,* and *d* respectively. A dot over *m, n,* and *q* means to add stress. *Q* without the dot is formed by the tongue in the back of the mouth and in contact with the root of the mouth; so with a dot add stress to this!

The vowels are basically *a, i,* and *u: A* as in English "alone," *i* as in English "inside," and *u* as in English *oo* in "hoot"—not as in "foot."

Today Kootenai leaders have adopted a method of writing their language which includes symbols we shall need to transcribe names in the parks. Here is the modern Kootenai alphabet presented by the Kootenai Cultural Committee:

a   as in English *about* and Kootenai *amak* (land, earth)

¢   as *ts* or *tz* in English *cats* and Kootenai *¢upka* (deer)

ȼ	the same sound with the tongue against the cheek
h	as in English *hat* or Kootenai *hanqu* (muskrat)
i	as in English *in* or Kootenai *inȼ* (mouse)
k	as in English *key* or Kootenai *kamin* (me, mine)
k̓	like English *k* but with more stress, or between *k* and *g*
l	as in English *lady* and Kootenai *kulilu* (butterfly)
ł	the voiceless *l* with the air forced out through the sides of the tongue
m	as in English *mother* and Kootenai *mak* (bone)
m̓	the same but with more stress, as in Kootenai *aklam̓* (head)
n	as in English *not* and Kootenai *ninku* (you)
n̓	the same but with more stress as in Kootenai *lan̓* (moccasins)
p	as in English *pass* or Kootenai *piłak* (spoon)
p̓	between English *p* and *b*, as in Kootenai *p̓iq* (nighthawk)
q	somewhat like *k* but with the tongue touching the roof of the mouth in the back, as in Kootenai *qala* (who)
q̓	the same as *q* but with more stress, as in Kootenai *q̓api* (all, everything)
s	as in English *same* and Kootenai *sina* (beaver)
t	as in English *tell*
t̓	between English *t* and *d*, as in Kootenai *titqat̓* (man)
u	as the *oo* in English *boot* and Kootenai *kupi* (owl)
w	as in English *water* and Kootenai *wu'u* (water)
x	like English *h* but more rasping, as in Kootenai *xapi* (camas)
y	as in English *year* or Kootenai *yuwa* (go away)
·	the glottal stop
·	a dot following a vowel makes the vowel longer, as in Kootenai *ka·kin* (wolf)

In Kootenai names I have simply accepted translations given by James Willard Schultz in *Signposts of Adventure*, but not his transcriptions. Schultz himself, no expert in the language, probably derived his translations from John Star, but even so Brian Reeves finds a disconcerting difference from the material presented by Claude Schaeffer and included here. Additional Kootenai material is derived from Franz Boas, Thain White, and Malouf and Phillips as cited in the bibliography. But the lion's share of the Kootenai language in this book has been worked out by the Kootenai Cultural Committee at Big Arm or Elmo, Montana.

Blackfoot

Blackfoot and Cree are easier to transcribe into the Roman alphabet. The vowels in Blackfoot are basically *a*, *i*, and *u*, and may be either long or short. *E* will occur as *ay* in English "day, say, pray." The diphthong *ai* sounds like *i* in "sigh" or *y* in "sky" but is variable to *ay* in "day." *H* is guttural except when it is initial, and then it is like the English *h*. *-W* is a verbalizing suffix and sounds like *-w* in "few." *K*, *p*, and *t* resemble the sounds in English "skill, spill, still" and have sometimes been mistaken for *g*, *b*, and *d*. There are also glottal stops, wavering vowels and even occasional tones that rise, fall or remain flat. The accent is ´.

I have also included virtually all Schultz's Blackfoot names as listed in *Signposts* but the transcriptions in this book correspond to those being printed by the Piegan Institute in Browning. Blackfoot is a relatively simple language to transcribe:

a	short as in English *above* or *Dakota*, or *u* in *up*
a	long as in *father*
i	short as in *it* and *in*
i	long as in *machine*
u	short, interchangeable with short *a*
u	long as *oo* in *moon*
e	long only like *ay* in *pay, say, day* (as spoken in the U.S.)
ai	as *i* in sigh or *y* in *sky*, but it varies to *ay* in *day*
h	guttural as in German or Gaelic *ch*, but like English *h* when initial
-w	a verbalizing suffix pronounced like *-w* in English *few*
k,p,t	(unless final) resemble the respective sounds in English *skill, spill, still* (and can be mistaken for *g*, *b*, and *d*)
x	*ks*
z	*ts* or *tz* (represented in Kootenai as *ł*)
w, y	sometimes semi-vowels as in English

Before an *i*, *k* often assibilates to *x* and *t* to *z*.

For the names of mountains, add *-istaki*. The word is really *mistaki* with the initial *m-* dropped in the combining form. For the names of lakes, add *omahkxikimi* (big water), and for streams some variation of *-étaktai* (*ai* as *y* in *sky*).

Some speakers us *ch* instead of *tz*, but that is dialectal. Other dialectal shifts common in Blackfoot include these: *ai* with *ei*, *x* with *z*, *w* with *y*. As in dialectal English, *ai* sometimes sounds like *y* in "sky," sometimes like *ay* in "day." There are no known rules to govern these shifts, but it is generally safer to use the *y* sound after *k-, p-, s-, t-* (*kai, pai, sai, tai*) and the *ay* sound in the verbal prefix *ai-*.

We can never forget that all or nearly all current studies of Blackfoot (including my own) are deeply indebted to the work of C. C. Uhlenbeck and his colleagues. And it is important to realize that Blackfoot (like Cree, Chippewa or Ojibwa, Virginian, Passaquamody, Delaware, etc.) belongs to the Algonquin (or Algic) linguistic stock. Kootenai has no certain affiliation at this time, not even with the neighboring Salish, a large group scattered from the coast to the interior. Other languages of the Pacific Northwest are Nez Perce, belonging to the Penutian stock, and Shoshoni belonging to the widely spread Uto-Aztecan stock.

Cree

The Cree language is close enough in origin to Blackfoot to use the same alphabet. In the pages that follow we shall generally use the system adopted by the University of Alberta for its courses on the Cree language.

The consonants in all dialects of Cree are *h, k, m, n, p, s, t* and *tz*. This last sound is written as *c* in the system of the University of Alberta and should be pronounced as *tz* or *ts*, not as *ch*. The *h* in Cree as in Blackfoot is usually guttural. In some Cree dialects *l* and *r* also occur. *K, p,* and *t* are not explosive and sometimes sound close to *g, b,* and *d* respectively (more so in Ojibwa than in Cree).

The vowels in both Cree as in Blackfoot are *a, e, i,* and *o. E* is always long like *ay* in *say*. The other vowels are both long and short: Long *a* is like *a* in *father*; short *a* is like *a* in *above* or *u* in *but*. Long *i* is like *ee* in *queen*, short *i* is like *i* in *pin, sin, thin*. Long *o* is like *oo* in *look, book*; short *o* is like *o* in *go, so*. The long vowels are indicated by ˆ: *î, â, ô*, except that *e* is always long so need not be capped. No diacritical mark is used for short vowels. Semi-vowels are *w* and *y*, much as in English, with final *-w* like that in *few*.

ADAIR RIDGE is named for Bill Adair who homesteaded on the west side of Glacier National Park in the wild North Fork country and in 1914 built the Polebridge Mercantile. He was also a packer and inn-keeper. But his Polebridge store introduced someone to Glacier history who has been almost forgotten. Robert Ray Vincent began his career in Glacier by keeping store for Adair and eventually rose through the ranks to the superintendency of Glacier, even in this world of political appointments. The Kootenai name of the ridge is Woman Mountain: *Pałkiy Akwukłi'it.*

AGASSIZ* CREEK and **GLACIER** are named in honor of the noted Swiss-American naturalist (Jean) Louis Rodolphe Agassiz (1807–1873). Inspired in his youth by the great naturalist, Baron Alexander von Humboldt, Louis Agassiz became one of the pioneering community of scientists at Harvard. Though he traveled a lot in both America and abroad, he did not come to the area here named for him. But his researches in the study of glaciers earned him his name on this list. The Kootenai names for these features are Red Woman River and Glacier: *Kanuhus Pałkiy Akinmituk* and *Kanuhus Pałkiy Akwiswitxu.* (See HUMBOLDT.)

AHERN* CREEK, GLACIER, PASS, and **PEAK** are named for Lt. George Patrick Ahern who conducted what must have been the most extensive and intensive of the early explorations of Glacier National Park. A remarkably kind and courageous man, he left a record of service hardly equaled by anyone else mentioned in these pages. (See *Who Was Who...* for more on Ahern.)

Ahern Pass has long been known as one of the most dangerous in the Waterton/Glacier country, but it was used by surveyor R. H. Sergent, packer Frank Valentine, and especially by Joe Cosley who made it his favorite route into his Belly River refuge. Once Joe's two horses slipped on the ice and hurtled a thousand feet into the abyss.

The Blood Indian name for the pass is *Soóix ozitamisohpi(iaw)* or "The Warriors, Where They Go Up or West." (West is the "up" direction for people who live on the east side of the Divide.) The Blackfoot name for the glacier is *Sisukkokutui,* "Spotted Ice."

AKAIYAN* FALLS and **LAKE** are named for *Akai-yan* or Old Robe, the hero of the Blackfoot story of the Beaver Medicine. Akaiyan is the younger of two brothers. His older brother wants to be rid of him and so maroons him on an island in a lake (Saint Mary?). But Beaver Chief and the other beavers take Akaiyan into their lodge for the winter, teach him their "medicine" and send him home in the spring as a new man. Obviously, this story shows a resemblance to the story in Genesis of Joseph and his brothers and also to the Egyptian tale of the Two Brothers.

Akaiyan Lake has an alternate name of Perry Lake after Robert Edwin Perry (1856–1920), who "discovered" the North Pole in 1909. But the name Akaiyan took precedence because of the project that was carried out by Dr. George Ruhle. The Board on Geographic Names in Washington, D.C., preferred Indian names for Glacier and even names in the original Indian languages. Though some of these names were not considered practical, Akaiyan was one of those accepted. (See BEAVER CHIEF, XIXTAKI.)

AKAMINA LAKE, TRAIL, BROOK, PASS, HIGHWAY, and **RIDGE** lie mostly in Canada, but the ridge dips into Glacier, and the trail is a portion of the old Kootenai trail running from the Flathead Valley via Crystal Creek and the North Fork. In Kootenai *akamina* or *kamina* probably means "valley, benchland" referring to the benchlands near South Kootenay Pass. The U.S. Northwestern Boundary Survey, headed by Archibald Campbell, spelled the word *A-kám-ina* and recorded the meaning of *kamina* as "watershed." The surveyors established their most easterly base at Camp Akamina on the border and apparently near Cameron Lake. The Continental Divide zigzags to and fro along the Akamina Syncline through most of Glacier.

The British team, under command of Colonel John S. Hawkins, left vivid records kept by Lt. Charles Wilson. His editor says that Wilson probably "ascended Akamina Creek, a branch of the Kishinena, which takes its origin in Wall Lake, not far from the boundary line and in Akamina Pass." He gives the elevation of this pass as 5,835 feet, while that of the South Kootenay Pass is 6,903 feet. On a stone cairn were engraved "sundry Anglo Saxon names."

The story of the boundary surveys of 1857 to 1861 is an epic that has escaped the spell-binders who make mini-series. The naturalist of the British team, John Keast Lord, wrote two books about it, while Lieutenant Wilson wrote only one but that one especially fascinating. The dark cloud of the incipient War Between the States haunted the U.S. team and partly obscured the records of the great adventure. But one remarkable record of the U.S. team consists of the paintings and sketches of James Alden, a descendent of John and his gentle Huguenot Priscilla. James had gained his reputation by his paintings of Yosemite and the Spanish missions of California. The U.S. team was also fortunate to include pioneering ethnologist George Gibbs.

Each team numbered perhaps two hundred men, officers, packers, masons, cooks, soldiers, Indian guides, and hunters. Lieutenant Wilson tells us that all the packers and muleteers of the British team were Mexicans (and the same may be true of the U.S. team). These Mexicans came up from California and many originally from Sonora, Mexico, by way of Los Angeles. Wilson stresses "the head swell, a wonderful hand at the lasso." His name was José, and he may have been the man of that name who went back with Lord to San Francisco to recruit more packers. Wilson gives vivid details about his skills at horse-taming. Three of the Mexican packers were drowned and one was shot by Indians but survived. José may be the same person as Pacheco, whom Wilson calls "a capital fellow." In March and April Pacheco was submitted to trial for assault at Port Douglas, British Columbia, but was acquitted by the famous and severe Judge Begbie.

The survey had to cover 410 miles from the San Juan Islands to Akamina through the most rugged sector of the forty-ninth parallel, across the North Cascades, over the Columbia and Kootenay Rivers to the headwaters of the Flathead. During the winters the work ceased and the teams relaxed at Fort Vancouver or at Angus MacDonald's at Fort Colville, even at San Francisco or Victoria. Special balls were held in Victoria, hosted by Governor Sir James Douglas and Lady Douglas and thoroughly enjoyed by Lieutenant Wilson. While it was especially important to keep the peace between the U.S. and Britain during this crucial venture, General Harney started the "Pig War" (for a quarrel over a pig) by occupying San Juan with five hundred U.S. troops. Sir James countered with two–maybe five–warships. But war was averted and the struggle to Akamina went on. (See *Who Was Who...* for more information.)

AKOKALA CREEK and **LAKE** were formerly called Indian Creek, Indian Lake, and also Oil Creek. They were renamed Akokala, which was originally the Kootenai name for Bowman Lake. The term probably derives from the word for swamp, "a place of red willows," in reference to the bog at the upper end of Bowman Lake. Schultz defines the term as "rotten" and lists it as the name of Indian Lake and Indian Mountain as well as of Bowman Lake.

ALBERTA: The province of Alberta was named by the Governor General of Canada, the Marquis of Lorne, for his wife, Princess Louise Caroline Alberta, daughter of Queen Victoria. Her first name was given to Lake Louise in Banff National Park. Since the Governor-General, a tall and handsome Highland Scot, was also a poet, he began a poem about the name "Alberta" with the verses: "In token of the love which thou hast shown / for this wide land of freedom."

In 1881 Lord Lorne made the first vice regal tour of western Canada, guided in part by the Cree chief Poundmaker. He consulted with leaders of the Métis and with tribal leaders, especially at one huge assembly where the Blackfoot were represented by Chief Crowfoot. Lord Lorne was so overwhelmed by the beauty of the Rockies near Banff that he swung southward following the eastern slopes of the mountains to Fort MacLeod. With a sizeable escort of the Northwest Mounted Police he approached what is now Waterton Lakes National Park. Whether he actually set foot inside the present park boundaries is hard to tell. But he continued southward along the eastern edge of Glacier National Park as far as Old Agency. Joined by an escort of the U.S. Army, he continued to Fort Shaw then on down to Ogden, Utah, to catch the Union Pacific for the east.

In 1883 Lord Lorne and Princess Louise made another tour westward to San Francisco and Santa Barbara, then up to British Columbia. In all his tours he was under threat for his life from the Irish Fenians. He stressed the need for famine relief for the Indians of western Canada, and if his orders had not been disregarded he might have prevented at least some of the tragedy of the Starvation Winter (1883).

Alberta became a provisional district in 1882 and a province in 1905. There is a Mount Alberta, 11,874 feet high, as well as a village and a river of that name.

ALDER CREEK and **TRAIL** are in the Granite Park area, once called Broken Arm Country. The creek is also called Granite Creek. (See GRANITE.)

ALDERSON, MOUNT, stands in Waterton Lakes National Park. Once named Bertha, it was one of the places in Waterton renamed to commemorate World War I. Lieutenant General E. H. A. Alderson was commander of the Canadian Expeditionary Forces in 1915–1916. The name Bertha is still retained for the creek, lake, and falls, and was reputedly assigned in the first place to the lake by Joe Cosley for one of his lady friends.

ALGAL CAVE is one of several known caves in or near Glacier National Park. Of its passageways, 628 meters have been mapped. It is thought to make contact with sinkholes near Granite Park. It occurs in the Siyeh limestone formation and is not typical of caves.

ALHAMBRA POINT is an old surveyors' landmark on Lake McDonald. It refers to the famous Moorish palace and fortress at Granada, Spain. Its walls have many shades of red (the Arabic name *al-hamra'u* means "the red" in reference to something grammatically feminine). A post office of this name in Alberta and a city in California could have provided a source for the name on Lake McDonald.

ALLEN CREEK and **MOUNTAIN** are named for Cornelia Seward Allen, granddaughter of Lincoln's controversial Secretary of State. (See SEWARD.) The Blackfoot name honors Pita Síxinam (Black Eagle or Eagle Is Black), father-in-law of Schultz. Black Eagle was a sub-chief proscribed by the Army, but was in the camp of the peace chief Heavy Runner when it was massacred in 1870. He escaped, wounded, to Canada, only to be murdered. His favorite horse, Crazy Gray, was slain at his funeral. (See NATAHKI, CRACKER, CRAZY GRAY HORSE.)

In 1891 George Bird Grinnell made one of his trips to the area accompanied by his classmate from Yale, Cornelia's brother William H. Seward, with J. W. Schultz as cook, Billy Jackson and Joe Kipp as guides, and also Henry Norris and Henry L. Stimson. This trip Grinnell could not get Jack Monroe to go along, since Agent Steele had caught Jack bootlegging. Grinnell did not at that time think that Schultz was good for much else than cooking. Following the "old Kootenay trail" along the west shore of Upper Saint Mary Lake, they began an exploration that led them to identify and name Mount Allen (for Seward's sister), Reynolds, Fusillade, Mount Wilbur, Mount Norris, Seward Ridge, Iceberg Lake, Jackson Mount and Glacier, and Blackfoot Mount and Glacier. According to L. O. Vaught, it was at this time that Grinnell bestowed Stimson's name on what is now Mount Logan. Grinnell shared notes with W. C. Browne (later General) who was leading a party in that region at the same time. Later Grinnell published his account of the trip under the title "Crown of the Continent." (See MERRITT.)

ALMIGHTY VOICE is the name of a peak on Bear Mountain in the northeast sector of Glacier. The name occasioned some misunderstanding when it was being considered about 1940. It was proposed for a summit 8,800 feet in elevation at T37N, R17W to commemorate a Blood Indian "who resisted the coming of the Red Coats." The Board on Names wanted to know the version of the name Almighty Voice in the native language, and apparently got no reply. There was indeed an historical person of that name, but of a later generation, and he was not Blood but Cree. The Almighty Voice of record was the son of Sounding Sky, and both father and son were champions of Cree self-determination. Though the son escaped into the wilderness with his bride, he came out in 1897 for a final showdown with the North West Mounties. As he and his mother sang his death song to each other back and forth across the line, he was shot many times.

"Almighty Voice" was one of six names for which in 1940 the Board preferred the original Indian term rather than the translation. But apparently the officials in Glacier had trouble getting the original Indian terms for these six place names. Perhaps a closer translation would be "He who talks like God": *(Ka)-Kihtzi-Manito-wew*. It's a good example of what happens when you try to interpret an Indian verb by an English noun.

ALMOST A DOG* MOUNTAIN at Saint Mary Lake is named for Imazí-imita, the Blackfeet name for Almost a Dog, a survivor of the Baker massacre of January 1870. With his parents, wife and little daughter, he was perhaps still asleep when the Baker's men opened fire. Though the rest of his family was killed and his child was shot dead as he was struggling to carry her to safety, Almost a Dog escaped but was crippled for life. During the Winter of Starvation (1883–4) he kept count of his fellow tribesmen who perished by cutting notches on a stick—555 notches.

ALPS OF AMERICA: a name proposed for the area of Glacier/ Waterton, but officially discouraged. The question is: How seriously should official approval or disapproval be regarded? New Zealand calls its principle mountain range the Southern Alps, and indeed they fit the description. Australia, considered (by non-Australians?) to be the only continent that has no true alpine mountains, still talks about her Alps and proudly labels the ranges near the source of the Snowy River as the Australian Alps—beautiful country whether or not "alpine" in the strictest sense of the term.

ALTYN PEAK used to be called McDermott Peak whereas Altyn was the name of the mining town at its foot. The town site is now partly covered by the impounded waters of Sherburne Lake. The name Altyn derives either from Dave Altyn or from the horse of prospector Jim Harris or both. About 1898 Harris is said to have named Mount Wynn after his horse Altyn, but the names were changed in 1927. The Blackfoot name for Mount Altyn is Crowfoot. (See CROWFEET.) Altyn is also the name of one of the prominent rock formations of this area.

The town site of Altyn was plotted in 1900. Mining corporations at once took root around the country from Butte to Boston. The role of the Copper Kings, Marcus Daly and William Andrews Clark, remains obscure. A stage line ran three times a week to Blackfoot, a station on the Great Northern. The Fourth of July was celebrated by a grand banquet at the Altyn Hotel. On the 1st of September the *Swift Current Courier* of Altyn published its first—and only—edition, seconded by the *Acantha* of Dupuyer. A ball team sprang up. Lumber was being cut right and left, and two saloons were ready for their grand openings. Then the troubles began: forest fires, dangers in the deep mine tunnels, and blackest of all, the officials of the national forest declared No Liquor Sales! "Cruel and iconoclastic man!" the Altynites shouted back at the Secretary of the Interior, drearily moaning that they faced "a boozeless winter" with nothing but "painkiller...and other North Dakota substitutes...." Altyn was doomed.

AMPHITHEATER MOUNTAIN's name is descriptive of the Twin Butte Peaks of Cut Bank valley and is compounded of the Greek terms *amphi-* (around) + *theatron* (theater). The Blackfoot name is Three Horns, *Niuóxkai-ozkina* for a warrior who captured a Nez Perce woman and lived with her happily (ever after?). This may be the mountain that has also been called Whalen for a former ranger of the area.

ANACONDA CREEK, HILL, and **PEAK**: The term *anaconda* is believed to derive from a crisscross in Sri Lanka of Singalese, Sanskrit, and Tamil or Dravidian. The roots are *hena* (lightning) + *kanda* (stem or bulb), and the composite refers to both the Asian python and the South American boa constrictor. The boa may exceed forty feet in length. The term was popularized by Horace Greeley when he used it to describe a serpentine or constricting maneuver of Grant's forces against Lee's. Then it was adopted as a name for mining claims. The Kootenai name for the features in Glacier is Kicking Horse or *Yakił Qanaqłiyki Kqłłaxa' łȼin* which is also the name for a mining claim of John E. Lewis of Lake McDonald.

However, the use of the name Anaconda in Glacier probably derives directly from the once powerful, despotic corporation of Marcus Daly often known as "the Amalgamated." The corporation had a project to exploit coal mines along the North Fork. According to Vaught, Anaconda Creek was named after the company because Marcus Daly was popular in the Flathead valley, where many of his former employees were settled. Ironically, a steamy conflict eventually developed between the park and the company over air pollution.

The struggle between the developmental Anaconda Company and the conservationists is personified in Glacier by Senator Wheeler and his wife Lulu who had a cabin at the head of Lake McDonald. The dispute had reached an early climax in 1917 when Wheeler was district attorney in Butte. A labor organizer named Frank Little, of Cherokee origin, appeared to urge unity among Butte laborers. When Anaconda officials wanted Wheeler to silence him, he refused because Little was breaking no law. One night Little vanished and was found in the morning dangling from the railway bridge with signs of torture on his corpse. Lulu Wheeler was a gentle church lady whose soft touch frustrated corporate giants and political tricksters alike. Franklin Roosevelt labeled her "Lady Macbeth."

ANDERSON PEAK is a lofty mountain of Waterton Park named for the astronomer Lieutenant (later Captain) Samuel Anderson, R. E. He was the only officer who served with both British boundary commissions, 1858–1862 and 1872–1876, and came to be regarded as an outstanding authority on questions of the forty-ninth parallel. Anderson Peak was once called Millionaire Peak.

ANGEL WING PEAK: See GOULD.

APGAR MOUNTAIN, RANGE, and **VILLAGE** are named for Milo B. Apgar who arrived here from Maine in 1892, crossing Marias Pass with a two-wheeled cart (maybe a Red River cart?). He and his Métis companion, Charlie Howe, homesteaded at the foot of Lake McDonald. Dimon and Harvey Apgar came later, and some of the family ran a resort. Many famous visitors came to Apgar in early times, and especially to the old summer home of cowboy artist Charlie Russell, built for him partly by Dimon.

APIKUNI CREEK, FALLS, FLAT, and **MOUNTAIN** were formerly labeled "Appekunny." This traditional Blackfoot name can be translated as "scabby or spotted robe." It was the name of James Willard Schultz which he sometimes used as a pen-name, claiming that it meant Far-Off White Robe, while the tribal name Pikani meant Far Robe(s). The roots involved would be *api* (white), *pi* (far) and *ani* (robe). The trouble with Schultz's translation of his own name is that it does not account for the loss of one of the two syllables *pi*, nor for the *k* in the middle. So we look elsewhere:

The root *apik-* sometimes refers to small pox, the disease that in one epidemic after another from the eighteenth century into the twentieth decimated the Indian tribes of Glacier country and beyond. The second root in the term is *-uni* is better spelled *-ani* with a short *a* as in "about" and means "robe." An alternate explanation of the name is less controversial and was used by old traders. It refers to the "spotted robe," a buffalo robe taken in a spring hunt, which is out of the prime season, when the hair has been rubbed off in spots before the calving period.

In any event, the name is an honorable one and may even be the original form of the tribal name Pikuni or Pikani (Piegan, Peigan). It was given to author James Willard Schultz by Running Crane, who owned it. In Schultz's honor, it was applied as a place name in 1886, probably by Lt. Samuel Robertson. (See ROBERTSON.)

Who was James Willard Schultz (1859–1947) who, right or wrong, had such an important impact on the place names of Glacier and Waterton parks? An up-state New Yorker, he hated Sunday school and the military academy, but loved operas and concerts in New York City. An uncle in Saint Louis introduced him to the Missouri River country and he followed the river to Fort Benton. Though a johnny-come-lately to the high Missouri, he quickly fitted into the company of Joe Kipp and the family of Hugh Monroe, and in 1878 he joined Joe as a trader at Fort Conrad. Joe's wife Martha Double Strike paved his way to marry Natahki. As the buffalo population decreased Schultz and Kipp moved their trade down to the Judith country, where they contacted leading figures in tribal history—Crowfoot, Eli Guardipee, Takes-Gun-First—and even employed Louis Riel. In 1883 Schultz was guided into the Saint Mary country by Oliver Sandoval. Thus began the Starvation Winter, which Schultz began to publicize in his writings. Allegedly, he and his family had to flee the tribal police and take refuge on Thunder Bird Island in Lower Saint Mary Lake. With Kipp and Charlie Rose (Otahkomi) he became a guide to hunting expeditions like those of Grinnell, the Baring brothers, Emerson Hough and Ralph Pulitzer. Charged with poaching, he fled again, this time down the Missouri and, as a widower, he took off to California.

In San Francisco he began to write his autobiographical novel *My Life As an Indian*, which he finished in Arizona, where he worked with archaeologist James Walter Fewkes. He became the literary critic for the *Los Angeles Times*. Though involved in a shaky second marriage with Celia, he returned in 1914 to Montana sponsored by Louis Hill in his project to give place names to the newly established Glacier National Park. The work took over ten years.

In 1927 at a powwow on Belly River he met anthropologist Jessica Donaldson and with her undertook research among the Kaina of Alberta. He divorced Celia and married Jessica. With Jessica he played host to the Count and Countess Bernadotte, probably on various occasions. Worn weary by addictions, he died on the Wind River Reservation in Wyoming.

A major rock formation of Waterton/Glacier is named "Appekunny." It is a greenish argillite. But the Board on Geographic Names approved the spelling "Apikuni" in 1976.

APPISTOKI* CREEK, FALLS, and **PEAK**: Though this name sounds like a good Blackfoot term, it has long been something of a puzzle. Schultz brushes the problem aside with a casual allusion to "*apustoki*," which can be interpreted as "behind the ears" or "north ears" (-*stoki* means "ears"). It also suggests something like "bag ears." Long ago Ranger Frank Guardipee objected to the present form used by the park service.

The present name was applied by the early surveyor R. T. Evans, who thought the mountain looked out over everything else around it and so asked his Indian guide for a term to describe the "overseer." Evidently, the guide responded with the word for God, *Apístotoki*, which is also the stem of the verb "to create." But who dropped the syllable out of the middle? Or was the guide using a form of the word not commonly known? At any rate, the book *Place Names of Alberta*, does list the word *Apistoki* as the Blackfoot name of the river in Alberta, Oldman River. (See NAPI.)

Schultz has an altogether different name for the mountain in Glacier: Iron Shirt or *Miskim-asokas(i)*. Iron Shirt was a warrior who went on a raid south into Spanish territory and brought back a coat of mail. His portrait was painted by Charles Bodmer, the artist companion of Prince Maximilian in 1833, and he was the one who resented the favor the traders showed to Bear Chief. When Iron Shirt died, his coat of mail was buried with him.

ARROW* LAKE was named Small Camas Lake, *Kɛaquna Xapí Akuȧnuk* in the Kootenai language. But the word for "arrow" in Kootenai is *aak* and occurs as the place name *Yaak* in the northwestern corner of Montana.

ASSINIBOINE: To avoid confusion, let's take note that this name is used for a Souian tribe, certain steamers on the Missouri River, a matterhorn-like peak on the Alberta-British Columbia line and a U.S. Army fort at Havre. The tribe, which is also called Nakota and includes the Stoneys of Alberta, usually spells the word as written here. The name of the steamers sometimes dropped the final *e*. The Army spelling for the fort uses a double *n* in the middle.

ASTER* CREEK and **PARK** were named by R. T. Evans.

ATLANTIC* CREEK: See TRIPLE DIVIDE.

ATSINA* FALLS and **LAKE** were given the Blackfoot name *Azina*, which refers to the Gros Ventre tribe whose French name means "Big Belly," *azi- (uzi-)* is "belly, guts," and *azina* as a verb means "to be paunchy." The Gros Ventres are an Algonquin linguistic group, occasional allies of the Blackfoot Confederacy but sometimes at war. They are an off-shoot of the Arapahos or at least closely related to them linguistically.

AURICE* LAKE is named for Aurice Tetrault, who belonged to a French Canadian family that came to the Flathead valley in a covered wagon. She became the wife of Dr. Rod Houston, a guide and dentist of the West Glacier area. The Kootenai name of the lake is Small Woman Lake, *Kuɛkuɛ Akuȧnuk*. (See MARTHA'S BASIN.)

AUTUMN* CREEK was named by R. T. Evans for its golden aspens of fall.

AVALANCHE* BASIN, CREEK, GORGE, LAKE, and **PARK** were named by Dr. Sperry in 1895. However, research indicates that Sperry was not the "discoverer" of Avalanche, that Charlie Howe and Libby Collins were here ahead of him and the Kootenais before that. The Gorge has also been called Royal Gorge (after the canyon in Colorado?), and there are Lost Lake and Glacier Lake. (See CATTLE QUEEN.) A Blackfoot name (which must be just a translation) describes the snowslides and is recorded as *Mistáki koni-awah-kaw-inítohzi* (with the orthography adjusted). The peaks around Avalanche basin were probably all named by Sperry or members of his party and include The Castle, The Dome or Cathedral Dome, Cathedral Spires, The Sphinx, and The Matterhorn. Here are the Kootenai names: *Sina Akłaṁ Akuq̓nuk* (Beaver Head Lake); *Sina Akłaṁ Akikq̓łała'mi* (Beaver Head Basin); and *Akłam Akinmituk* (Beaver Head Creek). (See CHANEY.)

The Kootenais may also have called the lake and creek "Avalanche" in their language. Chief Paul David, as a young man in the 1860s was in a party of Akanahonek and Akiyinak Kootenais who hunted goats in wintertime along Avalanche Creek and observed some avalanches.

AVION RIDGE in Waterton Park: *avion* is French for "airplane" and also a place in France taken by the Canadian forces in 1917.

BABB VILLAGE is named for Cyrus C. Babb, supervisor of the Saint Mary Irrigation Project that was intended to divert water from Saint Mary River before it slipped into Canada, and turn it instead into eastern Montana. Formerly the village was called Main after Orrin S. Main, who married Isabel, the sister of George Starr and the daughter of Frank Pablo. Or it may have been named for their son Henry. However, the settlement dates back to the old Kennedy whiskey post (probably 1874), and it became a trading center for Kootenais as well as for Crees and Blackfeet. The rumor runs that there were many confrontations between these rival tribal groups on the Babb flats. During and after the rebellion of Louis Riel in 1885, a number of Crees and Métis fled across the border from the present prairie provinces into Montana and Dakota. Among them were survivors of Big Bear's band, who, under his son Little Bear, wandered about Montana. They tried in vain to find a refuge on the Salish Reservation or some other settled areas, and eventually joined a Chippewa band under Rocky Boy, a chief from Wisconsin. Some of these Chippewas and/or Crees were rounded up like cattle by the military from Fort Assinniboine. Some too were shipped from Helena up to Browning and assigned to the Blackfeet Reservation, where the U.S. Census for 1910 shows 160 Chippewas in residence. This problem went on amid much hostility toward the refugees aired in the Montana press until 1916, when at last, through the help of Frank Linderman, Charlie Russell, Senators Dixon and Carter, and other socially-minded citizens, a reservation was opened for these "Chippwa-Crees" on the former lands of Fort Assinniboine at Rocky Boy. Some, however, have continued to live at Babb, descendents of refugees from the troublesome times of the late 1880s or perhaps even earlier.

BABY* Glacier's Kootenai name, says Schultz, means "Ice where the goats' children play"—a real gem of a name that should not be allowed to slip into oblivion: *Aq̇¢an Yakił Haq̇¢i'ki Akwiswitxu* (Ice where the kids play, slide, skate). Some of the Kootenais liked to slide down the ice here too, at least during the summer dances at Lake McDonald.

BAD MARRIAGE MOUNTAIN: This name was assigned by Superintendent E. T. Scoyen. Bad Married was a Blackfoot leader, and "Bad

27

Marriage" is a current surname. This mountain seems to be the one Schultz calls Elk Tongue. The name in its English form was not approved and a Blackfeet name or version of it was preferred but apparently never found.

BAD ROCK CANYON and **MOUNTAINS** are said to be named for a battle between Indian tribes, but what battle, what tribes? See SKELETON MOUNTAIN for a possible answer, even though the event there described took place farther east. More likely, the canyon was named for rocks in the river that jeopardized navigation. And then there was a man nicknamed Bad Rock Stanton of Demersville, evidently the husband of the famous Lottie.

There is, however, evidence of intertribal conflict at or near Bad Rock Canyon. In 1876, while other tribes in Montana were concerned with Custer, a Blackfeet war party headed the other way, westward, and encountered a Kootenai party on the South Fork of the Flathead in the Bad Rock Mountains. In the ensuing fight the chief of the Akiyinik band of Kootenais, Kałna, was killed, and so too was John Kelwa¢ or "Kilowatts." *Kałna* means roseberry or tomato, and this chief was also known as Baptiste. *Kelwa¢* was called in English (Good) Gambler. (However, there was a man named Kalna who succeeded to the chieftainship in 1887.)

Petroglyphs are reported in Bad Rock Canyon.

BALD HILL is near East Glacier. The name refers to the sparse vegetation on the summit. The Inside and Outside Trails that pass this way are old patrol routes used by the rangers.

BARING* CREEK and **FALLS**: The Blackfoot name for the creek is *apaoápspi* (weasel eyes), which signifies blueberries and huckleberries.

Baring Brothers of London is described as "England's oldest investment firm." It was established about 1770 by a family that traces its origins back to Bremen, Germany. In the reign of King George the mad, the House of Brunswick ruled both Britain and the kingdom of Hanover, and two grandsons of a Bremen minister took advantage of this bond to establish a banking house in London. By discreet marriages and financial support to the East India Company and to England's war with Napoleon, the firm of Baring Brothers spread its power through the Empire. It even helped finance the Louisiana Purchase.

Two descendents of the founders were Thomas and Robert who chose the Saint Mary country as a favorite vacationland. In 1886 with their nephew Cecil, they made a trip to Fort Benton, Montana, where Charles Conrad, a partner of the I. G. Baker Company, arranged a hunting and fishing excursion with Joe Kipp and James Willard Schultz as their guides and Jack Bean as their cook. The report that they came with Sir James Douglas, governor of British Columbia, must be mistaken since Sir James died in 1877. However, Thomas Baring may have toured with Sir James on one of his earlier trips into western U.S. and Canada.

It is a little difficult to identify all the members of the Baring family of whom Schultz speaks admiringly, partly because Schultz was not fully aware of their background. So it has been supposed that Thomas or "the Governor" of Schultz's account was really Thomas George Baring (1826–1904), once Viceroy of India and then First Lord of the Admiralty. But on the basis of material graciously provided for me by the Baring archivist in London, I am inclined to think that "the Governor" of Schultz's story was Thomas Baring (1839–1923), son of Henry Baring and grandson of the founder Sir Francis. He had business connections in the U.S. and made visits to both the U.S. and Canada. His brother was Colonel Robert Baring, also in Schultz's hunting party. The Colonel had spent many years in India and impressed Schultz with his comment that neither in the Alps nor the Himalayas had he ever beheld a scene comparable to Upper Saint Mary Lake.

The party enjoyed their trip to the fullest, while the Montanans relished the occasional nips of "the Governor's whiskey." They hunted and fished around Going-to-the-Sun Mountain where the various features were named for them. The name Baring on the glacier has since been changed to Sexton.

Schultz adds that the Barings returned the following autumn and then "sent us many English parties to outfit and guide." It must be remembered that in those days Lethbridge on the Canadian Pacific, partly financed by the Baring Bank, was the natural gateway to what is now the Waterton-Glacier country. The Lethbridge news adds that in the second trip young Cecil Baring, son of the first Lord Revelstoke, lingered behind the rest of the party in the country of Saint Mary and Waterton Lakes and got caught in a risky shift in the weather. Searchers were sent out to find him, but he got into Lethbridge of his own accord.

Cecil married into a French-American family of New Jersey and with his son Rupert, returned to Glacier at least once again. On this trip their guide was Jack Monroe, whose Blackfoot relatives accompanied the expedition with tipis to camp in. Since now the gateway to Glacier had become Midvale or East Glacier, this elaborate excursion took them from East Glacier up to Saint Mary, Slide Lake, and Chief Mountain.

Later Rupert Lord Baring wrote of possibly returning again. Revelstoke, British Columbia, was also named for one of the Barings. (See *Who Was Who...* for more information.)

BARRIER* BUTTES were so called by surveyor Evans because they hide Lost Basin. Their alternate name is Three Tops and their Kootenai name is Ground Grizzly Mountain: *Amak Kławła Akwukłi'it.*

BASIN* MOUNTAIN: This is a descriptive name. The Blackfoot name assigned by Schultz is Old Kutenai or *Kutonapi.* In spite of his name, he was a North Blackfoot chief who was notably hospitable to Prince Maximilian in 1833. The prince had come up the Missouri with Alexander Culbertson and was at the Marias seeking information on the Blackfeet with Isidoro Sandoval as his interpreter. Kutonapi impressed Maximilian as favorably as he had impressed David Thompson in 1787–88. He had led a war party south into Spanish territory, raided a Spanish silver train and come home with horses and mules. He had five wives and six children and was probably the man who signed the 1855 treaty.

BATTLEMENT* is another mountain named by Evans. The Kootenai name is Left Grizzly Mountain: *Kkułwiyat Kławła Akwukłi'it.* Here "left" means "(on the) left hand."

BAUERMAN MOUNTAIN is in Waterton Lakes and is named for Dr. Hilary B. Bauerman (1835–1909), a metallurgist, mineralogist, and geologist with the British Boundary Commission of 1858–1862. His research later carried him to far parts of the world, from Lapland to Arabia and Asia Minor, Mexico, Brazil, and Peru.

BEAR CREEK: The Blackfoot word for "bear" is *kyáiyo,* the Cree is *másqua,* and the Kootenai *kławła* (grizzly) and *nupqu* (black bear). Bear names in and around the parks are legion. This creek skirts Glacier's southwestern boundary and is said to have been called Bear Creek and Big Salmon Trout Creek by Indians. Among its tributaries are Devil Creek, Giefer Creek, and the spectacular waterfall called the Silver Stairs. When the railroad was first pushed through here about

1891 the turbulent history of Bear Creek went into full swing around a point now called Fielding Siding. Much of the drudgery of railroad construction was borne willy-nilly by countless Chinese coolies, many of whom perished along the way. (So we are told by the oral reports of the neighborhood.) The kitchens and graveyards of the Chinese are said to have dotted the railway every five or ten miles around Glacier. One of these kitchens with the usual conical oven stood at Fielding in the old loop of the tracks. Other Chinese ovens, now perhaps vanished, have been reported near Garry, Crystal, Wahoo, Stanton, and Cascadilla Creeks and around Coram. Also near Fielding (Blacktail) was the notorious boom town of McCarthyille, named for the raw youth who started it and became its mayor. Most famous of its gamblers was Slippery Bill, a gentleman and a scholar to boot.

The most popular gamble was mining. Among the claims around Bear Creek were the Santiago (which belonged to Sydney M. Logan, et al.), and the Giefer plot of 1910 (called Running Bear). Phil Giefer was the first track-walker for the sector. He and his wife Louise had many mining interests: Hungry Horse, Spotted Bear, Warbonnet, and a series of six called Iroquois.

BEAR* MOUNTAIN and **POINT**: See Almighty Voice, Crandell.

BEAR MEDICINE* FALLS is also called Crystal Falls and was named by Dr. Ruhle. It is four or five miles from McDonald Lodge. Bear Medicine is the surname of a Blackfoot family and artist.

BEARHAT* MOUNTAIN was named for a prominent Kootenai leader. He and his band camped with Schultz at Saint Mary when Schultz conferred his name on Hidden Lake. The name was switched to the mountain in 1934, replacing the name Davenport Mountain (for the hotel in Spokane?). Bearhat was the companion of Back-in-Sight, another chief who camped with Schultz on this occasion. (See Cerulean.) The Kootenai form for the name "Bearhat" can be *Nupqu-kayuka* (Black Bear Hat) or *Kławła kayuka* (Grizzly Hat). Schultz uses the latter for Hidden Lake and the former for Cerulean. (See Little Dog.)

BEARHEAD* MOUNTAIN is named for *kyáiyótokan*, a Piegan who went to war against the dreaded Assiniboine White Dog and who also was one of the survivors of the Baker massacre. He was the brother of Chief Heavy Runner and an informant of Schultz. His name, however, was applied to this mountain by Evans, while Schultz named it Eagle Ribs. (See Eagle Ribs.)

BEARS HUMP: an overlook that offers a favorite hill and view of Waterton Lake. (See CRANDELL.)

BEAVER CHIEF* FALLS (1,334 feet high) was named by Dr. Ruhle for the figure in a Blackfoot story, *Nínai-xíxtaki* (literally Chief Beaver). The Blackfoot term for "beaver" would be better written *xis-xtaki*. The falls has had other names: Lincoln and Diamond. (See XIXTAKI.)

BEAVER MEDICINE FALLS on Sprague Creek was probably named for the Bear Medicine story as retold by Walter McClintock in The Old North Trail. (See AKAIYAN for a brief version of the story.) This cataract has also been known as Crystal Falls and perhaps Bear Medicine Falls.

BEAVER WOMAN* LAKE is a lake in Martha's Basin named by Dr. Ruhle. Beaver Woman in Blackfoot is *Xisxtaki-aki*, and in Kootenai, *Sina Pałkiy. (See XIXTAKI.)

BELLEVUE*: The French name of a hill in Waterton Lakes Park and also of a ridge at the side of Gunsight Mountain in Glacier. *Belle vue* of course means "beautiful view."

BELLY* RIVER bears one of the oldest known names in the International Peace Park. In Blackfoot this river is called *Mokowánisz* (apparently an "inanimate" plural), referring to the digestive system of the buffalo. The river crosses from Glacier into Waterton Park and then flows by the Big Belly Buttes, for which it must have been named long ago. On the Arrowsmith map of 1802 the name appears as Moo-coo-wans. However, on David Thompson's map of 1814 it is called Bull Head. Its Kootenai name is *Akaȼimuk* (perhaps a goat's belly).

In Glacier Dr. Ruhle applied the Blackfoot term also to a cascade, a lake, and a river. The name is associated with the Gros Ventre tribe. Hugh Monroe informed George Bird Grinnell that the Gros Ventres had approached the Rockies shortly before 1814. Their name for Belly River or the South Saskatchewan was *Nut nitséh.* (See GROS VENTRE, ATSINA, MOKOWANIS.)

The river known as Belly River to the Hudson's Bay Company was also called Bull Pound. The Belly River Ranger Station in Glacier was formerly known as Sulphur Springs Station in reference to a nearby elk lick redolent with sulphur. The Mokowan Butte in Alberta lies partly within Waterton Lakes Park. It is a flat-topped mesa, only about six thousand feet in elevation but known to geologists because it seems to predate the glacial age.

BELTON* HILLS, STATION, CANYON, and **VILLAGE**: The village, just outside Glacier National Park, was once the site of park headquarters, housed in the Belton Chalets. It had its beginnings, like other stations or sidings, as a box-car on a side track. According to various accounts, it was named after (1) James Belton, a trapper; (2) a town in Missouri; (3) camp cook Andrew Bell; or (4) camp cook Daniel Webster Bell. Be that as it may, in 1949 the village was renamed West Glacier, though the railroad station and the chalets retain their old name Belton. Across the road, diagonally, from the railway station and next to the chalets stands the home Louis Hill is said to have built for himself and family. It is now privately owned and of course reported to be haunted. No old house of status would be worth its taxes without its pet ghost.

The Kootenais called the Belton Hills "Spotted Foot Mountains": *Kaɋɫiɫɫik Akwukɫi'it.* Several mining claims were staked out hereabouts: Belton, Monte Cristo, War Eagle, Wild Cat (belonging to Jack Monroe), and War House (belonging to L. F. Vinal.)

BENCH* LAKE: The name is descriptive.

BENTON, FORT and **TRAIL**: Fort Benton had been established by 1850 by Alexander Culbertson, head of the Upper Missouri fur trade for American Fur Company. It was the successor of other earlier trading posts for the Piegans (South Blackfeet) in the area around the mouth of the Marias River. Culbertson, who had previously been in charge of Fort Laramie, preferred adobe structures to logs. Fort Benton soon became the social and commercial center of Montana only to be supplanted by boomtowns of the gold rush. But it remained the capital of the merchant princes, profiting from the rising cattle industry, the whiskey trade, and the exploitation of the Indian population. For a while Fort Benton was the agency for the Blackfeet. Trails led from the fort up into the whiskey posts in present Alberta and Saskatchewan. The sheriff of Fort Benton was likely to be one of the chief bootleggers (a Montana tradition that endured into the twentieth century). Though not actually located in "Glacier country," Fort Benton played a decisive role in the history of both Waterton and Glacier. After the North West Mounted Police arrived in 1874 to close down the liquor trade, they were obliged to use Fort Benton, the whiskey capital, as their major supply depot. Because of the Canadian Shield, it was not practical to reach western Canada from eastern Canada except by descending into the U.S. and taking the steamers up the Missouri to

Fort Benton, then resorting to the Fort Benton Trail along the edge of Glacier Country.

BERTHA LAKE, CREEK, FALLS and **BAY** were named for a homesteader of Waterton village eventually charged with counterfeiting and sent to jail. The older name for the lake is Spirit Lake.

BIG CEDARS are near Avalanche Campground and were probably "discovered" by Fred Langerman, J. F. Vogt (Voght), J. H. Edwards, and their companions who were exploring the area north of Lake McDonald. A Scot named James Finley (Finlay) is said to have had a claim here. (See EDWARDS, COMEAU.)

BIG DRIFT is a seasonal snowdrift just below Logan Pass on the eastward side.

BIG PRAIRIE lies along the North Fork River north of Polebridge. Some people from Havre had private homes here, calling their settlement Haverville.

BIGHORN* BASIN, PARK, and **PEAK** are named for the mountain sheep, in Blackfoot called *ómahx-ihkini* (big horn). The Kootenai name for the peak is Red Horn, *Kanusqłi Akwukłi'it,* and the lake seems to have been called No Name. Joe Kipp was part owner of a Big Horn claim in the East Flattop area. A Piegan subchief named Big Horn was blacklisted by the U.S. Army and killed in the Baker massacre.

BIRD WOMAN* FALLS and **PASS**: The falls used to be called Trapper Falls, but this name was suggested by Dr. Ruhle. It has sometimes been assumed to refer to Sacajawea (Sakakawea), the young Shoshoni mother who accompanied Lewis and Clark with her newborn baby Pampi. Her Hidatsa name may mean "Bird Woman" though the word "Sacajawea" seems closer to the Shoshoni term for "boat pusher."

In fact, however, the famous falls were probably named for someone else, perhaps the wife of Old Sun or (more likely) the wife of Lone Walker of the Small Robes band. Bird Woman, wife of Lone Walker, had a son Red Crow and daughters called Mink Woman and Fox Woman (*Sinopáki*). Her son-in-law was Hugh Monroe. It may be that Three Suns was another of her children and that she herself was a sister of Red Eagle.

BISHOP'S CAP on the Garden Wall is a descriptive name of no recorded origin. Peaks reminiscent of a "bishop's cap" are usually called "mitre peaks," of which better examples occur in the Kintla region.

BISON* MOUNTAIN is near the southeastern portion of Glacier. It resembles the hump of a buffalo and bears the Blackfoot name *Stamik-otokan* or buffalo bull head. (See BULLHEAD.) There is also a creek and a railway station named Bison between East Glacier and Marias Pass, although the station was formerly called Talbot. There was at one time a project to locate a herd of buffalo nearby. Though this program was never realized, the Blackfeet tribe does have a small herd of buffalo today in another part of the reservation near the old Holy Family Mission.

BLACKFEET* GLACIER and **MOUNTAIN** were formerly called Blackfoot. The glacier is said to have been named Old Man Ice by the Kootenais, but was re-named in honor of the Blackfeet tribe by George Bird Grinnell and William H. Seward in 1891, or perhaps by Schultz and William Jackson. In fact, there is a possibility that Schultz named it in honor of William (Billy) Jackson rather than for the tribe. (See JACKSON.) But Grinnell's term "Crown of the Continent" (in the opinion of this author) refers primarily to this peak rather than to Glacier National Park in general as it is now interpreted.

In Canada the term Blackfoot is preferred to Blackfeet, especially for the northernmost branch of the confederation or alliance, now resident near Calgary, but in the U.S. modern Piegans have expressed a preference for the plural form. However, in more recent times, this distinction is less rigid. "Blackfoot" is often used for the name of the language and as an adjective, and the plural form for the name of the South Piegans. The question arises because the original name *Síxika (Síxikai, Síxikaw)* can be translated as singular or plural. The root *-ka* makes no distinction between "foot" or "feet." The sign for *Síxika* is to stroke the leg downwards and point to something black. The three tribes together are sometimes called *Nízitapi* or Real People, sometimes too *Saukitapi* or *Sokitapi* meaning Prairie People. (However, *Nízitapi* is also used as a generic term for "Indians." See ALLEN).

BLACKTAIL* HILLS and **CREEK** were probably named by railroad men in reference to the deer of the area. The Kootenai name is Magpie Mountain, *Anan Akwukli'it*. Near here once stood McCarthyville. This is also the site of the railway station Fielding. The blacktail is more commonly called the mule deer.

BLAKISTON CREEK, PASS, and **MOUNTAIN**: Mount Blakiston is the highest peak in Waterton Lakes National Park at 2940 meters. Blakiston Brook used to be called Pass Creek. These features were named for Thomas Wright Blakiston (1832–1891), explorer and ornithologist, second son of the second baronet Sir Matthew Blakiston and perhaps of royal descent. He was born in Hampshire and became a second lieutenant in the Royal Army in 1851, serving with his regiment in Ireland, Nova Scotia, and the Crimea during the siege of Sebastopol. In 1857 he was assigned to the expedition of John Palliser to explore what is now western Canada.

In the following year (1858) after a disagreement with Palliser, and with three "Red River half-breed voyageurs," a Cree hunter and ten horses, Blakiston turned southwestward into the Rocky Mountains. The men with him were Thomas Sinclair, Amable Hogg, Charles Racette, and the Cree guide James. They explored the North and South Kootenay Passes, down into the northwestern corner of what is now Glacier, and across the ranges to the Tobacco Plains. On the return they visited Waterton Lakes, not previously reported. Blakiston named the Galton Range for his contemporary and fellow scientist, Sir Francis Galton, Darwin's cousin. He also named the Waterton Lakes after the naturalist Charles Waterton, Darwin's friend. In the elastic sense, Blakiston may be regarded as the "discoverer" of the Waterton Lakes. (See *Who Was Who...* for more information.)

There is supposed to be a profile of an Indian face in the rocks of this peak, but such theories depend on imaginations engaged in identifying the elusive Indianhead Mountain of Waterton..

BLOOD INDIAN RESERVE TIMBER LIMIT Is a closed area inside Waterton Lakes Park designated to acknowledge tribal timber rights. (On the U.S. side no such rights are recognized.)

BLUEING LAKE: You may see it if you look down from Split Mountain.

BOMBAY: a station on the railway, no doubt named for the city and the former state in India.

BOSPORUS and the **DARDENELLES** are place names borrowed from Turkey for a narrow slice of Waterton Lake. The *Bosporus* in Greek means "ox-ford." It is the name of a strait that empties the Black Sea into the Sea of Marmora, which in turn runs into the Aegean through the Dardanelles.

BOSWELL MOUNTAIN, which straddles the U.S./Canadian border, is named for a veterinary surgeon with the British Boundary Commission that traveled from the Lake of the Woods to the Continental Divide (1874). It is also called Street Mountain after Jack Street.

BOULDER* CREEK, GLACIER, PEAK, and **RIDGE** are named apparently just for boulders. The Kootenai name for the glacier and the peak is given as Stilts Glacier, *Kaqa·ȼmuɫAkwiswitxu,* and Stilts Mountain, *Kaqa·ȼmuɫ Akwukɫi'it.* The creek and the ridge are said to have been called Blacktail by Hugh Monroe. The Blackfoot name for the mule deer is *áisikotuyi* (breaks the tail), which can easily be misconstrued to mean "black tail."

BOUNDARY* CREEK, MOUNTAINS, PASS, and **TRAIL** are located along the international line. The mountains are partly in Glacier and partly in the Provincial Forest of British Columbia. The pass has the more recent name of Kootenai Pass, one of the several by that name. Nearby looms Pyramid Hill, so called by the party of Lord Lathom. Highest of the Boundary Mountains is Long Knife.

BOWMAN* CREEK and **LAKE** carry the name of rancher Fred Bowman, who worked in the North Fork country in the 1880s. His Chinook wife was Kalsanooka, and probably we should name things after the wives instead of the husbands. The Kootenai name for the creek is "Big Strawberries," *Yakiɫ Wiɫ́ quku'ki Akinmituk* and for the lake *Aqukaɫa Akuq́nuk,* presumably with reference to the bog at the upper end. The French map of 1846 marks Bowman Lake and Creek as *Lac et Riviére de Point* after the Jesuit Nicholas Point, who wandered about with the Indians and painted many pictures of them. Local Democrats, says Vaught, called the lake Cleveland in early times, but the name did not take hold. (See AKOKALA.)

BOY LAKE: Boy has been known as a family name among both the Crees and Blackfeet, probably a shortened form of an older name. About 1869 the U.S. Army listed Piegan chiefs as "friendly" or "hostile," rating The Boy as friendly—maybe. But it is more likely that the name of this lake resulted from the blister-rust camps of the World War II era, and may have been applied by Dave Cavanina to round out the names of two other lakes in this area, Young Man and Old Man. For a legend of The Boy, see WATERTON.

BRADLEY, MOUNT: A mountain that rises south of Glacier in the neighboring Flathead Range may have been named for a forest ranger Richard Bradley. The name, however, also commemorates someone who was especially important to the history of the region and might have stepped out of "Gone With the Wind." Lt. James Bradley (1844–1877) was a short, wiry youngster from Ohio whose father, a colonel, did not want his son in the Civil War. But he was short enough to slip into the ranks unrecognized and got himself into the various battles in 1861 and various more when he re-enlisted the next year. Taken prisoner in 1863 he did time in the horrible Andersonville, was exchanged and pitched into another series of battles that culminated in the siege of Atlanta. That was the home of his future bride, a surgeon's daughter named Mary, but it is not certain whether he first met her at that time or after his duty in Wyoming. Anyhow, he was back at Atlanta seeking her hand from an intransigent father, who forbade the marriage. So off he eloped with Mary to put down a disturbance by the Ku Klux Klan, and then, in 1871, off again to Wyoming on the Union Pacific. But this was the time of the terrible blizzards that trapped the trains for two months near Cheyenne.

Somehow, James and Mary got a stage to Helena where he was isolated in a pest house with the smallpox. On his recovery, they were sent to Fort Shaw and Fort Benton. With the help of the Jesuits and Alexander Culbertson and probably various Blackfeet, James began to write his "Land of the Blackfeet," which is preserved in part as a foundation piece of Glacier Country history. He also composed a Blackfoot glossary and published articles under the pseudonym "Cavalier."

Transferred to Fort Shaw and dispatched under General Gibbons, he organized a corps of Crow Indian scouts, one of whom was the famous Curley. After the Custer massacre, he was sent to recover the remains and was evidently the first to report to Gibbons that he had counted 195 dead. He was still with Gibbon the next year when they joined General Howard against the fleeing Nez Perces. At the Big Hole he was one of the first to die. (See *Who Was Who...* for more information.)

BRAVE DOG* MOUNTAIN is named for the Blackfeet *Mazix* (Braves). The Braves or Brave Dogs are a division of the All Comrades Society. This peak was once called Little Dog. (See LITTLE DOG.)

BRITISH COLUMBIA: With the survey of the forty-ninth parallel begun in 1858, British Columbia became a Crown Colony with Sir James Douglas (1803–1877) as its governor. A native of the Caribbean, probably of Guyana, South America, he was a descendent of the famous Scottish hero, the Black Douglas, on his father's side and evidently of African descent on his mother's. Educated in Scotland and England and fluent in French, he joined the North West Company in 1819 and the Hudson's Bay Company on its take-over in 1821. He reached present British Columbia in 1826 and soon afterwards Fort Vancouver on the Columbia. There he befriended the young botanist (perhaps a cousin) David Douglas (of the Douglas-fir). In two years he married a Cree lady, Amelia Connelly. He soon won his reputation as one of the most remarkable figures in the history of the Pacific Northwest. His travels on company business took him to Russian Alaska and Mexican California. After founding the city of Victoria, in the midst of a land plagued with slavery, he helped ransom slaves and give them refuge. (These slaves may have come from California or elsewhere in the U.S., but there were also many Indian and South Pacific slaves even on the west coast of the U.S. and the east coast of Australia that historians usually don't mention.) He defied General Harney in the "Pig War," but took a lead in the Boundary Survey and was knighted in 1864. He and Lady Amelia were the center of a lively social circle in Victoria.

A large chunk of what became British Columbia (or on the French versions of the map *Colombie-Britannique*) had previously been known as New Caledonia. The section impinging on the Glacier/Waterton country includes the Akamina-Kishinena Recreation Area and also the headwaters of the Flathead River and therefore the uppermost Flathead Valley and Mounts Darrah and Saint Eloi. Two peaks with Chippewa names rise in this region not far from the border: *Miskwasini* (red rock) and *Kenow* (eagle).

BROKEN ARM COUNTRY: One would suppose that the Flattop Mountain area got this nickname because someone broke his/her arm. Or perhaps it was named after the chief of the Wetaskewin Crees during the project to give Cree names in the northeastern part of Glacier. Anyway, Broken Arm or Maskipiton pops up from Washington to Washington and many places in between. His early years were dedicated to fighting the Blackfeet. In 1831 he was one of the chiefs who visited President Jackson, and he paused in Saint Louis for Catlin to paint his portrait. In 1833 he met Prince Maximilian at Fort Union. In 1841 he helped guide James Sinclair and his caravan of Métis to Fort Vancouver. In 1850 and 1854 he led other emigrant parties across the Rockies.

A violent man and a hard drinker, he repulsed missionaries declaring "I'll never be a Christian so long as there are Blackfeet left to kill."

Then he went on a vision quest. The message he received was: "All men and beasts belong to the one family of the Great Spirit. Burn the black feathers of violence and wear the white feathers of peace." So he evidently attended the treaty of Laramie and again the Judith treaty of 1855, a guest of Little Dog. As "The Friend" he guided John Palliser, and he learned to read the Bible. He walked straight into Blackfoot camps armed only with the pipe of peace. But In 1869, in an attempt to end a fierce war between Crees and Blackfeet, he tried this strategy once more only to be shot down.

BROKEN STRAW MOUNTAIN, in Kootenai *Tiáhkat*, is reported but its identity and whereabouts remain a mystery.

BROWN*, MOUNT, is named for William Brown, a railroad man from Jacksonville, Illinois, who led a party here in 1894 to hunt and fish. They camped near Lake McDonald, and two of the party (one of whom was Charlie Russell) climbed and named this peak. The Kootenai name is Wolf Hat: *Ká·kinkayuka Akwukłi'it.*

BROWN* PASS was probably named for one of two men:

1) Louis Brun (whose French name was locally anglicized to "Brown") was a Qubequois who came into the upper Flathead valley very early and married the daughter of Kalispel Chief Goshea, perhaps becoming the first settler of the area in 1847. But since gold was discovered in California, the Bruns and other Métis families including Benetsee took off for that Mother Lode. It was not long before they drifted back to Montana—perhaps because people who were not Anglos were driven from the California mines as "foreigners." (Even Hispanic Californians born in California were excluded as foreigners by Anglos who had been there only a few months.) So back in Montana, Benetsee applied what he had learned in California and soon found gold in Montana too. But the Bruns re-settled first near Colville, Washington, until the Indian wars of the late 1850s when Métis people and French Canadians with Indian wives were subject to surveillance or arrest by Governor Isaac Stevens. Then the Bruns moved back to Montana.

The story goes that when Charles Conrad was authorized by Jim Hill to locate a new railroad town in the Flathead valley, Louis Brun's daughter Emilie suggested the name of her mother's tribe for the new town, Kalispel. (Conrad is supposed to have added the final "l" for emphasis or accent.)

2) The second (and more probable) candidate for the source of the name of Brown's Pass was George (Kootenai) Brown (1839–1916), something of a rascal but nevertheless a prime mover in the establishment of Waterton Lakes Park (though the pass is in Glacier). Born in County Clare, Ireland, and orphaned very young, he was raised by his grandmother and in 1858 shipped off to India as an ensign. (Legend says he was raised in the royal family and once punched the Crown Prince in the nose, so Victoria sent him to India, where a rajah made him a gift of an elephant.) But in sober truth, his service in India was quite routine at Kanpur, Calcutta, and other points, and in 1860 he returned to England. Selling his commission, he took ship to Panama, San Francisco, and the gold fields of British Columbia. After a stint as a lawman, he moved to the Flathead country and then to Waterton lakes (1865). On his various trips between the Flathead and Waterton, he is said to have used both South Kootenay and Browns Pass. (But the Blackfeet name for the pass, *Kutenai Apikoan ozitámisohpi*—where Kootenay Whiteman went up—sounds rigged.) Near Medicine Hat he once caught an arrow in his backside and medicated himself with turpentine. Then he joined the Métis of Duck Lake and Fort Garry (Winnipeg).

In Dakota he became a pony express rider with his companions Joe the Spaniard and Guardipee the Métis. In 1868 he was captured by the Sioux (by Sitting Bull, he claimed). Next year at Pembina he married a Métisse named Olive Lyonnais. In 1873 he guided U.S. Army soldiers in a search for a wagon train attached to the Northern Boundary Survey, and thereafter joined the last buffalo hunts in Montana and the Cypress Hills. (How much of this story to believe, I leave to the alert reader.)

In 1877 he killed a man at Fort Benton but was acquitted in Helena for self-defense. Then he took refuge at Waterton (in those times called Kootenai Lakes)—but why take refuge if he had been acquitted? Anyhow, he and Olive ran a trading post for Kootenais, Salish, Blackfeet, Stonies, and Nez Perces until the Mounties closed the border. Olive died here at the birth of a son during one of her husband's absences. Her other children called out to her corpse, "Maman, get up!" In time, Father Albert Lacombe helped place her three children in school.

During the rebellion of Louis Riel, Brown served as a scout in the Rocky Mountain Rangers and met a Cree lady named "Blue Lightning," *Sepihko-waskotesiw.* She was a fine cook and a sharp shot and took many trips with him out of Waterton and the Flathead. Crees and Métis camped with them at Waterton along with Joe Cosley and the Mounties Street and Rouleau. Brown often served as a packer for the Mounties and accompanied Sam Steele into the Kootenay country in 1888. Though he has been accused of smuggling into Glacier via Flattop, he eventually became the first warden of Waterton Lakes Park and died there in 1916. His Blackfoot name was "Long Hair," *Inóspi,* which is now used as the name of a campground at Waterton.

Brian Reeves suggests that a Kootenai name discovered by Schaeffer may apply to the area of Brown Pass and the Hole-in-the-Wall. The name is "Hand-Standing-in-the-Middle-of-the-Mountains," also translated as "Hand-Up-in-the-Mountain" or simply "Hand Peak." Schaeffer himself could not decide just where this name applied except that it was somewhere near the Montana-Canadian boundary. And it was a place of great "power, that is, it conferred power on those who climbed these peaks, especially a young man named *A'kinu* (?) [*sic*]." Reeves also cites Ambrose Gravelle who stated that it consisted of five peaks called Hands of the Mountains, "east of Kintla between the headwaters of Waterton and Flathead drainages." It does not seem clear whether it was in Canada or the U.S. or partly in each, but at least it was a place which the Kootenais scaled hand over hand. If they were horseback they circled around the Hand. If they were on snowshoes they plodded between the thumb and the forefinger. The name for this mountain in Kootenai is said to be *Kaiyakawalin Kalaxi.*

BROWNING is the Blackfeet (Piegan) Indian Agency on Highway 89 east of Glacier and the town which clusters about the Agency Square. The post office there dates from 1900. The agency had previously been located at two points along Badger Creek and earlier on the Teton River (near modern Choteau), along Sun River, and at Fort Benton. Gradually and in disregard of the Treaty of 1855, the U.S. Government yielded to the demands of stockmen and restricted the reservation boundaries. The present site used to be called Fort Browning, probably after old Fort Browning, a subagency of the Gros Ventres and other tribes on the Milk River near where Dodson is today. The "fort" lasted from about 1869 to 1871. The name Browning probably was intended to honor Orville H. Browning, Secretary of the Interior. But the Blackfeet call it, among other things, *Itún'niopi* (Where we have our father). Is the irony intentional?

BUCHANAN RIDGE and **MOUNTAIN** are in Waterton Park, named in honor of Senator Buchanan, newspaper publisher of Lethbridge, first Provincial Librarian, Minister of Municipal Affairs and founder of the YMCA camp on Knights Lake (lower Waterton Lake).

BUCHER CREEK in Waterton Park is said to have been named for an Indian tribe, but no such tribe is listed by Frederick W. Hodge, whose compilation is regarded as authoritative in both Canada and the U.S. But there was a very early trapper in the vicinity sometimes called Bouch . Maybe the creek was named for him. Or it may have been named for Bucher or Busha, a leader of the Cree Métis who in vain sought shelter for his people on the Flathead Reservation. In this quest he had to make a heroic crossing in the deep snow over the Continental Divide. (See MARIAS.)

BUFFALO PADDOCK (*l'enclos des bisons*) lies near the northern edge of Waterton Lakes Park. Note that the French uses *bisons*. The word "buffalo" comes from the Italian which comes from the Greek *boubalos*, and that refers to an ox.

BUFFALO WOMAN* LAKE: This name was on the list for approval but seems to have remained in limbo, neither approved nor rejected. In any case, it is in Martha's Basin.

BULLHEAD* LAKE is also known as Ladyhead and Jealous Women's (or Woman's) Lake. (See SWIFTCURRENT.) The Bull's Head group of mining claims were on the slopes of Mount Wilbur with a camp called Harrisville huddled on Bullshead Lake. There is also a Bullshead point on Mount Wilbur. (The locals got the two forms—Bullhead and Bullshead—mixed up, and there is no way to straighten them out now.) The Blackfoot form of this name, *Stamik-ótokan*, appears at various places about Glacier, and there was a Piegan called Bull Head whose name was sometimes used for Mount Logan. This was also the name of Colonel MacLeod of the Royal Northwest Mounted Police at Fort MacLeod, a man widely respected by the Indians and by Chief Crowfoot in particular.

BULL'S HEAD LODGE was the summer home of Montana's cowboy artist Charlie Russell. The name is reminiscent of Charlie's signature on his paintings and sketches. The house was built for him near Apgar by Dimon Apgar in 1890 with additions in 1916 and 1917. Russell lived here with his wife Nancy each summer until snowtime. Here or nearby he entertained Will Rogers, Irving S. Cobb, Frank Linderman, and Mary Roberts Rinehart. A greenhorn from Missouri, he had tried his hand at sheepherding and cowpunching, had resided for a time with the Kaina Blackfoot, and succeeded mostly as a brilliant portrayer of these life styles. In later years the Russells and Lindermans spent their winters at Santa Barbara and Ventura County, California.

BURNT ROCK CANYON and **FALLS** are in Waterton Park. The name refers to black lichens.

BUTTE WELL was an early oil well on Lower Kintla Lake, maybe the first in Montana (1901). But attempts to get oil out of it or elsewhere in the area did not prove worthwhile. (See KINTLA.)

BUTTERCUP* CREEK and **PARK** were named by R. T. Evans.

CALF ROBE* MOUNTAIN is the source of Coonsa Creek. However, it is not certain which man named Calf Robe is referred to. One of them could have been Calf Robe or Calf Shirt, a son of the Blood chief Man'stokos and so probably a brother or half-brother of Natawista Culbertson. He was a notorious bully, held in awe by his own people. Finally, a group of traders at a whiskey post (now in Alberta) killed him. They had a hard time doing it, and even after he was dead and his body stuffed into a hole in the ice, women fled from the corpse as it bobbed up to the surface. The other Calf Robe seems to have been a much more congenial person, and his story is told in the entry MEDICINE GRIZZLY. One way to say Calf Robe in Blackfoot is *Onistaiayi*.

CAMAS* CREEK, LAKE, and **RIDGE**: The camas is the *pomme blanche* of the French-Canadians. It has an exquisite blue flower and an edible bulb and is arguably the showiest flower of the Waterton/Glacier country, if not for size, at least for delicacy. A small lake named for Billy Ackerman is part of this creek. The term camas or *quamash* derives from the Nootka language of British Columbia, probably meaning "sweet." The Kootenais seem to have named this area for the camas, *xapi* in their tongue. Camas Lake was once called Langerman for Fred Langerman, and someone on the Ahern expedition called the stream Mud Creek. Still another variation in names arose when a local guide named Geduhn led S. W. Morgan of Chicago, his wife, and her brother from London to the third Camas Lake and called it Lake Morgan.

At the junction of Camas and Dutch Creeks, a lonesome young man found his home, which has long since fallen away and even the man's name has been forgotten. But it was Louis Fournier. He was an electrician, born in Detroit in 1882, perhaps an orphan because he was adopted by Arthur Glen, brought up as Lewis in the Methodist Church and transformed from a French Canadian to an ardent Yankee. In 1900 he joined the U.S. Army in Wyoming and was shipped off in a cavalry unit to San Francisco and the Boxer Rebellion in China. Perhaps he was involved in the famous relief force to raise the siege of Peking (Beijing). He also served in the Philippines and in 1903 at Fort Assiniboine, Montana.

About 1910 he filed claim to farmland on Camas Creek and endured the forest fires only to find his farm surrounded by the new national park. A special bill in Congress for veterans secured his claim. So he got married only to be sent off to Mexico with the National Guard. From sergeant he rapidly advanced to lieutenant and captain and was dispatched to France and Germany from 1917 to 1919. Was it France that helped him find himself? Anyhow he changed his name back to "Louis," but shortly after his return to Belton and Camas Creek he became "mentally ill," probably from the effects of lethal gas, and died at Warm Springs in 1921.

CAMEL'S HUMP: A descriptive arabesque term: "camel" is one of the most ancient words in the language. But the Kootenai name is Young Man, *Niʤtahal*, which now appears transferred to a lake not far off. (See TINKHAM, BOY.)

CAMERON* CREEK, FALLS, LAKE, and **CAMERONIAN MOUNTAIN** are all in Waterton Lakes National Park, except for the portion of the lake that lies in Glacier. They are named for Donald R. Cameron, who headed the British contingent of the Northern Boundary Commission of 1874. Cameron Lake seems to be identical with the lake sometimes called Cannon and so must be the one listed by Schultz under the name of *Paiótaki* in the Blackfoot language. This name belonged to Mrs. Charles Phelan, for whom the Blackfeet felt a special respect, and also for a Piegan lady of long ago who was a holy woman of the Medicine Lodge. Reginald Daly (1910) refers to the lake as Summit and the creek as Oil Creek. The lake, however, also was labeled Oil Lake. On Oil Creek once stood "Oil City," derricks and all. These may not be the most euphonious names in the Waterton-Glacier complex, but a name more musical was bestowed by Staveley-Hill. He refers to Cameron Falls as Louise Falls, which, like Lake Louise in Banff, was presumably bestowed in honor of Princess Louise, the Marchioness of Lorne (1883).

Kootenai Chief Paul David claimed that his people used a pass on snowshoes in winter, Akamina Pass, but it was too muddy for horse traffic in summer. So the upper reaches of Cameron Creek were probably called Red Mud Creek.

CAMP* CREEK: No reason is known for this name, but someone must have camped here to get the name approved.

CAMPBELL* MOUNTAIN: Though there is a report that in 1904 this peak was known as Intersection Mountain, the U.S. Board on Geographic Names evidently has no record to show which Campbell left his name on this mountain. However, two candidates for the honor present themselves:

(1) Fred C. Campbell whose Blackfoot name was Red Head or *Máhkihkini.* He was superintendent of the Blackfeet Reservation during some of the difficult years after World War I, famous for his agricultural program and his method of visiting person to person. He is probably the best remembered of all the agents for the Blackfeet. James Willard Schultz named this mountain after him.

(2) Archibald Campbell who headed the U.S. contingent for the International Boundary Survey of the forty-ninth parallel, 1860–61, from the San Juan Islands to Akamina, (see AKAMINA). He was noted for his stubborn grouch. In spite of his disposition, he was again in charge of the second boundary survey of 1874.

CANNON* CREEK and **MOUNT** in Glacier were named for a couple of honeymooners who in 1901 climbed the peak which was then called Goat Mountain. Dr. Walter Bradford Cannon was only a year out of Harvard Medical School, where he would return to become professor of physiology. His bride Cornelia James Cannon was a writer of children's literature. They were taken by boat to the head of Lake McDonald and guided from there by Denis Comeau. Near one of the summits they left a note in a bottle naming the mountain after themselves. The couple remained locally unknown until the bottle and the note were discovered in 1985 by James Best of Kalispell and Ted Steiner of Whitefish. The Kootenai name for the mountain is Old Man Dog, *Nuł'aqna Xa' l- ¢ in,* and in 1894 Sperry called it Goat Mountain, a bland name for one of the spectacular guardians of Lake McDonald.

CANYON* CREEK empties Cracker Lake. Another Canyon Creek on the opposite side of Glacier flows into the North Fork.

CAPER* PEAK: R. T. Evans sighted over thirty goats here and so gave the name which means "goat" in Latin. The Kootenai name is Sacred Gun: *Knupkaqawu't.*

CARCAJOU* LAKE is named for the wolverine, though the name is sometimes applied to other animals. This word is a French adaptation of the word for the wolverine in the Montagnais Cree dialect of Quebec: *karkajou*. It was assigned by Dr. Ruhle to one of the North Lakes.

CARDSTON: Founded by Mormons in 1887 and named after their leader Charles Card. The Blood Indian Agency is at Cardston, and the Blackfoot name is *Ak-óhkimi*: Many Wives.

CARIBOU, a French adaptation of Algonquin *khalibou* for the reindeer, is a favorite name for mining claims, notably for one belonging to Joe Kipp, O. S. Main, et al., in a series that included Big Horn, Grinnell, Merritt, Alice, Ahern, Emma, and Cora. They were located on the west slope of the Divide opposite the head of the south fork of Belly River.

CARNELIAN* CLIFF: Descriptive. The Kootenai name is recorded as "Gyrfalcon Mountain," *Aknuqɫuɫaṁ Akwukɫi'it*, but the name has now been transferred to a lake and really means "bald eagle." (See GYRFALCON.)

CARTER* GLACIER and **MOUNTAIN:** The glacier was once called Culver Glacier, presumably after Professor G. E. Culver of the University of Wisconsin, who in 1890 accompanied Lt. George Ahern and the African-American troopers in their explorations of the present park. The Kootenai name for the mountain and nearby lakes is "Weasel Collar," *Mayuk'ana*.

While the name Carter could have been applied to this mountain after a local trapper named Charles Carter, a hunting companion of J. W. Schultz, it is more likely that the name derives from Senator Thomas H. Carter of Montana. It was he who introduced the bill of 1907 to establish Glacier National Park and who also gave the park its name. Others who pushed the project, and probably pushed Carter in the process, included Senator Joseph Dixon, Senator Boies Penrose of Pennsylvania, George Bird Grinnell, Lewis Hill, and Congressman Charles Pray. The irony is that Carter seems to have been motivated by his desire to promote industry—in particular, the mining industry. He was a friend of Marcus Daly, a champion of Anaconda Copper, and a political opponent of William Andrews Clark, the richest of the "copper kings." He also opposed the leading conservationist George Ahern, whose name lies close to Carter's on park maps. So why, with such developmental interests, should he promote a national park? For whom was he saving the wilderness? The mystery has never been solved. However, there is a story that Carter's wife, the former Ellen Galen, paid a visit to the Saint Mary country and was so deeply impressed with the scenery that she may very well have provided the motivation for preserving it as a national park. We have to recall that there was at that time no definitive notion of what a national park should be, and the National Park Service had not yet been established. It may be that the mountain should be named Ellen Carter Mountain.

CARTHEW CREEK, LAKES, and **MOUNTAIN** are in Waterton Lakes Park and were named for Lt. William R. Carthew, a surveyor, who was killed in Ypres in 1916.

CASCADILLA CREEK forms one of the series of waterfalls that spill into Nyack valley, making it into a miniature Yosemite. Cascadilla is the creek farthest south of this series and has a river access named for it. The name *cascadilla* means "little cascade" in Spanish. There are two or three Chinese ovens here.

CASSIDY CURVE is named for Mike Cassidy, an Altyn miner who drilled for oil and gas.

CASTLE MOUNTAIN, RIVER, and **DIVIDE** were named by Blakiston in 1858. The Castle River Divide is on the northern edge of Waterton Park. The Ptarmigan Wall in Glacier is also sometimes called Castle Mountain.

CATARACT* CREEK and **MOUNTAIN** received their name from George Bird Grinnell (1887). But their Blackfoot name recalls a warrior named *Iníkokaup*, Buffalo Painted Lodge, in reference to the tipi of a medicine man. The tipi is painted with two black buffalos, male and female, each with a mystical red life-line. (Cf. Schultz, 1926.) For a late summer flower garden along Cataract Creek, Morton Elrod gave the name Garden of Heaven.

CATHEDRAL* PEAKS: Descriptive. The name Calf Robe has also been used here but is now applied elsewhere. Sometimes Calf Robe is called in Blackfoot *Onistaiyi*, which may really mean Manito Robe, since words for "calf" and "spirit" are homonyms, and *-yi* is uncertain. It is not known to which of the two Calf Robes this name referred, if either. (See CALF ROBE, MEDICINE GRIZZLY.)

CATTLE QUEEN* CREEK is named for Libby (Elizabeth) Smith, later Mrs. Nat Collins, known as "the cowboys' mother" and "the Cattle Queen of Montana." She had a ranch near Choteau and worked mining claims at the top of the world with but little success. She acted as boss and cook of her outfit. A movie based (loosely) on her story starred Barbara Stanwyck and Ronald Reagan. One of her claims was the Wake Up Jeff. (See MONTEZUMA.)

According to her autobiography (for which I give no guarantees), she left Illinois at age ten and came west to Colorado. On the trip, she slapped the cheeky son of a tribal chief and received a pony from his father in compensation. In New Mexico she saw an Indian pueblo, mistakenly attributing it to Navajos. Her brother joined "Colonel" J. M. Chivington against the Indians. (This sounds like the appalling massacre of peaceful Cheyennes at Sand Creek in 1864.) She herself was captured by Indians who burned a young Mexican alive, but the chief who had given her the pony came to her rescue. (Can we believe all this?) She made trips to the Missouri and Yellowstone Rivers and at Helena married Nat Collins (1874). From her ranch at Choteau she and her brother Chan came to Belton and "Glacier Lake" (McDonald or Avalanche?) where, said she, "A glacier slowly slides down these surrounding cliffs" and melts in the lake, cooling the hot summers. But to escape the cold winters, she would go to California. So it appears that the first person known to find Sperry Glacier was not Sperry, but Libby.

Note also the strangely sexist practice of naming mountains only for men and lakes or perhaps creeks for women.

CEDAR CREEK: In 1902 ranger Frank Liebig built the first ranger station here. The Trail of the Cedars follows Avalanche Creek.

CEDED STRIP: This term refers roughly to what is now the eastern half of Glacier and adjacent fringes of the reservation and National Forest. This area was "ceded" by the Blackfeet tribe to the U.S. government by the Agreement of 1895–1896. Or was it? The term may be a misnomer since the land in question was ceded *conditionally*. It is ironic that it was also land assigned by the U.S. government to the Blackfeet by the Judith Treaty of 1855. Primal people usually regard land as communal property, and this attitude has caused endless misunderstanding by Euro-Americans and Europeans.

The three commissioners who arranged the Agreement of 1895–1896—Grinnell, Pollock, and Clements (especially Grinnell)—believed that the only way the Blackfeet could make a living off their bleak reservation was by raising stock. Therefore, they concluded, the government should keep the reservation as open range and never cut it up into allotments like pieces of pie. So in Article V of the Agreement they inserted a proviso that if the government ever allotted the reservation of its own accord the Agreement would be terminated. Though the government paid the price for this "ceded strip," it defaulted on the condition (probably under political pressure from stockmen who wanted the land) and began to allot the reservation about 1907 or 1908. So it would seem that in so doing without the consent of the tribe, the U.S. nullified or terminated the Agreement.

So insistent were the commissioners on this point that on December 14, 1895, all three reiterated their opposition to allotments in a letter to the Commissioner of Indian Affairs (who was not happy about it). They pointed out that they had inserted this proviso against allotment "upon the earnest request of the Indians" in order that the reservation be held "as a communal grazing tract."

One would suppose that the "ceded strip" should revert to the Blackfeet. But by 1899 the government had turned some of it into a Forest Reserve. The idea of making it part of a national park did not arise till later.

CERULEAN* LAKE, MOUNTAIN, and **RIDGE:** Descriptive for the lake. The Kootenai name is "Black Bear Hat": *Nupqu·kayuka*. (See BEARHAT.)

CHANEY* GLACIER is named for L. W. Chaney, a geologist from Minnesota who in 1895 was in Dr. Sperry's party exploring this glacier. According to Vaught, Chaney named several lakes: Emerald, Glacier, Center, Long, Summit, and Sue. The Blackfoot name for the glacier is that of the wife of Old Sun, *Siszáki* or "Little-Bird Woman," who is one of the persons for whom Bird Woman Falls may have been named.

CHAPMAN* PEAK is named for topographer Robert H. Chapman, acting superintendent of Glacier from May to November of 1912. A student of nature rather than an exploiter of nature, he does not appear to have been a favorite of the Hills and did not last long in office. He worked on survey crews and climbed peaks in the park including Carter, Kintla, Rainbow, and Vulture. The Blackfoot name for Chapman Peak honors Eli Guardipee. (See GUARDIPEE, CHIEF LODGEPOLE.)

CHEWING-BLACK-BONES CAMPGROUND is a tribal enterprise dedicated in 1977. It lies on Lower Saint Mary Lake within the reservation and was named for *Síkawhkika*, a Blackfeet elder. Chewing-Black-Bones was born in 1859 on Two Medicine River near the traditional Sun Dance site, and became a warrior and counselor to his people. Blind in his last years, he lived to the age of 104.

CHIEF LODGEPOLE PEAK is named after Francis X. Guardipee, for many years a park ranger and especially at Two Medicine. As the son of Eli Guardipee, he probably knew more of the lore of Glacier than anyone of his time. Frank claimed a relationship with Sacajawea, whose waterfall tumbles off the east face of Rising Wolf. Shortly after he was born on the reservation, his grandmother named him *Makski*, "Ugly Face," but his adult name was conferred on him by Two Guns, Bird Rattler, and other tribal leaders during a trip to a Shriners' convention in Atlanta in 1914. It was the name of his grandfather who was said to have killed the noted Assiniboine White Dog. Frank's name *Ako-inistámi* does not mean the person so called is a chief but rather refers to the chief or principal pole in the tipi on which the temple home depends. Frank was educated at Carlisle, drove a taxi in New York, acted in the movie "Covered Wagon," worked for the American Museum of Natural History, took great interest in the Boy Scouts, and traveled to Mexico and France.

CHIEF* MOUNTAIN: This is one of the few authentic or original Indian names in Glacier and Waterton Parks: *Nináistaki* or the archaic form *Nináistako*. It is the name of the mountain and also a personal and family name. (See MOUNTAIN CHIEF.) The Crees call this rock tower *Okimaw-wazi* which has the same meaning as the Blackfoot term. So too the Kootenai name, *Nasu'kin Akwekli'itá*. Bloods, Piegans, Crees, Salish, and probably other tribes regard this landmark as a shrine and traditional mecca for the vision quest. Many are those who come here to pray and often return. White tourists who approach this mountain should bear this fact in mind, especially as about half the mountain rests on reservation land. Chief Mountain is visible a hundred miles or more in three directions, considered to be the home of the Thunder Bird and the Wind Spirit. Long ago a Salish or Kootenai brave scaled this peak to find his vision, bringing up a buffalo skull for his sacred pillow. In 1892 Henry Stimson, then a young outdoorsman, did notice a decomposed skull on the summit. His party for this climb included Dr. Walter James and an Indian guide.

Chief Mountain is sometimes believed to have a twin on the Alberta side of the border, both of them isolated monarchs on the Lewis

Overthrust. This story could be a reference to Crowsnest Mountain. Others have seen it as one of a family group with a Squaw Mountain and a Papoose following behind the Chief on his march out into the prairie. Still others cite a legend that has circulated in Alberta: according to this story, Old Man or Napi wanted to prove his strength or cleverness to the Great Spirit and so tore pieces out of Chief and scattered them over the plains to the east forming the Sweetgrass Buttes. Such a story may have arisen because of the great avalanches that have broken loose from the Chief, several in 1993 (not unlike those that tore loose from Mount Cook in New Zealand in December of 1991).

In 1992 Glacier Country was jolted with earthquakes, none severe but all ominous. Two occurred in the area of Swan River and three near Glacier. On July 2, 1992, an earthquake centered south of Browning was rated 4.6 on the Richter scale or 4.2 at Saint Mary where it cracked a window at the entrance to the park. Milder quakes shook Hungry Horse and the North Fork. Soon afterwards a great block split off the north face of Chief Mountain, spreading havoc over five hundred acres. The land kept moving for some time, cracking and popping and uprooting trees. Both the Park Service and the Blackfeet tribe closed access. This slide recalled the last previous slide on the north face of the Chief in August 1972.

At any rate, Chief is a "focal mountain," that is, it has been used by Indians on a vision quest since prehistoric times. The quester climbs either the focal mountain itself or another from which he/she can get a clear view of the focal peak. Other focal mountains in the area include Heart Butte to the south and Mount Assiniboine in the north.

Chief Mountain was sighted December 31, 1792, a hundred years before Stimson's climb, by a surveyor for the Hudson's Bay Company named Peter Fidler. He collected data for maps issued 1795–96 by the British cartographer Aaron Arrowsmith, which show both Belly River and Chief Mountain here labeled the King. This was Fidler's translation of the Blackfeet name, adding that other Indians to the south called the landmark "the Governor of the Mountain(s)."

Other names for the peak include Tower Mountain, Kaiser Mountain, and The Altar. The name Kaiser may be for Lee Kaiser, a local bullwhacker, or perhaps because "Kaiser" (from Caesar) is another term for "king" or "chief." The name The Altar is descriptive; as seen from the Alberta side of the border it does resemble a huge table. This is the name used by the Governor General of Canada, the Marquis of Lorne, when he visited this area in 1881 and wrote a poem about Chief Mountain that well deserves to be called to the attention of other visitors. "The Tooth" is still another name, that began with Peter Fidler and was echoed by Kootenay Brown, but it is not clear which peak it designates. (See NINAKI.)

It was not until many years later that its relationship to the Lewis Overthrust was recognized by geologists. To someone standing out on the prairie, like Captain Lewis, the Rockies appear to form a great concave bow between Chief on the north and Heart Butte, *Móskizipáhpi-istaki*, or perhaps Spotted Eagle and the cluster of peaks on the south. Old-timers knew this feature as the Great Bend, which encompassed virtually all the eastern extension of Glacier National Park. No wonder then that the Lewis and Clark map shows both "The King" and "The Heart" in the "Rocky or Shining Mountains."

In 1845 Father DeSmet made a long trip up the western side of the Rockies (which probably resulted in the French map of 1846) via Lake Columbia and then across the Divide somewhere near Lake Louise en route to the Bow River. He was looking for the Blackfoot people and eventually turned south with a guide and a Cree Métis. How far south he came is a matter of dispute, though his map shows he stopped near the present border. Near the point where he turned back north, he recorded the "mountain of Quilloux." This was a landmark and may have been Chief Mountain by still another name. (See QUILLOUX.) In 1858, still another explorer sighted Chief Mountain. This was John Palliser of the British North American Expedition. Palliser and his guide Baptiste Gabriel paused before the Chief to marvel at the sunset beyond him. But Thomas Blakiston explored the area more closely.

The legend usually associated with Chief Mountain claims that a young chief, very fond of his wife and baby, was reluctant to leave them for the war trail. But leave he did—never to return. Mad with grief his wife eluded her guardians, scaled the heights of Chief Mountain and flung her baby and herself over the precipice. I must add that tossing oneself off cliffs seems to be a favorite climax to non-authentic native legends.

On his vice regal tour of 1881 the Marquis of Lorne was so impressed by Chief Mountain that he made a sketch of it and a poem, which he titled "On Chief Mountain, a Great Rock on the American North-West Frontier." Here it is:

Among white peaks a rock, hewn altar-wise,
Marks the long frontier of our mighty lands.
Apart its dark tremendous sculpture stands,
Too steep for snow, and square against the skies.
In other shape its buttressed masses rise.
When seen from north or south; but eastward set,
God carved it where two sovereignties are met,
An altar to His peace, before men's eyes.
Of old there Indian mystics, fasting, prayed;
And from its base to distant shores the streams
Take sands of gold to be at last inlaid
Where ocean's floor in shadowed splendour gleams.
So in our nations' sundered lives be blent
Love's golden memories from one proud descent!

Not the least remarkable thing about his poem is its foresight of the International Peace Park. (See *Who Was Who...* for more information.)

CHINOOK COUNTRY: In tourist promotional literature the southwestern cut of Alberta is called Chinook Country, stretching from the U.S. border to Calgary and Banff and bounded on the west by the Continental Divide. It of course includes Waterton Lakes National Park and numerous provincial parks and tourist meccas, probably more than in any other part of Alberta and the neighboring portion of Montana. The Great Bear Trail runs through it (See GREAT BEAR TRAIL). Among the many attractions, Head Smashed In Buffalo Jump is regarded as a World Heritage Site, and the heritage it preserves is largely that of the Blackfoot people. There is also a Dinosaur Provincial Park. The major city is Lethbridge. Crowsnest Pass is especially noted for a town partly buried under an avalanche called Frank Slide. Nearby are sulphur springs.

Chinook is the name of an Indian "tribe" at the mouth of the Columbia River. It is also the name of the language spoken by these people and a form of it much corrupted by English, French, and whatnot that became the Chinook Jargon spoken by traders, it is said, from California to Alaska. Chinook is also the name of the southwest winds that blew over Astoria, Oregon, and eventually much farther inland into Montana and Alberta. There are wet chinooks and dry chinooks, and they can melt the snow so fast you cannot believe it. So, often, a chinook means a thaw in the winter weather.

CHOUTEAU COUNTY is one of the original counties of Montana (1864). Encompassing the eastern slopes of Glacier, the county was named for the French Creole family that founded the city of Saint Louis and also the American Fur Company. The matriarch of the family was Marie-Therese, who kept slaves even after slavery was forbidden by the Spanish law of the Louisiana Territory, and generally made up her own rules in other matters too. Her son Pierre le Cadet was a charmer who also made his own rules even when they were forbidden by U.S. law. It was Pierre who built the fur trade of the Missouri till his reign passed to his more moderate son Charles.

Chouteau County has by now shrunk in size, but its county seat is still Fort Benton. In 1893 a portion of the county including eastern Glacier was broken off to form Teton County, which was split again to form Glacier County. The seat of Teton County is Choteau—the same old family name but in a new spelling.

CHRISTENSEN MEADOWS: Ernest and Theodore Christensen were subsistence farmers in this North Fork country.

CHURCH* BUTTE: Descriptive. The Kootenai name is Three Moons: *Kqaɫsa Natanik.*

CITADEL* MOUNTAIN looms over Upper Saint Mary Lake. It was named by Grinnell and Schultz (1885–7?). It has a large cirque in the middle of it so as to form a double mountain. The second peak is now called Heavy Runner, while the southwest side of the cirque is Two Guns. Coram Village was called Citadel in 1933. (See DUSTY STAR, WHITE CALF, HEAVY RUNNER, TWO GUNS.)

CITADEL* PEAKS near Waterton Park are called "the Needles" in Blackfoot: *Ataniáwxis.*

CLARKE RANGE: This is the Canadian name for the western range in both Glacier and Waterton Parks. (See LIVINGSTON.)

CLEMENTS, MOUNT, at the top of Logan Pass, is named for Walter M. Clements, who worked on the agreement with the Blackfeet to buy or lease the eastern half of the present park. Tourists may think of this peak as the Gorilla Head since guides often point out the resemblance. There is also a Clements Glacier (sometimes called Museum Glacier).

The Blackfoot name for this peak recalls a person of greater historical significance, Alexander Culbertson or Xixtaki-poka, "Beaver Child"

(1809–1879). King of the fur traders, he was only a clerk when he came up the Missouri in 1833 with Prince Maximilian. When a Cree-Assiniboine army attacked the Blackfeet camp at Fort McKenzie, Culbertson manned the fort gates trying to drag Blackfeet victims to safety within the walls. The Prince's artist Bodmer painted a masterful picture of this battle. Culbertson had the support of two Mexican hunters but both were killed. He took to wife Natawista of the Kaina aristocracy and began a life that was a rollicking good time one day and a trauma another. He gave help to scientists of the Smithsonian Institute, especially his own brother Thaddeus. He founded the adobe Fort Benton as the commercial and social focus of Montana, dedicating the fort with a Christmas ball in 1850. While Natawista presided as queen, he played the violin. They both helped Governor Stevens in 1853 and 1855. Later, they withdrew to their estate at Peoria, Illinois, and sent their children to private schools, but when their fortune collapsed in the Civil War, they returned to Montana. In the mounting hostilities that ensued, Culbertson tried in vain to keep the peace, and Natawista fled back to her own people. Their sons Jack and Joe were friends of Sitting Bull, and Joe became an Army scout and a friend also of Louis Hill.

CLEVELAND*, **MOUNT** and **CREEK:** This peak, the highest in Glacier, was named by Grinnell for President Cleveland in 1898 because Cleveland had established the Lewis and Clark Forest Reserve the year before. This reserve included modern Glacier. The mountain had previously been called Kaiser Peak by the U.S. Northern Boundary Survey of 1872–76, whether for someone in particular or as the title Kaiser, derived (like Czar) from Latin Caesar. Or perhaps the peak was named for a bull-whacker Lee Kaiser. (See Lee.) A well-known Shawnee guide and mountain man of western Montana was Ben Kiser, and persons of this family name appear in the 1900 Census for both the Blackfeet and Salish-Kootenai Reservations. Schultz assigns the name Napi to this peak after the trickster and demi-god of northern Indian traditions. (See Napi, Logging.) From the summit of Cleveland you can see the mighty spire of Mount Assiniboine on the Alberta-British Columbia border.

CLOUDCROFT* PEAKS: The old Anglo-Saxon word croft means a small hill or a tenant farm. Here the clouds appear to be the tenant. The Kootenai name is "Grizzly Mountain": *Kławła Akwukłi'it*.

CLOUDY RIDGE: A descriptive name of a ridge in Waterton Park.

CLYDE PEAK, 8,610 feet high, near Mount Logan, is named by climbers to honor Norman Clyde, a champion mountain-climber associated with the Sierra Club. He is credited with scaling thirty-eight peaks in Glacier plus others in the Sierra Nevada and elsewhere.

COAL* CREEK: There is—or was—some coal, not much, near the mouth of this creek. Its Kootenai name is "Bull Robe" or "Bullrobe." Abraham Bull Robe was an aide to ethnographer Turney-High and again to ethnographer Claude Schaeffer. A photo of him and his family appears in Turney-High's book. Bull Robe River is *Niɬsikɬa'maɬ Aknuxu'nuk.*

COBALT LAKE was named by R. T. Evans for its color.

COLUMBIA FALLS was established in 1890 or 1891 with the coming of the railroad. This area, perhaps a part of a reservation for the Kootenai Indians (though the question has never been legally clarified), was attracting attention for its coal deposits. A cable raft with a donkey engine brought samples from the upper North Fork to be transshipped at Flathead Lake. Probably in the interests of the Anaconda Company and/or other entrepreneurs in Butte, James A. Talbott tried to push a railroad line up the North Fork to the coal fields. He is said to have bought up land at the mouth of Bad Rock Canyon from a Kootenai lady named Mrs. La Fromboise at five or six thousand dollars. The transaction seems odd in view of the law against unauthorized contracts with Indian "wards of the government." Perhaps we could clarify the issue if we knew the identity of Mrs. La Fromboise. Persons of that name (which means "the raspberry") were quite numerous along the frontier. General Sully had a favorite scout Francois La Fromboise during the Great Sioux Uprising, and Francois, Michel, Thomas, and Joseph La Fromboise appear in the Oregon Country. Michel was probably the most noted because of his various trips from the Columbia down into California. Perhaps the Mrs. LaFromboise of Columbia Falls was the wife of one of these men or their sons. As Métis they would not be wards of the U.S. government and so free to buy or sell land. At any rate, Talbott represented a group of speculators in Butte calling themselves the Northern International Improvement Company of Columbia Falls, Montana. So at least by October 1893 the town already had that name. (Records Flathead County Courthouse, warranty deed 626.) They are said to have assumed that this place would become a division point on the railway. Jim Hill refused to pay such prices for the land and moved the division point to Kalispell first, then to Whitefish, with the much-reported remark "Here

Columbia falls!" However, a more likely story is that the original name of the town was just Columbia, said to have been suggested by the postmaster's wife, Margaret Kennedy, because the town was near some of the headwaters of the Columbia River. The river of course was named for the ship, though it had earlier Spanish names already on maps, for example San Roque. (See CHANEY.)

COMEAU PASS is named for Denis Comeau, a French Canadian from Nova Scotia and a favorite guide of Dr. Sperry. He settled near Lake McDonald about 1892 and had a mining interest near the South Fork in 1899. About 1906 he returned to Canada but remained in contact by mail with his daughter who stayed in the Lake McDonald country. He died in British Columbia. Sperry attached his name to a peak and also to "Comeau's Horn." (See GUNSIGHT, LITTLE MATTERHORN.)

CONTINENTAL* CREEK is close to the Continental Divide.

COONSA* CREEK: The Glacier map spells this name with a *c* while almost every other source spells it with *k*. The Salish or Kootenai Indian by this name is mentioned in a number of original sources: Peter Ronan's tribal census reports for 1886, 1887, and 1888; General William Carey Brown(e)'s account of John Stevens' reconnaissance of Marias Pass in 1889; Stevens' own accounts (which omit the name); Deputy Dan Mumbrue's manuscript; Frank Linderman's Montana Adventure; and newspapers like the Missoulian.

The mystery is that all these accounts evidently deal with the same person yet each one represents him differently: as a criminal, as a witness for the law, as a trustworthy partner, a champion, a victim. Which was he?

His story runs something like this: Koonsa, whose Salish name was *Kwil-spu'ús* or "Red Heart," is an orphan, but by the time we meet him, he is in his early thirties. He has a predilection for the color red that appears even in his name. With his Grecian physique, he aspires to be a ladies' man and perhaps has killed a man over one of the ladies. So he takes refuge across the mountains with the Blackfeet. When he returns to the Flathead country, he becomes Linderman's trapping partner and likes to ride about with a red blanket, a breechclout and moccasins on a white charger. Challenged to a wrestling bout on the lake shore near Polson, he drops his red blanket and cleans up the beach with Cock-Eyed Kelly, winning enough cash for a celebration. But he is stabbed and is nursed back to health by Linderman—only to be mysteriously murdered. Now, according to propagandists for

Great Northern, at some time during this sequence he becomes the companion of John Stevens in the trek into Marias Pass with whiskey and a red blanket as a reward. Besides the detail of plying an Indian with liquor, there are other problems with the Great Northern's story. I give you the worst one: The trek into the pass takes place on the 10th and 11th of December, 1889, by which date Koonsa had already been dead over a year. *The Missoulian* for September 19, 1888 and the *Helena Weekly Independent* for the day following have articles on how he was murdered. No wonder Stevens complained that he was not very cooperative.

COPPER CREEK: This seems to have been confused with Valentine Creek when Dutch Louie prospected here as early as 1885 or 1889. Louie was a mining partner of Joe Kipp and had interests with Charles Aubrey in the North Star, Ibex, Minerva, Summit, Marmot, Wolverine, and Badger mines (1892), all near the head of Belly River but on the west side of the Divide. There is also a Coppermine Creek in Waterton Lakes Park.

COSLEY* LAKE, CAVE, and **RIDGE:** This name was formerly spelled Crossley, which is still the name on the benchmark. The ridge is also called Bear Tooth Mountain, and the peak called Pyramid by Joe Cosley himself may be the present Pyramid Peak or another one on Cosley Ridge.

Joseph Clarence Cosley (1870–1944) was a trapper, ranger, guide, last of the hippy mountain men, and apparently the one figure in the history of the Waterton/Glacier country who attracts the most popular appeal. Born perhaps on a fishing boat in Lake Huron, he was one of a dozen children, educated largely in convents. Their mother was of Indian and Spanish descent. When their father, a Frenchman (Métis?), was drowned, young Joe took off for Arizona, wandered about the West, and turned to cow punching in Montana. He is alleged to have got himself into a duel on horseback with a Sioux warrior and carried the scar over his right eye. He and Dutch Louie Meyer probably accompanied Lieutenant Ahern and about 1900 became a ranger at Belton for the Forest Service. With a yen to be a romantic poet, he was more expert at trick riding, sharp-shooting, and botany, and wrote verse and short stories. Charming and courteous, he won friends among the ranchers and settlers: the Howes of Lake McDonald, the Henkels of Babb, the Browns of Waterton, and was delighted by the cooking of Blue Lightning. He named lakes in Glacier after his lady friends and carved arrows through hearts on a trail of trees. His loss of two horses that slipped off Ahern Pass dealt him a severe shock. Tall and good-looking, he sported mustachios and a goatee, a red voyageur's sash and earrings, and the fanciest clothes his trapper's skins would buy. His long flowing hair earned him his Indian name (which seems undecipherable). Quite a Beau Brummell but forever a bachelor!

One of the original rangers of Glacier, Cosley was also one of its first poachers, but merely one of many. In those days the U.S. Government itself was poaching and wolfing.

In World War I, he was with the Canadian Mounted Rifles in England and France, where he gained his reputation as a sharp-shooter. He also acted as a guardian for a young soldier named John Orville Bates, later a resident of West Glacier who provided recollections for this writer among others.

He came home via Michigan to visit his mother and returned to Belly River but not to his old job of ranger. When he was no longer the young tiger, he was tracked down and arrested by Ranger Joe Heimes, tried, fined, and released at Belton. Crossing on snowshoes via Ahern Pass, he fled to Canada. After recuperating in a hospital at Edmonton in the care of his niece, he retreated to a lonely cabin near Isle a la Crosse (which he thought had a curse on it) and died of scurvy. There the Mounties found him. (See *Who Was Who...* for more information.)

COTTONWOOD CREEK in Waterton is named for the trees on its banks.

CRACKER* LAKE, FLATS, and **MINE:** The lake was once called Blue Lake, but in 1897 two prospectors ate a lunch there of crackers and cheese. Or at least, such is the tale, but the mine was sometimes called the Cracker Jack Mine. The Blue Lake and Snowshoe lodes were patented in 1905. Schultz's name for the lake is Patáki (Carrier Woman), his mother-in-law and (says he) a woman of great kindness. Though her name derives from the root for "to carry," it also means "a potato" and that was how she was listed in the census reports.

CRANDELL LAKE and **MOUNTAIN** in Waterton Lakes Park are named for E. H. Crandell, an oil man lured by the seepage on Cameron Creek. The lake has also been known as Blue Lake and the mountain or part of it as Bear Mountain, Black Bear Mountain, and Bears Hump.

CRAZY GRAY HORSE MOUNTAIN: See Ptarmigan, Olson, Cracker, ALLEN.

CROOKED CREEK: Descriptive for a creek in Waterton Lakes Park.

CROWFEET MOUNTAIN is near Mount Altyn, which Schultz listed by the name of Crowfoot. But Dr. Ruhle saved the name from oblivion by transferring it to this neighboring mountain, though in pluralized form. The original name, *Isapo-Omahxi-Ka*, "Big Foot of a Crow Indian," does not distinguish singular from plural. (See CROWFOOT.)

CROWFOOT (c.1830–1890) Most famous of all the Blackfoot Confederation that we have any record of is Crowfoot or *Isapo-omahxika*. Though he was evidently related to both Red Crow and Natawista, his immediate origins among the Kaina or Bloods were humble. His father was killed in war when he was very young and his mother was left a poor widow with himself and a younger brother to raise as best she could. When he was five years old, a warrior of the Sixika or (North) Blackfoot branch of the confederation came to visit the Kaina and took his mother back with him as his wife. Baby Crowfoot (then called Shot Close) was supposed to stay behind, but he toddled along after his mother, unbidden but not rejected. In later days he is supposed to have been named Bear's Ghost. (If that was *Kyaiyo-sta'aw* as I think it may have been, it was not a very pleasant label to carry through life.) One story among the Sixika is that he took the name Crowfoot because he bravely walked up and touched the tipi of an enemy chief and left footprints in the ground. Another story, perhaps more reliable, has him acquiring the name from a warrior who was making a peace visit to the Shoshoni but was slain during the trip. At any rate, it means the Big Foot of a Crow Indian (not the raven which is *maisto-wa.*) Probably bearing this name, he went warring down into Montana, was shot two or three times and was blacklisted by the U.S. Army. But he cherished a dream of becoming the *manístokos* or guardian of all his people, Sixika, Kaina, and Pikani.

Never a great warrior, he was more of a peace chief with a self-contradictory crosscurrent in his make-up, famed for wisdom and restraint and a fiery temper, yet a statesman of one loyalty—to his own people.

Although not a teetotaler himself, he was quick to recognize the tragic results of the whiskey trade. In 1874 he welcomed the arrival of the Mounted Police, determined as they were to put a halt to the bootlegging and smuggling from Fort Benton. His relations with Colonel MacLeod of the Mounties and especially with Cecil Denny were cordial as were his contacts with the missionaries John MacDougall and Father Albert Lacombe and even with the eccentric ex-seminarian Jean L'Heureux. But he did resent the Mounties' policy of "divide and rule," which divided the Blackfoot confederacy and blocked the rise of any *manístokos*. When Treaty Seven was negotiated in 1877 in order to corral the Indians into reserves, Crowfoot insisted that the council be held on the Blackfoot Crossing of the Bow River. In that traditional site around five thousand Indians gathered with the mounted police, tribesmen from the Kaina, Sixika, and Pikani, and from the Stonies and the Sarcees as well. With the buffalo and other big game vanishing, what hope remained for the native people but Treaty Seven? Crowfoot had his doubts. But he "signed" the treaty in his own way, that is, by not touching the pen, he avoided transferring his *manitu* to the paper. Instead he gestured and added "I trust the Great Spirit...." And according to Ben Calf Robe (in his book *Siksiká*), Crowfoot did become the head chief who could say, "All the people are my children," as the *manístokos* was supposed to do. But it was only for that one occasion: the signing of the Treaty Seven, which became a prelude to disaster.

Though he had ten wives, none of Crowfoot's children was adequate to become his heir in the chieftainship, handicapped one way or another, except one boy, the chosen of his father. But alas, in 1873 this youth of promise had been out on the war trail and was slain by Crees. In his despair, Crowfoot led a counterattack that killed a Cree.

So what became of his chances for a successor? There are at least two stories or theories. One is that the Kaina captured some Cree women, and Crowfoot took one as his wife. In time, when she was pregnant by him, her people stole her back and the son of Crowfoot was born and brought up among the Crees.

A more complicated story claims that the mother of Crowfoot's son who had been slain in 1873 had a half-sister, a Cree Métisse, who had a son by a Stoney father. She was also the sister of Big Child, a chief of the Crees in the Eagle Hills. One day, when Crowfoot went spying on Crees, he came upon this boy. Not only was this lad now an orphan, but he so closely resembled Crowfoot's lost son, that the chief resolved to adopt him. In any case, whether in accord with one of these theories or some other, a constant that runs through the theories is that the young lad looked much like the dead son reincarnated. So under Crowfoot's tutelage, the young Cree or half-Cree grew up to become the tall and handsome Poundmaker, *Pitukwahanapiwiyin* or *Pito-kanow-apikin* or even *Opeteka Hanawaywin.*

Such was his Cree name, referring to the impounding or corralling of the buffalo. The Blackfeet, however, called the young chief Wolf Shins or *Mahkuyi-kohkin.* The symbol of his charisma was not so much his name but rather his magnificent long black hair.

It is not possible to tell the story of either Crowfoot or Poundmaker without reference to them both. And both were in a sense peace chiefs, not war chiefs. Officials in the governments of both the U.S. and Canada have had trouble understanding this distinction. In times of emergency the peace chief could be superceded (not deposed) by the war chief or even by tribal "soldiers" or police. A leading "soldier" of the Crees was Wandering Spirit, and it was a fatal mistake for officials to ignore him. He caused much misery in the story of Crowfoot and Poundmaker.

Though on the Indian calendar or Winter Count the year 1875 was The Year When the Whiskey Was Stopped, 1879 was The Year When First There Were No More Buffalo. That spelled utter disaster to tribes on both sides of the Medicine Line. When Poundmaker became a Cree chief (about 1878) the prairie ecosystems had been shattered irreparably and the buffalo and other wild game were on the wane on the Canadian prairies. Crowfoot and his son or foster son faced the problem of governing hungry and desperate people.

When the Sioux under Sitting Bull fled into Saskatchewan after Custer's defeat, Sitting Bull urged Crowfoot to join him. But Crowfoot knew better that to entangle his people into more trouble. Instead, joined by Jean L'Heureux and the Cree chief Big Bear he followed the retreating buffalo herds south into the Judith River country of Montana. Louis Riel with his Métis followers and maybe some of Sitting Bull's Sioux slipped over the border and down to the Judith also. There they traded at a fly-by-night post set up by Joe Kipp, J. W. Schultz, and Eli Guardapee, who employed Louis Riel as their agent. But as the game ran out, the hunts ended in famine. Soldiers came to chase the Piegans back to their reservation, and Crowfoot had to lead his hungry, hopeless people back into their homeland.

In 1881 Poundmaker was called upon to guide the Marquis of Lorne on the first-ever vice regal tour of western Canada. Entertaining the Queen's son-in-law by campfire tales, Poundmaker brought the vice regal party to a great council with Crowfoot. Hundreds gathered, but Crowfoot appeared in his shabbiest clothes to impress Lord Lorne with the poverty of his people. From Chief Mountain, Lorne with an escort of Mounties skirted the present Waterton and Glaciers to the Old Agency. U.S. soldiers brought him down to Fort Shaw and on to the railway. Lord Lorne had been well impressed by Crowfoot and his people and gave orders at Ottawa that the famine among the western tribes and the Métis must be relieved. The officials in Ottawa chose to disregard orders from the Queen's viceroy. But Lord Lorne crossed words if not swords with the U.S. Secretary of State over the American attempts to harass the Indian refugees in Canada.

In 1883 the Canadian Pacific was violating the Sixika reserve with its tracks and its "poisonous" fumes, and young warriors were itching for a fight. Crowfoot might have turned them loose had not Father Lacombe persuaded the government to compensate the Blackfoot for the damage the railway had done.

When Louis Riel led some Crees into the 1885 revolt against the administration in Ottawa, Crowfoot refused to join it, but Poundmaker joined it reluctantly. On the one hand he opposed the attempt of the Mounties to interrupt the sacred Thirst Dance in order to make an arrest. On the other, he openly regretted the atrocities committed by Wandering Spirit and his followers at Frog Lake. But when Colonel Otter and his militia attacked his camp at Cut Knife Hill, Poundmaker outsmarted the Colonel but, as victor, had the grace to let vanquished militiamen escape alive. Crowfoot compromised by opening his camp as a sanctuary for Cree and Métis refugees and even sent runners to bid the Kaina and the Piegans to do the same.

When Louis Riel surrendered to trial (and ultimately the noose), Poundmaker and the other peace chief, Big Bear, surrendered to the arrogant General Frederick Middleton.

Arrogant indeed! At a big council a Cree woman arose to speak. Middleton told her, "We do not listen to women."

"Then what about the Queen?" demanded the Crees.

"She," declared Middleton, "has men to tell her what to do."

In spite of the testimony given in his behalf by Father Cochin, a witness at the battle of Cut Knife, Poundmaker was thrown into prison. Since prison to him as to many natives was the cruelest punishment, he asked to be hanged instead. His plea was denied but his long black hair was not cut off. At the intercession of Father Lacombe among others, he was released early and went west with his family to join Crowfoot. Troubled by an old gunshot wound and a musket ball that was still in his body, and broken in spirit as well, Poundmaker reached Crowfoot but soon collapsed in death.

In an effort at conciliation Father Lacombe escorted Crowfoot, L'Heureux, and Red Crow on an official visit to Ottawa and Quebec.

In 1887–88 the aging Crowfoot took treatment at the U.S. hospital at Old Agency, Montana, and made visits to Bloods, Piegans, Gros Ventres, and Assiniboines, urging peaceful co-existence. Sometimes he was greeted with hostility or even the chiefs' lash. So he had no successor to his chieftainship from among his own offspring and nevermore would there be a *manístokos*.

As he lay dying Crowfoot said (prompted by L'Heureux?) "What is life? It is the flash of a firefly in the night. It is the breath of a buffalo in the winter. It is the little shadow that runs across the grass and gets lost in the sunset." (See *Who Was Who...* for more information.)

CROWN OF THE CONTINENT: This name seems to have originated with Grinnell around 1900. Whether Grinnell got the concept from the Triple Divide or (as I suspect) from Mount Jackson and Blackfoot Glacier, or even whether the name was an attempt to honor the Blackfeet tribe, is a moot question.

A similar concept, however, had occurred in 1858 to Lt. Thomas Blakiston when he crossed what he called "Kooteany Pass" and regarded it as "the culminating point of North America" because it was near the headwaters of the rivers Missouri, Columbia, Saskatchewan, and MacKenzie. It is hardly necessary to add that both concepts completely disregard the triple divides in Banff and Yellowstone, the various divides in Alaska and Mexico, etc. Perhaps these names make better poetry than geography.

CROWSNEST PASS and **MOUNTAIN** lie between Waterton and Banff. Some suggest that the mountain is the twin of Chief Mountain and also a sacred peak. However, the mountain called Crowsnest by the Indians may be a peak about eighteen miles east of the one which now carries the name. The Blackfoot term for "crow's nest" is *maistó-uís*, of which the final element seems to derive from the word *owa* (egg), coincidentally very like the root in Latin. The Cree name is *Kakakíw-wuchistun*, and the first term is onomatopoetic.

CRYPT LAKE and **PALE** are in Waterton Lakes Park, though the lake reaches the border. The name is a Greek word for "hidden," usually applied to a burial area under a church.

CRYSTAL FALLS, FORD, and **POINT:** The crystals at the Point are pyrite: fool's gold or iron disulfide. It is halfway on the Logan Pass Road between West Glacier and Saint Mary. For the falls, see BEAVER MEDICINE. There is a Crystal Creek southwest of Glacier (see AKAMINA) and another just south of the park where an old Chinese oven is reported. It is or was near the railroad with some mysterious circular masonry walls (see STANTON).

CUBA LIBRE MINE: a quartz mine located in the Swiftcurrent or Many Glacier area, probably named during the war fever of 1898, the name means "Free Cuba." Other local Spanish mining names: California, Mexico, Caltana, San Jos, Santa Rosa, and El Cid.

CUMMINGS CREEK and **MEADOW** were named for an early settler or his family.

CURLY BEAR MOUNTAIN: Curly Bear, *Yokih-kyáiyo* or *Kyáiyo-xusi*, was a noted warrior and a walking treasury of tribal lore as well as owner of the Beaver Medicine. He was one of the Blackfeet who worked with J. W. Schultz in the project on park place names. His own name was applied by Schultz to Hudson Glacier but was suggested for the mountain that now bears it by H. A. Noble in 1928. (See AKAIYAN, HUDSON, KOOTENAI, RED CROW, YELLOW, KUPUNKAMINT.)

CUSTER MOUNT is probably not named for General Custer, who had nothing to do with Glacier. But even Schultz uses the translation of the General's Indian name, "Long Hair," *Inúspi*, which was also the name of Kootenai Brown and is now applied to a campground in Waterton Lakes Park in honor of Brown, not Custer. The most probable explanation for the presence of the name is that this mountain was named for Henry Custer, a topographer who worked in this part of the present park about 1860 or 1861 with the U.S. Northwestern Boundary Survey.

CUT BANK CREEK and **PASS:** The Blackfeet term is *Ponákixi*, of which the English is a translation. This pass was a favorite route across the Rockies and was also called the Upper Marias Pass and Flathead Pass (depending, I suppose, on which way you were heading). The Salish and Kootenais from the West climbed the pass via Nyack Creek. The mouth of Cut Bank Creek was named *Inóhpisi* (Dangle Down), to describe the way some Gros Ventres let themselves down over a cliff with ropes and caught the Piegan camp unawares (*in-* = down; -*ohpi* = dangle, fall). Dr. Ruhle located Red Blanket Butte on Cut Bank Ridge, named for Red Blanket, *Mahk-áipiszi*, who was laid to rest here in a tree burial. Chief White Calf was also buried here.

DANCING LADY MOUNTAIN: This peak looms behind the big hotel at East Glacier. The big rock on its east slope with smaller rocks below it reminded someone of a woman climbing the mountain followed by her dogs. This illusion may have been the reason the mountain was once named Squaw Mountain. But the name has recently been changed in agreement with Blackfeet tribal officials. Though the word "squaw" derives from an Algonquian root *squas* in the Massachusetts dialect, it has become in English usage a racist and sexist pejorative.

The summer powwows and Sun Lodge ceremonies feature sacred dancing, and the name Dancing Lady is based on information from Donald Little Dog and Joe Eagle Child. Schultz reports that the mountain used to be called *Íkaki* (Small Lady), after the mother of Curly Bear. She was regarded as a visionary and a participant in the summer rites.

DARDANELLES: The Bosporus and Dardanelles of Waterton Lakes parallel in miniature the features of those names in Turkey.

DAWN MIST* FALLS is also called Morning Mist and Morning Dew. The Blackfoot name is Little Falls: *Kinuk-Ohtokui*. Dawn Mist is the name of the fictitious heroine of the novel *The White Quiver*, by Montana historian Helen Fitzgerald Sanders and copyrighted in 1913. As the author assures us, it is a work of fiction but does attempt to portray life among the Blackfoot people realistically (?) as it was before white contact, with factual descriptions derived from informants Helen and Horace Clarke, Oliver and Richard Sandoval (Sanderville), and others. Louis Hill provided photos posed by tribal members, so probably the book was a part of his project to attract public attention to the new national park.

So the story may be pure fiction, but Dan Whetstone, for many years editor of the *Pioneer Press* of Cut Bank, has just as good a story coupled with both the novel and Louise Hill's project, and whether more or less fictitious, who knows?

About 1910, shortly after Dan has set himself up in a printing office in Cut Bank, Nick the cook discovers the body of an Indian girl in a snowdrift, lovely but apparently lifeless. When Nick and Dan carry her inside, she begins to show signs of life. So Nick sets off for the

Cree camp on Cut Bank Creek, while Dan attends to the girl, keeping her under some restraint so that she does not bolt in panic. Two Crees arrive and identify her as Lizzie White Beaver of the Rocky Boy band (which, by the way, was historically a Chippewa band, not Cree). The Crees take Lizzie home.

Not long afterwards, a young Cree from Cypress Hills named Mike Crazy Colt appears with his fiddle. Mike and Lizzie are married. Come summertime with the Fourth of July at the Blackfoot powwow at Browning, Mike and Lizzie are there and Mike's fiddle probably adds melody to the merriment. Another at hand is "Hoaxer" Smith, a tourism promoter for the Great Northern. With help from a taxidermist in Whitefish and the hide of a muskrat, Hoaxer concocts the monstrosity of "the fur-bearing trout of Iceberg Lake." When his eye fall on Lizzie he sees his career sealed in triumph. He declares Lizzie to be none other than Dawn Mist herself, daughter of Chief Going-to-the-Sun. And he packs Lizzie, Mike and the fiddle off on the railroad to tour the great cities of the land.

"Hoaxer's" name is suspiciously like that of a government official of that day, and in fact there probably were other Indian girls who posed as Dawn Mist for GN adds. (See WHITE QUIVER.)

DAWSON* PASS was named by surveyor Evans for Thomas Dawson, son of Andrew Dawson and his Gros Ventre wife Pipe Woman. Andrew was a Scotsman who succeeded to the management of the Upper Missouri fur trade on the retirement of Culbertson. Thomas was born in the adobe Fort Benton but at age five was whisked off to school in Edinburgh, Scotland, and later in Liverpool, England. As a young man he wandered to New York and Winnipeg. During the "Riel Rebellion," he served as a scout for the Royal Northwest Mounties. Then he became a partner of Joe Kipp in a store at Old Agency, Montana. At Saint Peters Mission he married Isabel, a daughter of Malcolm Clarke. He was a guide in Glacier for Jim and Louis Hill, the Baring brothers, Dr. Sperry, and Henry Stimson, and also an interpreter for Mary Roberts Rinehart in 1916. There was a Mount Dawson in the vicinity of the Dawson Pass, but the name on the mountain has disappeared from the map. When he sat for a portrait by Winold Reiss, he donned a coon-skin cap for the first time, and at least looked the part of a mountain man. His Blackfoot name was "Little Chief," *Inuxina*, and the pass is *Inuxina ozitasmisohpi*.

DEAD HORSE POINT on Upper Saint Mary Lake. A Bar X 6 horse was lost there. *Bar X 6* is the name of the ranch that used to be operated by the Park Saddle Horse Company.

DEADWOOD FALLS: Probably descriptive. (See DEBRIS.)

DEBRIS* CREEK: The forest fires of 1910 and others left unsightly debris. The Kootenai name is "Sacred Rock," a woman's name: *Kauknam Nu'kiy.*

DEER LODGE COUNTY is one of the original counties of Montana (1864) and once included a huge chunk of what is now Glacier. Later it was subdivided into portions of Missoula and Chouteau Counties. The name Deer Lodge is probably of Shoshoni origin, referring to the hot springs and deer lick that became known in French as *La Loge aux Chevreuils*. The *chevreuil* is the white-tail or roe deer. The Shoshoni term, reconstructed, would be *Teheya-kahni* (deer house or lodge). The area was settled by Hispanic and French-Canadian pioneers with their Indian wives, and their settlement was alternately called Spanish Fork, Cottonwood, Labarge City, and finally Deer Lodge. The name LaBarge honored the Missouri steamboat captain, Joseph la Barge.

DEL ORO LODE: Four claims near Stanton Creek. The name means "of the gold" in Spanish.

DEMERS RIDGE, just west of Glacier, was probably named for Telesphore Jacques DeMers, who was commonly called "Jack." Born near Montreal in 1834 or 1835, he grew up with a longing to go west, perhaps inspired by his uncle Modeste DeMers, a priest in the Oregon Country. So eventually he went to San Francisco, then up to Forte Colville, Washington. In 1857 he married a Métisse, Clara or Claire Rivet, daughter of Antoine Rivet and *Xixitelixken* of the Kalispel or Pend d'Oreille tribe. Clara's grandfather is said to have been a veteran of the Lewis and Clark expedition, while Clara's brother Michel was the well-known interpreter for Peter Ronan of the Flathead agency. The DeMers moved to Frenchtown, Montana, from which point Jack ran pack trains into Idaho and the Wild Horse mines in British Columbia. Jack's brother Amable came west and joined Jack in business at Frenchtown, and another brother Alexandre took up trade at Sainte Ignatius. Jack's son, Telesphore Gar on DeMers lived at Camas Hot Springs and left his name on nearby Gar on Ridge. Elzeor Demers, nicknamed Ed, is reported to have driven a herd up from Frenchtown in 1888 with Ovide Peltier and Frank Desrosiers. Elzeor's father was

Alexandre Demers who ranged over most of the West. (Cuffe, pp. 107–8). By 1878 Frenchtown was still quite French but also a-bustle with Indians of the surrounding tribes, Germans, Irish, Spaniards, African-Americans, and Chinese. (Carle O'Neil p. 26)

After Clara died in 1879, Jack remarried, to a teacher, Leonie Garnot, and set out on a honeymoon in Quebec. Returning, Jack and Leonie started a second family. Among their guests in Montana were the famous churchmen, Father Ravalli and Archbishop Seghers. Jack's pack-trains traced the route of the later Fort Steele Road up through the Flathead Valley and the Stillwater River to the Tobacco Plains, and perhaps to strengthen this trade Jack established Demersville about 1887 at the head of navigation on the Flathead River. Perhaps it was just as well that Jack did not live to see what would happen to his new town. He died at Butte in 1889.

DEMERSVILLE stood on the southern outskirts of what is now Kalispell. On the death of Jack DeMers, the reins of power fell into the reckless hands of his handsome son-in-law John Clifford. In Demersville, incorporated in 1891, the social center was the "Cliff House," named for Clifford. In fact, Clifford came close to renaming Demersville after himself. His fondness for celebration began innocently enough with champagne but ended in general drunks—which no doubt added to Clifford's popularity. When the railroad came through, Clifford expected it to pass via Demersville and perhaps to protect the railroad, troops were summoned to Demersville from Fort Missoula. This was a company of the 25th Infantry of African-Americans troopers, commanded by white officers. One of the lieutenants was James Ord, nephew of General Edward Ord and probably great-grandson of the King George IV of England.

But the railroad did not reach Demersville. Jim Hill swung it a few miles north, started the town of Kalispell and doomed Demersville. And, the daughter of Jack and Clara divorced Clifford on the grounds of physical abuse.

DESPAIR*, MOUNT, was named by R. T. Evans (with his usual flair for dramatic names) because he had to climb the mountain four or five times in the smoke of the forest fires. The Kootenai name is "Bear Dog" or "Grizzly Dog Mountain": *Kławła Xałćin Akwukłi'it.*

DEVIL'S ELBOW: A narrow piece of trail at the diorite sill near Swiftcurrent Pass where a number of horses have been lost.

DIAMOND FALLS: See Beaver Chief.

DIVIDE* CREEK and **MOUNTAIN**, near Saint Mary junction, were probably named by Schultz about 1883 with reference to the Hudson Bay Divide. There used to be popular confusion about the location of the international line through this area. Some thought it coincided with the Hudson Bay Divide and put all the headwaters of the Saskatchewan into Canada, and whiskey runners took advantage of that theory, which of course is wrong.

DIXON* GLACIER is named for Senator Joseph M. Dixon, who helped push the bill for establishing Glacier National Park. Dixon and Carter, both Republicans, worked on this issue. On New Year's Day, 1921, Dixon became the sixth governor of Montana; he is noted for his honorable service. The Blackfoot name is "Gros Ventre Ice": *Azina Kokutoi.* (See Carter, Ahern.)

DOODY*, MOUNT: The Kootenai name is "Bull Feather": *Niḱsik Aquḱł -upqa Akwuḱłi-it.* But Dan Doody was a trapper and prospector in the Nyack area who later became one of the first rangers. He seems to have been popular with everyone from Kootenay Brown in the north to the railroad people in the south and famous for his handlebar mustache. In McCartyville near Marias Pass, he fixed his eye on a dance hall girl named Josephine Gaines who reportedly was wanted by the law in Colorado. She had come west from Georgia in a wagon train and in Colorado had bought opium from the Chinese. After shooting a man in Pueblo, perhaps in self-defense, she had found it convenient to keep a few steps ahead of the law. She may have met Dan in Colorado. Short and feisty, she showed her mettle in McCartyville by demanding at rifle point that the railway boss get the infirmary cleaned up.

Well, Dan wanted that sort of woman and riding into McCartyville, strapped Josephine onto a mule, carried her off to his cabin, and locked her up. At least that's the story, and it adds that she got desperate for her opium.

But she calmed down and grew used to Dan and his Airedales. Dan provided her with a small secret cabin on a cliff near Nyack over the Middle Fork to which she could flee if the law came around. (I hear talk that the cabin is still there.)

Life was lonely, but soon people came for Dan to guide them and

Josephine to feed them. Jim Hill himself got injured on a hunting trip, so the story goes, and had to be crossed over the river by Dan and then put onto one of his own trains. Supposedly, Jim Hill directed the trains to stop at Doody Siding in case the Doodys needed a lift. (One has to wonder if this story refers to Louis Hill rather than to his father. Louis is reported to have brought his children to stay at the Doodys' 160-acre cattle ranch.)

The Doodys had three stills on their ranch, and their booze became so popular that railway men would stop trains at Doody Siding and blow the whistle to number the quarts they wanted. Josephine would row her merchandise across to the siding and sometimes have the railway men to dinner.

Dan did not remain a park ranger long. He was more interested in his mine and poaching and even led poaching expeditions into the park. Cougars were a favorite prey for the Airedales.

Josephine is still recalled around the village of Nyack for her spirited cussing and her huge earrings with gold nuggets. Her huckleberry pies drowned in fresh whipped cream lured people from Belton to jump onto their little handcars and pump their way up to Nyack.

But Dan had heart trouble and died suddenly in 1921. Josephine lived on for another ten years, then moved across the river to Deerlick Creek, where she kept house for 3 or 4 dozens of cats and cooked them beans. After a car accident, she died of pneumonia in January 1936 in a hospital at Kalispell. She was buried in the Conrad Cemetery—without the gold nuggets in her earrings. (Cf. John Frayley.)

DOUBLE* MOUNTAIN was named by Evans. The Kootenai name is *Kupumqamik*, which has now been transferred and misspelled to another mountain still called *Kupunkamint*, said to mean "He Shakes Himself".

DRAGON TAIL, near Comeau Pass, is a ridge or spur to the southwest of Mount Reynolds. The curious thing about dragons, which are not numerous among the fauna of Glacier or Waterton, is that in European tradition they represent chaos, whereas in Eastern thought they symbolize the power that brings order out of chaos.

DRY* FORK may be identical with Spring Creek.

DUCK LAKE lies on the Hudson Bay Divide within the Blackfeet Reservation. The Blackfoot name for duck is "red feet": *mexikázi*. Schultz says he named the lake, but Vaught regards it as a local popular name. An old name on record is Helen's Lake. Bear Head called Duck Lake "the Lake of the Drumming" because a water sprite comes out and drums on the shore. Its water could flow into the Saskatchewan or the Missouri.

DUNGARVAN PEAK and **CREEK** in Waterton Lakes Park has a Gaelic name supposed to mean "rugged mountain" after a place in Ireland. Dungarvan Creek was once called Pine Creek.

DUNWOODY* BASIN and **PARK**: No explanation for the name is known. The Kootenai name is "Coyote Basin": *SkinkuɛAkikqɬaɬa'mi.*

DUTCH* CREEK, LAKE, POND, and **RIDGE** are named for "Dutch Louie" Meyer, one of the earliest known prospectors in Glacier. However, there were other men in the area who may possibly be the person here alluded to: John Elsner, Fritz Schultz, Frank Geduhn, Frank Herrig, Frank Liebig, Joe Henkel, and Black Jack Reuter. The term "Dutch" is an anglicization of the German *Deutsch*. (But Fred Herrig was an Alsatian and considered himself French.) "Dutch Louie" had his surname spelled different ways, but the form used here is the one accepted by the Montana Historical Society (Spring, 1976). He had been a partner of Pike Landusky back in the Little Rockies of eastern Montana, when that country was the hangout of some pretty desperate characters. Some of them became the "Curry Gang." Dutch, Pike, and Frank Aldrich re-discovered gold in the Little Rockies in 1884, but before long the beautiful friendship came to an abrupt end when Pike shot Dutch in the chest. Dutch survived but moved on. He was probably with Ahern in 1890.

At Fort Benton or another post, he fell under the spell of Schultz and Indian Agent George Steele. Schultz says they were playing around with a coquina board teasing the agent's gullible clerk into believing that the ghost of Bedrock Jim had found gold on Swiftcurrent Creek. Dutch Louie got dragged into the game, unwittingly, and set out to find the gold. He did find a little copper, and news of that started a flow of prospectors onto the reservation and led to the sale or lease of the "ceded strip" in 1895. When the strip was thrown open to boomers, April 15, 1898, Louie was one of the boomers.

Schultz and Ralph Pulitzer, in their flight from the law for poaching, cruised down the Missouri River about 1903 and met Dutch Louie on a ranch near Round Butte. Evidently, he died there soon afterwards.

L. O. Vaught claimed that Dutch Creek was named for Fritz Schultz, a prospector locally nicknamed "Fool Hen Schultz" from his trick of snaring fool hens with a copper wire.

The Kootenai name tells of Big Belly Man, *Kwiłwum Akanuxunik*. He was a paunchy giant who made a trail through Dutch Creek country. So huge was he that he did not feel the sting of arrows.

The Myers and Dunlap(?) Glaciers may have been named by the Ahern party.

DUSTY STAR MOUNTAIN: Dr. Ruhle applied this name to the northeast side of the cirque of Citadel. The Blackfoot form is *ísziká-kakatósi*, which refers to a meteor and may be translated "smoking star". The concept of star dust or moon dust occurs in proper names among the Blackfeet and the Kootenais. Some Blackfeet associate meteorites with the fungus called puffball and often depict them around the base of their tipis. (See CITADEL.)

EAGLE NEST CREEK flows into Upper Kintla Lake. An eagle's nest was found nearby.

EAGLE PLUME* MOUNTAIN is named for a Blood (Kaina) chief whose poignant story is told by Long Lance.

Eagle Plume and his wife were a happy couple with only one great sorrow to mar their happiness: they had no child. One winter Eagle Plume took off alone through the western slopes of the Canadian Rockies. On snowshoes he followed the trail of a wolf that led him on and on. When, during a blizzard, he tried to shoot at the wolf, his gun misfired. Was the wolf fleeing from him or leading him on?

At last he felt he had gone far enough and built a brush shelter in the snow but still under the wolf's eye. Then he heard a strange cry through the woods. Tracing it on his snowshoes, he came upon the corpse of a woman. From above he heard a plaintive cry, and there, in the branches of the tree, he found a tiny baby hanging in a cradleboard. Eagle Plume hugged the little boy all night to keep him warm, then brought him home and presented him to his wife.

At last they had a son. They called him *Mahkuyi-uskun* (Wolf's Little Brother), and vowed never again to shoot at a wolf.

This little gem is Native American short story at its best. This story, and that of Almighty Voice, are derived (in part) from Buffalo Child Long Lance. His real name was Sylvester Long, and he was not a Blood but was partly Cherokee and Lumbee from North Carolina. He was something of a hero in World War I and prominent in Hollywood. With Antonio Moreno, he starred in a movie about the Riel uprising of 1885. His friends include the dour humorist of Lake McDonald, Irvin S. Cobb, and Canon Middleton of Waterton Lakes. When he died mysteriously in Hollywood, he left his fortune to Canon Middleton's school for Blood boys at Cardston.

Adolf Hungry Wolf also tells about Eagle Plume, probably the same man, born about 1850 and also named *Natosina* or Sun Chief. His family was evidently Kaina with traces of French and Mexican. If you want to know more about Eagle Plume, you must read it for yourself in Hungry Wolf's book since there is more detail than this present book will allow.

EAGLE RIBS* MOUNTAIN, once called Beadhead: *Pitaw-pikis* (Eagle's Rib) was a Blood warrior, said to be a relative of Natawista Culbertson and also of Red Crow. He was noted for his blondness. In 1832 he was painted by George Catlin at Fort Union, garbed in an elaborate costume that dripped with scalps.

When he and his party (including young Mountain Chief), set out for the Three Forks of the Missouri, he was entrusted with letters for Henry Vanderburgh, a trader who attended the trappers' rendezvous at Pierre's Hole (Idaho). They met on the Jefferson River—Eagle Ribs' party and Vanderburgh's—but did not recognize each other. Vanderburgh was probably the one who fired first and so was killed and his bones were defleshed. Soon afterwards the rival brigade of Jim Bridger showed up, and you can take the story from there if you turn to the entry on Spotted Eagle.

Eagle Ribs was reported dead by 1859, so he cannot have been the man of that name who is alleged to have taken part in the murder of Malcolm Clarke in 1869.

EAGLEHEAD* MOUNTAIN is named for *Pitaw-otokan*, a friend of Schultz, but the name is said to have been applied to this mountain by R. T. Evans. Schultz gives the name Eagle Head to Cosley Lake and Ridge. This warrior was noted for leading two parties down into Spanish territory. The Kootenai name for this mountain is Wolf Head: *Ka·kin Akłam Akwukłi'it.*

"Eaglehead" was also the name the Kaina people bestowed upon visiting Governors-General of Canada as they were initiated into the "Kainai Chieftainship" as honorary chiefs. In 1936 Lord Tweedsmuir was so honored on his visit to Saint Paul's School, fulfilling (as he said) his romantic dream as a boy wandering the hills of Scotland. In 1951, near the Belly Buttes, Viscount Harold Rupert Alexander of Tunis was accorded the same honor. Born in London of the Irish aristocracy, he had commanded in the Army in France in 1940, in Burma and the Mediterranean two years later, and later in Churchill's government. His two sons, aged twelve and sixteen, were initiated with the names Eagle Speaker and Many Fingers. The motto of the honorary chieftainship is *Mokokit ki aikakimat*: Be wise and persevere.

EAST FLATTOP*: See FLATTOP.

EAST GLACIER STATION and **VILLAGE** is the traditional eastern gateway to Glacier, corresponding to West Glacier on the other side of the Divide. It used to be called Glacier Station and before that, Midvale. And Midvale is still the name of the creek that flows by the village.

The name East Glacier was formerly attached to the present Rising Sun but was transferred to the railroad town in 1950. The premier hotel of Glacier is located at East Glacier, on the Blackfeet Reservation and not within the boundaries of the park. This anomalous situation has been the occasion for conflict between the tribe and the hotel company (GPI), since the unemployment rate on the reservation resembles that of the Third World. The Blackfeet call the hotel the Big Tree Lodge. It stands on property once owned by the family of Malcolm Clarke.

EATON* **TRAIL**: Howard Eaton was one of four brothers and a sister who pioneered in dude ranching near Medora, North Dakota. One well-heeled dude who was befriended by Howard was Theodore Roosevelt and another was the Marquis de Mores. When many others resented the handsome French Marquis as a foreign intruder, Howard stood by him. Later on, Howard moved to another ranch at Wolf, Wyoming, became active in the conservation of the American bison and led parties of dudes and dudines in Yellowstone National Park. From Yellowstone he conducted tours to Glacier in its green year. But customers became so numerous as to be an exotic threat to the east and the west sides of Glacier. The tours centered at Lake McDonald Lodge and Saint Mary. Participants included artist and raconteur Charlie Russell and novelist Mary Roberts Rinehart. Eventually Eaton led tours into New Mexico, Arizona, California, and northern Mexico.

EDWARDS*, **MOUNT,** used to be called "Horseshoe Mountain" and, in Kootenai, "Crane Mountain": *Qaspiłu'k Akwukłi'it.* There is also a Horseshoe Basin nearby. There are two versions of the name Edwards: (1) the mountain was named for Professor John H. Edwards; (2) the mountain was named for Mrs. John H. Edwards, supposedly the first lady tourist to reach Avalanche Basin. (See BIG CEDARS.)

EL DORADO and Silver King were mining claims of James Kennedy (1894) on the North Fork between Quartz and Logging Creeks. El Dorado is Spanish for "the golden or gilded man," originally referring to a Chibcha chief of South America, later used in California and elsewhere for a mining bonanza.

ELIZABETH* LAKE was named "Jean" by Lieutenant Ahern on the map of 1891 for Jean Gil, his bride of the previous year. It is also said to have been named Elizabeth for a surveyor's daughter. The Blackfoot name is "Otter Lake": *Amonisi-omahxikimi*. There is a curious story that the lake was named by Joe Cosley for a daughter of Theodore Roosevelt. Now, it is certainly possible that Joe did name this lake for a lady friend, and it is also possible that Joe did guide a daughter of Roosevelt in Glacier. But, alas, Roosevelt's daughters were named Ethel and Alice.

Chivalrous Joe is also supposed to have named lakes for Bertha, Lois, and Helen. (See Cosley, Roosevelt.)

ELK* CREEK and **MOUNTAIN:** Named for the wapiti. And *wapiti* is a Shawnee (Algonquin) word. In New Zealand, where deer are raised commercially on animal farms, the name *wapiti* is often applied to a cross-breed of American elk and European red deer. The Blackfoot term for the elk is *ponoká(w)*. The Kootenais called Elk Creek "Beaver Hat": *Sinakayuka Aknuxu'nuk* and the mountain *Kyaqi Akłałku Akwukłi'it*. Or perhaps the Kootenai name is just "Broken": *Kyaqi*, which may refer to Elk Calf Mountain just outside the southeastern corner of Glacier. On the Canadian side of the border the elk is a favorite theme for place names: Elk River in southeast British Columbia, the town of Ponoka in Alberta and the Red Deer and the Little Red Deer River. The "red deer" is used to translate the Cree word *(wa)wákasiw* + *-sipi* or *-osipi* for "river." In Blackfoot the Little Red Deer River is *asinoka-sisahtai* (*asi-* for little + *(po)-noka* for elk).

The difference in the use of terms like "elk" and "red deer" in Europe and America is confusing. In scientific terms the elk or wapiti is *cervus canadensis* and the red deer is *cervus elaphus*. For another complication see Ibex.

ELLEN WILSON* LAKE was named for the first Mrs. Woodrow Wilson, but it used to be both Lake Louise and one of the Little Saint Mary Lakes. Its Kootenai name is "Handling Bones": *Kaniłkin Akuqnuk*. It may refer to gambling or "the hand game." See Lincoln, for the Little Saint Mary Lakes.

ELLSWORTH*, MOUNT: Surveyor R. T. Evans is said to have named this mountain for an early packer, Billy Ellsworth. Glacier records, however, list the origin of the name as unknown. But there was another Ellsworth associated with the park, Lincoln Ellsworth, the financier who took part in the aerial expedition of Roald Amundson over the North Pole. Though he was in the park as early as 1911, Lincoln returned to the area with the expedition of 1926 on its way down from Alaska. Schultz assigns the name of "Buffalo Child," *Inókos*, to this mountain in honor of the Blackfoot man who was painted by George Catlin (though Catlin got his name wrong).

EMERALD BAY is in Waterton Park, but Emerald Lake in Glacier has been lost. (See CHANEY.)

ESSEX STATION and **VILLAGE**, on the railway, lie just outside the southern portion of Glacier. They get their name from an eastern county (once a kingdom) of England. The reason for the English name is not clear unless it was supposed to fit in well with the neighboring name of Izaak Walton. Several mining names lay in this area, including the Alabama, Alps, Avalanche, Florence, and Phoenix. Essex Creek, however, drains the lake called Almeda, which is normally a Hispanic-Arab name. A lady named Almeda Durham is listed as a mine claimant. (See SHIELDS.)

EVANGELINE* LAKE commemorates the heroine of Longfellow's narrative poem. The name may have been applied by the surveyor Sargent or his crew. If an Acadian or Cajun name seems out of place in Glacier, it will fit better if you recall that many of the earliest pioneers in the Rocky Mountain West were of Louisiana Creole origin by way of Missouri. The Kootenai name is "Shells Woman Lake": *Kumȼaknana Paⱡkiy Akuq̓nuk.* (See LONGFELLOW.)

FALLING LEAF* LAKE lies on Mount Allen. It was named for the month of October, which in the Chippewa language is called "the moon of the falling leaves," *Pinakwi-kisis.* A Blackfoot name for October is "when the leaves dry up." But see SNOW MOON for further explanation of the names of months. The Kootenai name for the lake is *Kupaquɬaqpi'k.*

FALSE SUMMIT is a point on the railroad near Summit and just beyond the Glacier boundary.

FEATHER PLUME* FALLS used to be called Bridal Veil (like other falls in Yosemite and Waterton). For a while it was known as Horsetail Falls. The lower falls is Morning Eagle.

FEATHER WOMAN LAKE: *Mamínyaki* (Feather or Wing Woman) is a figure in Blackfoot oral literature. Her lake lies near Sperry Glacier Trail. Sperry called it Nanson Lake.

FERN CREEK flows from the Apgar Mountains. The name must be descriptive.

FESTUBERT, MOUNT: It lies partly in Waterton and is named for a village near La Bassee, France.

FIFTY MOUNTAIN CAMP: From this place you are supposed to see fifty mountains. In the late 1920s, this camp was a favorite rendezvous, located as it is in the center of Glacier National Park, for the horseback trips called the Triangle and the Great North Circle. (See FLATTOP.)

A series of mining claims from a century ago were located in the Fifty Mountain area, which was accessible from both the west and the east sides of the Divide and lay just outside the boundary of the Indian Reservation. Claims located here belonged to Joe Kipp, Frank McPartland, the Cattle Queen, Louis Meyer, and others. Joe Cosley did some prospecting here for Joe Kipp. The claims of this area included the Akamina, Alpine, Blackfoot, Glacier, Humboldt, International, Northern Light, Pumpelly, and Saskatchewan—all on the headwaters of McDonald Creek and filed in 1894. Notice that the name "Glacier" was used for a claim and in various other places of Glacier long before the park itself existed or could have been named.

FIREBRAND* PASS was known as "the Bad Road" to the Blackfeet, *Makap-ohsokoi*, perhaps because of the dangers in crossing between two tribal territories. Its present name derives from the forest fires of 1910, when a firebrand is said to have been blown across the pass carrying the blaze to the forest on the east side.

FISH* CREEK and **LAKE** both feed Lake McDonald, which in 1846 had the old French name of *Lac de Poissons*. This may explain the "Fish."

FISHERCAP* LAKE was named for George Bird Grinnell, whose Indian name was "Fishercap." It has also been called "Elrod Lake" for the author and naturalist Morton J. Elrod. (See GRINNELL.)

FLATHEAD RANGE fringes Glacier on the southwest in the Flathead National Forest. It lays between the Lewis Range on the east and the Columbia (or Bad Rock) Mountains on the west. These three ranges comprise the Rocky Mountains in the strict sense at this latitude. Some geologists restrict the term, "Rockies," to the ranges between the Great Plains and the Rocky Mountain Trench, which in this region runs down from around Columbia Lake in British Columbia via the Stillwater to the Flathead Valley and possibly on through the Bitterroot Valley.

The Flathead Range is dominated by Great Northern Mountain. Other prominent mountains are Mount Grant with its lingering glacier, named for miner Dan Grant (?), and Stanton Mountain with its glacier and creek. Felix Mountain Creek and Basin were probably all named for prospector Felix Droullette. There are mountains with names Cameahwait and Baptiste that are bound to challenge the toponomist but we can handle them if we recall Cameahwait or Kame-ah-wah (meaning "reluctant to go"), the Shoshoni chief and the brother or cousin of Sacajawea. He aided Lewis and Clark across the Divide but was killed in battle about 1840. And Mount Baptiste, near Cameahwait may be named for the baby son of Sacajawea, Jean Baptiste Charbonneau, who as a babe was called Pampi. However, a more likely explanation attributes the name of both Baptiste Creek and Baptiste Mountain to Baptiste Zeroyal, a big man even among old-timers, who was buried on Hoke Creek and the South Fork road. (See SPOTTED BEAR.)

FLATHEAD RIVER is named for a Montana branch of the Salish called in French *Têtes Plates*, and in Blackfoot *Kotóxpi*. The Flathead River has three forks above Flathead Lake (four if we count the Swan coming in at the head of the lake). Two of these forks entwine themselves around western Glacier and all three drain the territories of the Kootenai and Salish peoples. The Kootenai name for the portion of the Middle Fork between Coram and the park is *Aqnisał*. The U.S. border survey of 1861 called the Flathead River at the latitude they saw it *A-kin-is-sáhtl*, presumably a Kootenai name and perhaps a form of *Aqnisał*. Schultz gives the name as "Liar River" transcribed as *Kkuktqananmituk* in reference to the treacherous currents. Lewis and Clark recorded other names for the Flathead River in its lower reaches: *Pahkee* by the Nez Perces and *Tushe-pah* by the Shoshonis. This name appears on Clark's map of 1814 and is translated as "summer water" with reference to the climate of the Bitterroot country of the Flatheads, and that is said to be the Shoshoni name of the Flathead people as well. (The Shoshoni dictionary of Wick R. Miller gives "summer" as *tatsa* and "water" as *paa*.)

The French map of 1846 goes into more detail for the upper sources: The Middle Fork of the Flathead is *Rivière de Smet* for Pierre-Jean DeSmet, S.J. The South Fork is *Fourche á François*, while the North Fork is *Fourche á Charles* (Francis Fork and Charles Fork). So who were Francis and Charles? Father DeSmet had brothers in Belgium of these names. However, it is more probable that these streams were named for the two sons of Old Ignasse La Mousse, the Iroquois voyageur who joined David Thompson near Thompson Falls about 1810. He married a Salish woman and was notably zealous in spreading Christianity among his wife's people. He was one of those who traveled all the way to Saint Louis to request missionaries, and in 1835 he brought these two sons east to be baptized. Charles and Fran ois Saxa continued their father's dedication and became guides, interpreters and companions-of-the-trail to DeSmet. It is possible that they were the sources of information on the maps of 1846, which seem to have been prepared at least in part by DeSmet himself. These maps reveal a hot springs west or southwest of Flathead Lake described as *Fontaine chaude* and *Belle Fontaine sulfureuse et bouillante*.

But now we switch from clerical names to military names. Another name for the South Fork is Gibbon's River, conferred on one or all of the three streams by Lieutenants Woodruff and Van Orsdale about 1873. Col. John Gibbon (eventually General) would attack the Nez Perces under Looking Glass, White Bird, and Joseph at the Big Hole in 1877, killing fifty women and children but losing a battle no one could "win."

The name Flathead has spawned a number of theories about its origin. The most fascinating story relates the name to "Shining Shirt," *Piél'xaɫ'ks* (a coat of mail?), and still used as a surname among the Salish. Shining Shirt and his "mystery people" came out of the West, maybe two hundred years ago, not recognizable as either white people or Indians. They claimed that they or their fathers had come from beyond the sea in a great boat which wrecked and cast them ashore. They took wives among the women of the coast but later wandered inland and settled with the Kalispels on Flathead Lake. These castaways taught the Montana Salish new ways to make fire and medicines, new practices of sanitation, and new ideas about God and the coming of the Black Robes. Eventually these people were absorbed by intermarriage with the Salish. And though the Montanans did not flatten the heads of their babies in cradleboards, some of the coastal people who came inland with Shining Shirt did have this custom. So the nickname—not the practice—is supposed to have become current in Montana. In support of this story there is some evidence of Spanish galleons from Mexico and/or Manila shipwrecked off the mouth of the Columbia River. However, versions of this story will differ and the version here given is not definitive.

So too the versions of the aftermath of this story, one of which may have become identified with the worldwide "Orpheus myth." Shining Shirt's beloved wife dies and leaves him bereaved. So he sets out to seek her, climbing the tallest mountain in the Kalispel country (not specified in the story but Mount Stimson on the maps). Though various animals try to dissuade him, he continues his ascent "to hear the Great Spirit speaking in the mountain tops." And what the Great Spirit tells him amounts to this: "Go home and leave the rest to me. Prepare your people for the coming of strangers, some of whom will bring good and some evil." In this story ethnologists may recognize a connection to the Prophet Dance and the Dreamers. (See MARIAS, NORTH FORK, NYACK, STIMSON.)

FLATTOP* CREEK and **MOUNTAINS**: West Flattop Mountain may have been so named by the Indians, and East Flattop by J. W. Schultz about 1883. In that year Oliver Sandoval, son of the New Mexican Isidoro Sandoval and his Piegan wife, first guided Schultz into the Saint Mary valley. Schultz probably went up East Flattop hunting for goats to get white hides like those he had seen Stonies bring into Fort Benton. From a Kootenai friend Oliver knew of a game lick apparently at the base of Flattop, and this too he revealed to Schultz. The Blackfoot name for East Flattop means "on top prairie," *Itóhkisawki*. Vaught says (East) Flattop was the name given by local people.

West Flattop includes the Broken Arm country. Joe Kipp and many others had mining claims here. There are also Flattop Crag, Flattop Creek, and Flattop Falls. The falls is also called Casami Falls, but the name Casami remains a mystery.

FLINSCH* PEAK is named for Rudolf Ernst Ferdinand Flinsch, a young German immigrant who came to New York from Frankurt-am-Main when he was twenty-two years old. Like Grinnell, he became a friend of the New York physician, Dr. Walter James, and in 1892 he set out with Dr. James to hunt goats around Two Medicine. They got aboard a work train of the new Great Northern, just then making one of its early runs to Glacier Country and took a pack trip with Billy Jackson. Up Cut Bank Creek they went to the Divide, where they passed three weeks on both sides of Pitamakan Pass. Then they came east down Two Medicine Creek to Two Medicine Lake. About ten years later Rudolf Flinsch looked at a government map of the area he had hunted in and was surprised to discover his own name attached to the peak, presumably given to it by the Indians. (The information about Rudolf Flinsch comes from his son, Roland Flinsch of California, kindly shared for this book.)

The Blackfoot name for this peak, no doubt conferred by Schultz, is that of a great warrior "No Chief" (or "Never a Chief"), *Kutáina*, whose sad story has been preserved by Schultz. Kutáina had a younger brother whom he greatly loved. But when they went together on the war trail, the younger brother was killed. Kutáina went home with his brother's bones in a sac, which he kept ever afterward in his tipi—much to the chagrin of his wife. When he died, the bag of bones was buried with him.

FLORAL PARK: Descriptive. It is located near Sperry Chalet. Mary Baker (or Myra Baker) Lake is here. (See MARY BAKER.) Luding Lake is nearby, named for the family that for years conducted the chalet.

FLORENCE* FALLS may be named for Senator Dixon's daughter or perhaps after a mining claim. Schultz lists these falls under the name *Paióta*.

FOLLETT CREEK is a place of refreshment for weary hikers on the Avalanche Trail.

FORD* CREEK and **STATION**: The name probably refers simply to the river crossing. There was a local family named De Ford and in 1908 Mary De Ford married a neighboring rancher Charles Schoenberger, but it seems unlikely that this surname was the source of the place name. The Kootenai term for Ford Creek is "Little Kintla," *Kinła Nana Akinmituk.*

FORTY MILE* CREEK is near East Glacier, but forty miles from where? Perhaps from the Canadian line by old roads.

FORTY-ONE MILE* CREEK is one mile nearer East Glacier, and this fact suggests the starting point is in the north.

FORUM PEAK, with its grand old Roman name, rests on the three corners where British Columbia, Alberta, and Montana all come together. There is also a Form Lake just over the line in British Columbia.

FRANCES* LAKE: This lake used to be called Francis (the masculine form) and that spelling was approved by the Geographic Board on Names in 1929. Perhaps it was named for Francis Herbst. (See HERBST.) But in 1970 the board changed the name to the feminine form. The Blackfoot name commemorates the wife of J. W. Schultz, daughter of Black Eagle, under her formal name of *Mazi-awótan(i)*: "Fine Shield" or "Pretty Shield." She was commonly called *Natahki*. (See NATAHKI.)

FUSILLADE* MOUNTAIN, once called Foresight (?), was reputedly named by Grinnell to poke fun at his companions, Henry Stimson and W. H. Seward, for firing a barrage at some goats and failing to score. Another story, however, credits Billy Jackson with giving the name for a similar reason. Schultz lists the name as Many Shots, adding that Fusillade and Gunsight were named together.

GABLE* MOUNTAIN and **PASS:** Probably descriptive for the mountain, but how do you get a gabled pass?

GALEN'S LADDER: The switchbacks on Swiftcurrent Pass were constructed under Superintendent James Galen, 1912–1914. The "ladder" may have been built during the year he was still only a ranger. You will not be surprised to learn that he was the brother-in-law of Senator Carter.

GALWEY, MOUNT, in Waterton Lakes Park was named for Lieutenant Galwey, an astronomer with the British Boundary Commission.

GARDEN WALL*: A party of tourists guided by Grinnell was camped at Grinnell Lake in the 1890s and gathered for an evening songfest around the campfire. A song then popular was "Over the Garden Wall." Someone joked about the Divide: "There's one wall you won't get over." (Would it were so!)

GARDINER CREEK in Waterton Park has a name of unknown origin.

GARDNER POINT* MOUNTAIN: G. Clinton Gardner was assistant astronomer and surveyor on the U.S. Boundary Survey of 1861. Later he was a civil engineer in Peru. Charles T. Gardner was also on the U.S. survey of 1861. Presumably, one of these men, or both, has his name on the mountain. The Kootenai name honors Chief Back (Coming) in Sight, *Kakawieɋyułak*. He used to lead his band from Canada to camp at Saint Mary, where he met Grinnell in 1885 and Schultz in 1887. This last time Back in Sight came with Bear Hat. At sunset he rang a bell to call his people to prayer in the manner taught by the Jesuits. Does this incident suggest an origin of the name for Saint Mary Lakes?

Schultz says that Back in Sight was brother to the wife of the old Piegan chief Big Lake and tells a story I would not vouch for: Back in Sight had a son who went off to war on the Great Plains and never came home. Years later old Back in Sight was still waiting for his son's promised return. Leaving his people camped at Saint Mary Lakes, he ventured far out onto the prairie alone calling for his lost son. At last he sighted a war party and ran toward it with shouts of joy and welcome. He was shot dead.

GARRY STATION and **LOOKOUT** may be named for Chief Spokane Garry or Fort Garry at Winnipeg. Perhaps it doesn't matter which one because Spokane Garry was named after the fort.

As a mere lad in 1825 he was sent there to school by Sir George Simpson, head of the Hudson's Bay Company in Rupert's Land. He returned home to Spokane Falls and passed on some of his Anglican training to his Salish people to lead them during the trying times of the wars and the hanging colonel, George Wright. He was "Sun Chief," *Ilumhu Spokanee.*

In his colorful career, Chief Spokane Garry covered a lot of western territory and crossed paths but not swords with most of its leading characters. On one of the various expeditions made by Indians of Oregon Country to California, Garry went along with his wife Nina in 1844. It was a caravan of Spokanes, Cayuses, and Walla Wallas bent on horse-trading. At Sutter's Fort (Sacramento), an American in cold blood shot and killed the son of Walla Walla chief Peopeomoxmox and precipitated hostility for years to come. In the winter of 1859-1860, Lt. John Mullan got Garry the job of mail-carrier between Fort Benton and Spokane Falls by way of the Clark Fork by snowshoe or horseback. Garry opposed Governor Stevens attempt to push his people onto a reservation and take over their lands, but he tried to keep the peace during the warfare of 1858 even though his own brother was one of many hanged by the Army.

GEDUHN, MOUNT, is named for Frank Geduhn, a guide of German origin. He was one of the earliest settlers on Lake McDonald. The Kootenai name is "Chased in the Woods Mountain," *Kaǫananutka Akwyukłi'it.* "Chased in the Woods" is a personal name.

GEM CREEK: Descriptive.

GIBRALTER POINT: This promontory at Piegan Pass is named after the famous rock on the coast of Spain, crossed by the Moor Tarik in 711 A.D. with his troops. So Gibraltar is a Spanish form of the Arabic *Jabal al-Tarik*: the mountain of Tarik.

GLACIER* BASIN: Descriptive.

GLACIER* CLIFF: It is remarkable how often the term "glacier" is used in names that may pre-date the naming of the park.

GLACIER NATIONAL PARK: Named by Senator Carter, or at least that is the official account. If Carter (or whoever) had known more about the area, he might have chosen a more appropriate name: for instance, Glacier Lakes, since it is the complex of glacial lakes that distinguishes this park from various others. But since tourists wanted glaciers, Sperry and Great Northern tried to provide them, thus creating the myth. No one then understood the degree or the process of deglaciation in the park. As glaciers diminish, glacial lakes evolve in their distinctive fjord-like settings. The Canadian Rockies have more impressive glaciers, while Glacier can boast its fabulous fjords or finger lakes.

In both Glacier and Waterton there are people important in history and often mentioned in these pages but not commemorated in place names. To redress this imbalance, I am including brief mention of forgotten ones under the entries of Glacier and Waterton National Parks. (See *Who Was Who...* for more information.)

Among the forgotten in Glacier's story is one of its superintendents, **Robert Ray Vincent.** In the catalogue of Glacier's superintendents, Vincent's page is almost a blank. We meet "Ray" first as a soldier from the Far West in France during World War I. That's where he met a man from Dutch Creek. Whatever the man told him left a lasting impression, and Ray resolved that when he got home from the war he would seek out the the North Fork. In 1917 he did just that, went home to Yakima, married Ruth, and moved her and their baby to Red Meadows Creek. Their first winter in the wilderness was miserably cold, with nothing to live in but a primitive log cabin and little to eat but rabbits. Ray began his career by keeping store at Adair, but in 1920 he became a clerk for the park service and soon moved to the Dow Hotel at Belton—a questionable improvement. From clerk he jumped to ranger and from ranger in one leap to assistant superintendent. In that status he remained from 1926 to 1948, with military leave during World War II when he was sent to the Aleutians and to Italy.

James Doty (1827?–1857) explored the eastern edges of Glacier with Hugh Monroe in 1854 and penetrated Marias Pass to the summit. Something of a puzzle, even though his father was well known as superintendent of Indian affairs in Wisconsin and in later years governor of Utah, James the son was born (for the record) at Green Bay. But encyclopedist Dan Trapp says he was an "Indian man" born in Michigan, and an Indian background could explain his remarkable success in dealing with the Blackfeet. Well educated and a specialist in "natural history," young James was assigned to the Northern Pacific

Survey to make meteorological and astronomical researches for Isaac I. Stevens, first governor of Washington Territory. But West Pointer Stevens had a fanatical genius for manipulating other people, and young James became his prime target. Stevens left Doty with three men to remain with the Blackfeet while he himself explored farther west. Loyal to the bone, Doty served as Stevens' right-hand man during the negotiations for the Judith Treaty of 1855. When Stevens assumed the governorship at Olympia, Washington, Doty became his secretary and his emissary to propose treaties with various tribes. But as Stevens became increasingly tyrannical, hostile to Jesuits and Frenchmen with Indian wives, Doty grew frustrated and got drunk. Stevens fired him, then relented and made him a clerk. Doty shot himself. "He is now no more," eulogized Stevens, too late, too late, "but he was my friend and companion—unwearied, indefatigable and able." For his high-handed methods, Stevens was recalled.

An Indian agent who had a direct impact on the Glacier-to-be was *George Steele* (1837–1916). Quebecker by birth, George was the son of a mother from England and a father from Scotland but moved to New York and Boston to enter business. In 1857 he came up the Missouri to Fort Benton and worked for the American Fur Company in Helena and in seven years formed a partnership with Matthew Carroll at Fort Benton. Named *Isziumaiokat* (Sleeping Thunder) by the Indians, evidently for a trait of character, he was famous for his black stallion Puhpoom, stolen (by Eagle Ribs, says Schultz) but recovered by Joe Kipp. His "country wife" was a daughter of Lame Bull by whom he had two daughters. Carroll and Steele, along with I. G. Baker and T. C. Power, became the famous "merchant princes" of Fort Benton. Since Steele, like Power, was a Republican, he stood in the good graces of the powerful Carter and in 1867 became one of the first commissioners of Chouteau County. As behooved a rising Republican, he took a legal wife in Ticonderoga, New York, Eva Treadway, and brought her to Helena where she soon died. (His Indian wife Mary married another white man, Peter Lukin.)

Carroll and Steele, employers of greenhorn J. W. Schulz, also joined C. A. Broadwater in freighting enterprises, probably along the Whoop-Up Trail. After a whirl at business in Salt Lake City, Steele returned to ranching on Sun River and married Annie Dias(?). He served on the territorial legislatures in 1877 and 1879 and took part in the constitutional convention of 1884. In 1890 he was appointed agent for the

Blackfeet. A high point in his career as agent was the trip he took with Joe Kipp and a group of chiefs to Washington, D.C. Another was the role he played in the negotiations for the "ceded strip" of what is now Glacier. He was chosen because after so many years of contact the Indians trusted him—in spite of his neuralgia and addiction to opium and his communication with Indians through the keyhole. But he had much trouble with the railroad, whose crews illegally cut hay and and timber on the reserve, introduced whiskey wagons and helped themselves to excessive right-of-way. And though his Republican affiliation won him the support of Grinnell and Carter, it cost him any favor of the Democratic Hills and Marcus Daly's Anaconda. In 1897 he ranched at Dupuyer.

And while we catch up on people important to Glacier but left uncommemorated, we cannot forget the brothers *Sandoval*. They were the grandsons of old Isidoro Sandoval, the Mexican *engag* who became an informant to Prince Maximillian in 1833. Isidoro was murdered in cold blood at Fort Union, leaving by his Piegan wife Catch For Nothing a son Isidoro II and a daughter who married Malcolm Clarke. Among the children of Isidoro II and his wife Margaret Red Bird Tail were Oliver (born at Fort Union, 1860) and Richard (born Fort Benton, 1866–7). Oliver must have been one of the earliest explorers in the Saint Mary valley and introduced Schultz to that country in 1883. Richard was a treasury of lore and history on early Glacier, and an active informant to Louis Hill and others. He changed his name to "Sanderville." (See *Who Was Who...* for more information.)

Allen Duvall was the co-worker of anthropologist Clark Wissler and the source of much of the professional knowledge of the Blackfeet. He descended from a white man Charles Duvall and a Piegan Yellow Bird. Tragedy stalked his family. Charles soon died and his 3-year-old daughter Lillie was kidnapped and brought down to Missouri. There she grew up and married in 1898 to George Bennett. After a ten-year search in vain for her origins, in 1907, she came to Montana and found her mother.

George Alexander Grant was the first official photographer in Glacier-Waterton. Photographers like Marble and T. J. Hileman are better known locally, but professionals, I believe, would give the laurels to Grant for his avoidance of special effects and for his "straight photography." Born in Pennsylvania, he served as a second lieutenant in the Army in Wyoming and acquired a special love for the West and a special yearning to photograph it. In September 1922 he was hired by Horace Albright to work in Yellowstone and it was not long before Albright discovered Grant's special genius for photography. In Yellowstone there was a charming young lady named Bernice, daughter of Judge Finney of the Department of Interior, and both Grant and Ranger Eivind Scoyen fell in love with her. But alas, poor Grant had a graceless walk and a lot of trouble riding horses. So Scoyen won out (partly, it is said, by assigning Grant to duties on horseback).

In 1929 Grant received his appointment as National Park Service photographer, a job perhaps designed for him by Albright, along with instructions to photograph all the national parks in the U.S. He also became noted for his pictures of the Navajos in Canyon de Chelly (Chelly is pronounced "shay"), and was assigned to Glacier, where Scoyen was now superintendent and where he had to do a lot of work by riding horses but also where he was known as the "Master Photographer."

In October 1935, he was photographer on the Sonoran Mission Expedition. Since he often traveled in Mexico and spoke Spanish well, his work on this venture is among his most famous. This in spite of the violent persecution which was at that time raging against the Catholic church that had built the very missions he was commemorating. In the late 1930s he used his photography to expose the environmental disaster that Hoover Dam was creating. He retired from the Park Service and spent ten years in ill health before dying in 1964.

Before we leave Glacier, we must note that a Blackfoot name for Going-to-the-Sun Road is *Stunatap-Ohsoko* (Scary, Awful Road) and for Glacier itself *Awhká-xahkui* or Fun Land—fun for white tourists but not for Blackfeet.

GLACIER WALL: This may be the original Kootenai name, since Schultz gives it as *Ahkwaiswílko* and the word for "glacier" as *Akwiswitxu*.

GLADSTONE MOUNTAIN stands southwest of Pincher Creek.

GLENDOWAN MOUNTAIN in Waterton Lakes Park, was named in 1915 by a surveyor named M. P. Bridgland after a mountain or range in Ireland.

GLENNS* LAKE is named for T. C. Glenn, an assistant to surveyor Sargent. Grinnell's map labels this and Cosley Lake the Lansing Lakes. The Blackfoot name given by Schultz is *Nizítapi* (Lone or Real Person), also suggesting "Indian" since Indians are called "the Real People" or *Nízitapi.*

GOAT* MOUNTAIN and **LAKE**: The mountain may have been so called by Schultz. "Goat" in Blackfoot is "white big horn," *apomahkihkini.* The Rocky Mountain goat is not a true goat and in early days was called an ibex. So the name Ibex became a name for a mining claim in Glacier. There is a Goat Lake in a remote part of Waterton Lakes Park, and Mount Cannon was formerly called Goat Mountain. (See IBEX.)

GOAT HAUNT* LAKE and **MOUNTAIN:** This name was applied by Sargent on the suggestion of Bailey Willis (later of Stanford University). The Blackfoot name is given as (1) "Where there are a lot of goats," probably *apomahkíhkini ozitakaiihi,,* and (2) "Moose Mountain," according to Schultz. A moose is *sikziso* (black entering or vanishing). The Cree word is *môswa.*

GOATLICK is on Highway 2 as it crosses a corner of Glacier, where there is a display and observation point.

GOING-TO-THE-SUN* MOUNTAIN, POINT, and **ROAD:** This most unforgettable name in Glacier turns out to be a bit disappointing. Or at least, if we follow James Willard Schultz who bluntly told the Geographic Board on Names and also Dr. Ruhle in 1929: "I myself named Going-to-the-Sun Mountain….There is no Indian legend in connection with its name." And it does appear that in 1887 Schultz and Tail-Feathers-Coming-in-Sight-Over-the-Hill were butchering a ram on Red Eagle Mountain. Over a smoke, Tail Feathers remarked that the peak across the lake would be ideal for a vision quest. So the two agreed on the name, and in that case the credit for the name should be shared with Tail Feathers. (Cf. John Willard.) Schultz tells a similar story but makes the date 1885 and the place of the hunt is at the foot of Sun Mountain. He adds that the original name was *Natái-ispi-istaki* or Lone High Mountain.

Since all this comes directly from the man who had the most to do with naming features of Glacier, it should settle the question for good. But nevertheless, there's more to the story. The Blackfoot version of the name can be *Natósi-áitapo,* "to the sun he/she goes," or also *Natósi-pokomiw.*

The legend associated with the peak may be a fake, but it runs like this: Sour Spirit (?) or Napi or Old Man comes to save the Indian people in a time of trouble and, when his work is accomplished, goes back to the sun. He leaves his portrait on the peak from which he takes off.

Ella E. Clark recorded another version from the lips of an elder, "Chewing Black Bones:" Napi has angered some of his people and is fleeing to the mountains. He passes Saint Mary Lakes and scales the highest peak, where he ducks into a lofty ravine with just his face peering out. He turns into a rock and is up there still, looking over his people, errant as they may be, turning his face this way and that. The profile on the mountain top, however, is clearer as a snowfield than as a rock, and because of it, the peak has also been called Face Mountain and its spur is Matahpi Peak (*matápi, -tapi*: "person, people," short *a* as in "above").

Though the connection is not certain, a name also associated with this peak is a personal name, *Natósi-inipi* (Brings Down the Sun). The idea appears in Grinnell's account of the young Hugh Monroe who amazed the Piegans under Lone Walker by lighting a fire with a magnifying glass.

Well, J. W. Schultz may have named this peak Going-to-the-Sun because (as he claims) of its uplift into the blue, but the name is an old one. In Bad Head's Winter Count, as recorded by Hugh A. Dempsey, the year 1845 is remembered for a Kaina or Blood of this name, *Natosipokomiw*. He had to hide from Crees by crawling into a hole (something like Napi peering out from the mountain top).

GOLDEN STAIRS and **GOLDEN STAIRS FALLS**: This name refers to the cliffs of the Lewis Overthrust just above Rising Sun and is no doubt a quote from the old hymn "Climbing Up the Golden Stairs."

GOULD*, MOUNT, is one of the most often photographed peaks in Glacier. It was named for George Huntington Gould of Santa Barbara (1851–1926), a friend of Grinnell, Jack B. Monroe, J. W. Schultz, and probably Theodore Roosevelt. He graduated from Harvard Law School in 1872 and practiced law in Santa Barbara, California. Like his brother Charles, he made his home in the suburb of Montecito on the old Romero land grant with an East Asian houseboy and a gardener, Teofil Romero. A confirmed bachelor, he also joined the social whirl. Though Schultz says he was an invalid, he was evidently quite a sportsman or sports fan nonetheless, and he was active with Grinnell in defense of Indian rights. He and Grinnell took the liberty of inspecting the Blackfeet reservation and the manner in which it was administered, and ended up with severe accusations against the government agent.

A northeastern spur of Mount Gould is called Angel Wing, while another name for part (or all?) of Mount Gould is Mount Monroe—probably for Jack Monroe, not Hugh. Jack was also married into the Blackfoot tribe and had a mining claim at Belton and three claims at Bad Rock Canyon in 1893: Caribou, Deer Path, and Great Divide.

GOVERNOR'S POND is named for Montana's Governor Hugo Aronson. The pond is also called Hugo Lake, Aronson Lake, and Mary's Tear—yes, and even No Name Lake! And the Governor was also called the Galloping Swede. His wife was the former Rose McClure, a long-time superintendent of schools of Glacier County. So the Aronsons had a special connection with Glacier. When Count Folke Bernadotte of the Swedish royal family, the Countess, and their sons came to Glacier in the summertime, Hugo Aronson joined them at the piano for a Swedish songfest. After the Count was assassinated in 1948 by Israeli terrorists, his family continued to come to Glacier, so I suppose the Aronson visits were in earlier years.

GRACE* LAKE: No one seems to know Grace, but the Kootenai name is "Skunk Robe," *Xaxasła'mał Akuqnuk.* (See LOGGING.)

GRANITE PARK*: Old-time prospectors looked over the rocks around here and (as some wag put it) took it for granite. So much for punsters, because the "granite" here is really a kind of basalt or Purcell Lava which occurs in various places in the International Peace Park and in the ranges of the Cordillera to the west. Purcell is the name of one of those ranges, so called in 1859 or earlier for the physician Goodwin Purcell. Geologist Daly observes: "Many of the higher peaks in the four ranges of the Rocky Mountain system...owe their special heights to the strength of the Purcell Lava, which is more resistant to the forces of weathering than the massive Siyeh formation underlying." In the Clarke Range at the head of Starvation Creek, Daly found twenty-five miles of outcrop on the boundary map and two vertical dykes of Purcell Lava north of Lower Kintla Lake. Various dykes and sills occur elsewhere, and the so-called diorite band, sixty to one hundred feet thick, is especially noticeable on Gould, Wilbur, Grinnell, Stimson, and other peaks. In the vicinity of Granite Park you will also find Granite Creek, Little Granite Creek, and Rosenwald Point.

Brian Reeves tells us that this lava is regarded by Indians as having a special spiritual value and a view or the close presence of the "diorite band" is sought by vision seekers who want to share this *manito.*

GREAT BEAR TRAIL: The Trail of the Great Bear is the name of travel routes between Yellowstone National Park (or even Grand Teton National Park) via Glacier and Waterton to Banff and Jasper National Parks.

GREAT SAND HILLS: In Blackfoot *Omahkspaziko (-koi)*, the supposed abode of the dead, located physically in southern Saskatchewan and the Alberta border. To the living it does seem a notably dreary region, but still a tourist attraction.

GREEN LAKE: Descriptive.

GREENSBORO CREEK is named for Charles K. Green, a realtor of Coram who had property here in the southwestern corner of Glacier.

GRINNELL* FALLS, **GLACIER**, **LAKE**, **MOUNT**, and **POINT** were all named for George Bird Grinnell, author, ethnologist, naturalist, and the "father of Glacier" (1849–1938). His name is of French origin and his ancestors were Huguenots from Burgundy who came to Rhode Island in 1630, but he also descended from the Alden family (perhaps again Huguenot). Born in Brooklyn, he was raised both in New York and at his grandfather's home in Massachusetts. His father bought a piece of the estate of John James Audubon, and young George was taught by Mrs. Audubon at her home. From her he may have learned something of the high Missouri country, for the Audubons were friends of the Culbertsons. The thrill of George's youth was skinny-dipping with the other boys in the Hudson River for the benefit of customers on passing trains. When he was hauled before Judge Quackenbush for this frenchified fun, the Judge scolded the policeman instead and sent the boy home exonerated.

George had a rough time at Yale, even with tutors, but he was graduated and admitted as a volunteer on the expedition of paleontologist Othniel Marsh to the wilderness of Nebraska (1870). This expedition helped substantiate the theory of evolution and was applauded by Charles Darwin. From Nebraska it went on to the Great Salt Lake, Yosemite and the Sequoias. In 1872 Grinnell joined another expedition, this one with Major Frank North to the Pawnee Indians, and later he made other trips with North, learning the need to conserve buffalo and other wildlife. He began to write for *Field and Stream*, the magazine of which he later became editor. He also worked for the Peabody Museum. Marsh recommended him to General Sheridan, who sent both Grinnell and North on Custer's expedition to the Black

Hills of South Dakota. There Grinnell made friends with scout Charley Reynolds. While Grinnell discovered elephant bones and other fossils, others discovered gold and so precipitated the Indian wars. Grinnell had the unusual opportunity to see those wars from both sides.

As his studies of birds and mammals were attracting the attention of other naturalists like C. Hart Merriam, Grinnell set out with William Ludlow to the Judith Basin of Montana and Yellowstone National Park, checking on poachers and exploiters. After he got his PhD in 1880, he traveled to San Francisco, British Columbia, and the Columbia River. He published articles by Schultz on the starvation of the Blackfeet in 1883 and then was drawn to Fort Benton. There he met Schultz and *Otahkomi* (see OTOKOMI), and paid his first visit to Glacier Country, where he became enraptured with Saint Mary and Many Glacier.

So began the many adventures in present Glacier recalled in these pages. As he befriended the Blackfeet, he was adopted into the tribe with the name "Fisher Cap," *Pinotuyi Izúmokan*. Though his reluctant wife could not abide mountains with joy, he kept coming to them and urging a national park status for the Glacier Country. In 1885 he helped persuade the Piegan Blackfeet to lease to the government the eastern slopes of what is now Glacier, stipulating as part of the bargain that the government would not force the allotment system onto the tribe before the termination of the agreement. He accompanied an expedition to Alaska in 1899 and founded the Audubon Society, naming it for his boyhood schoolteacher, Mrs. Audubon. And, best of all, he at last saw his goal of Glacier National Park achieved.

But alas! Before long he began to realize that his grand success was a Pyhrric victory. Dismayed to find his wilderness turned into a tourist trap of roads, chalets and huge hotels, he quarreled with one of the main concessionaires and finally refused to set foot in Glacier again. For his last years he remained in New York and wrote nostalgic letters to old friends in Montana he would never see again.

"Grinnell" is also the name of a local rock formation, a reddish argillite.

GRIZZLY* MOUNTAIN: This name, applied by Evans, may be a translation of its Kootenai name, "Big Grizzly Mountain," *Kwiłqa Kławła Akwukłi'it*.

GROS VENTRE FALLS is in the northeast section of Glacier. (See ATSINA.)

GUARDHOUSE*: Descriptive.

GUARDIPEE FALLS is the lower falls on Flattop Creek. The name may refer to Frank or to his father Eli or to the extended family among the Blackfeet and Crees. Schultz says that Guardipee's Crossing of the Saskatchewan was named for Eli's grandfather and that Eli's branch of this large family joined the Blackfeet about 1867. If so, such a move may have been motivated by a need for protection against feuds. Eli Guardipee's Blackfoot name was *Isi-namahkan* (Taking the Gun First or Counting Coup First) and was applied, probably by Schultz, to Chapman Peak. Eli was one of Schultz's main informants about the buffalo days and worked with him on the committee for place names in Glacier. Though of French, Cree and Shoshoni origin, Eli married into the Blackfeet tribe and became one of its principal authorities on tribal lore and history. Born near Fort Benton in 1857, he knew and outlived more frontiersmen than almost anyone else mentioned in these pages. In 1937 I met him still enthusiastically chasing horses at Holy Family Mission on the Two Medicine. (See CHAPMAN, CHIEF LODGEPOLE.)

GUNSIGHT* LAKE, MOUNTAIN, and **PASS**: The pass was so named by Grinnell about 1891 because it resembled the sight on a rifle. Fran ois Matthes called the peak Mount Comeau, a name suggested by Dr. Sperry, and this mountain may also have borne the name Glacier Peak. (See COMEAU.)

GYRFALCON* LAKE: *Gyrfalcon* is said to be the Kootenai name for Carnelian Cliff now transferred to this lake, while a quartz ledge here is the source of the name Quartz attached to another lake. What a mixup! However, the Kootenai name put on Carnelian Cliff by Schultz has required reconstruction by modern Kootenai scholars who make it mean "bald eagle," *Aknuqɬuɬamɩ*.

HALFMOON* LAKE: The Kootenai name is Crow or Raven Lake: *Qukin Akuq̓nuk*. These waters are near Nyack, while another lake of the same name is near West Glacier, outside Glacier, and a third locality of this name is the junction on Highway 2 west of Columbia Falls.

HAND MOUNTAIN: Its Kootenai name is *Kaiyakawalin Kalaxi* (Hand of the Mountain(s) or Hand in the Middle of the Mountain). Here for once we seem to have a noun-dominant name. Brian Reeves discovered it in the papers of Claude Schaeffer, but nobody identifies the mountain precisely. It is known to be close to the international border, east of Kintla and near the divide between the Waterton and Flathead Rivers. If a vision-quester climbed all five peaks he attained great power. This feat was accomplished by a young man named *A'kinu* and so he escaped snowslides. According to Ambrose Gravelle, Kootenais climbed hand over fist on this mountain, though they could ride horses all around the Hand and could pass on snowshoes between the thumb and the forefinger. Some believe this mountain is the one we call Citadel Peaks. (See CITADEL PEAKS.)

HANGING GARDENS*: This name may be descriptive, but it is reported by veteran hiker John Muff and others that the name derives from the Hanging Gardens of Babylon, that is, the gardens on the terraces of the ziggurats or Towers of Babel. They were one of the Seven Wonders of the Ancient World. Schultz says the Blackfoot name for at least part of this area was *Omahk-siszin izínitaw:* Where the Bigfoot was killed. The Bigfoot was a caribou, not a yeti or sasquatch. The presence of caribou was reported in and near Glacier by Dr. Ruhle in 1930. Ruhle says that "Big Feet Was Killed" was the Kootenai name for Logan Pass. But see LOGAN.

HANGING GLACIERS: These are Ahern and Old Sun Glaciers.

HARRIS* GLACIER: Joseph S. Harris was the general assistant in the U.S. Boundary Survey of 1861 and later became president of the Reading Railroad. The Kootenai name is "Long Bow," *Yakił Wuqa'ki Ťawu Akwiswitxu.*

HARRISON* CREEK, **GLACIER,** and **LAKE**: It has been suggested that these places were named for President Harrison (but which one?

Benjamin? William Henry?), but there is no evidence for this theory. A more likely namesake is Frank Harrison, a rancher near Babb and a long-time resident of Saint Mary. His interview, preserved in Glacier library, gives us rare data about the old Saint Mary settlement. According to Ace Powell, the western artist, Frank was one of the few Indians employed by the Park Saddle Horse Company, which was run by the Noffsingers of Bar X 6 Ranch. Frank played the fiddle and rode broncos. The Kootenai Indians named Harrison Creek and the lake after *Kwiłnukak* (Large Ribs) and probably knew the glacier as *Qutapҁik Akwiswitxu* (Coyote's or Old Man's Daughter).

HAWKINS MOUNTAIN stands in Waterton Lakes Park and is named for Lt. Col. John Summerfield Hawkins (1812–1895). He commanded the British Survey Expedition and reached the Waterton/Glacier region in 1861 to confer with his U.S. counterparts. He was knighted in 1881.

HAWKBILL POINT: The Hawk's Bill is an overhang on the wall of Brown's Pass.

HAY CREEK was named in 1890 because some hay was cut nearby to feed stock at a logging camp.

HAYSTACK* BUTTE and **CREEK**: Descriptive for the butte.

HEAD*: Descriptive. This mountain on the southeast edge of Glacier carries the Blackfoot name of "Under Bull," *Stáhzi-stamik*. It may refer to some prehistoric or Ice Age animal like the mastodon or the mammoth. Under Bull may have been present at Fort McKenzie on the Marias during the visit of Prince Maximilian and the battle with the Assiniboines in 1833.

HEAVENS* PEAK: This name appears already on Ahern's map of 1890. The mountain is said to have been named by the prospector Dutch Louie Meyer, who accompanied Ahern. The Kootani name is *Kanuhus Tuqҁqamna* (Red Bird) and the Blackfoot name is *Apistotóki ozitawpíhpiw* (Where God Lives). This last must be a paraphrase of the English. I am not aware that this is considered an especially sacred mountain by the Blackfeet. A funeral parlor in Whitefish from which a mountain in the park is clearly visible, used to sport a sign to reassure its customers, "Viewing Heavens Peak." The peak in view from that point, however, is Mount Jackson.

HEAVY RUNNER* PEAK: The Blackfoot form is *Isok-omahkan* (heavy running), a family name derived from a well-known chief, probably this one. It was originally assigned to the peak now called Citadel, perhaps by Schultz. Later, in honor of this chief, Dr. Ruhle rescued the name from oblivion and transferred it to the mountain next to Reynolds.

About 1869 the U.S. Army divided Piegan chiefs into two categories, peaceful and hostile. Heavy Runner (though no saint) made the peace list, and he had no part in the murder of Malcolm Clark. But white settlers clamored for retaliation, singling out the band of Mountain Chief. The rest of the sad story you already know if you have read in the historical preface about "the Baker massacre." Many persons whose names are now associated with Glacier were in the camp that was destroyed, among them Red Horn and Big Horn (who were killed), Black Eagle (who escaped), Almost-a-Dog (who was maimed for life), and Natahki (Schultz's wife-to-be, who was wounded). A tiny daughter of Heavy Runner survived to grow up and become the wife of Joe Kipp. Among the dead there was evidently one Mexican. While some soldiers apparently took pity and helped to save victims, there is also evidence described in French and never translated into English that soldiers killed pregnant women.

HELEN* LAKE and **MOUNTAIN**: The mountain stands in the southern portion of Glacier, and the lake is in the north, at the headwaters of the Belly River. The Kootenai name for the mountain is "Bull Elk Mountain," *Kiłqałłi Akwukłi'it*. There are at least three stories about the name for this lake: (1) This and Lake Elizabeth were named by a surveyor for his daughters; (2) They were both named by Joe Cosley for lady friends; (3) This lake, according to Schultz, was named for Helen Clarke, eldest daughter of Malcolm Clarke by his Piegan wife Kakokima and born in 1846 on the Judith River. Malcolm was a hot-tempered, talented, controversial trader brought up the river by Culbertson and eventually elevated to an executive in a fur company. At Fort Benton he was married by Father DeSmet in 1862 to his second wife, the daughter of Sandoval, and soon thereafter retired to a ranch near Helena. There, in a quarrel with relatives of his first wife, Malcolm was murdered in 1869. Helen, her sisters Isabel and Judith, and two or three Indian women and children were all spared. "We did not come to kill women and children," declared one of the intruders. But this affair precipitated an outcry from influential whites that ended in Baker's devastation of Heavy Runner's camp on the Marias in which at least fifty-three women and children were killed by whites.

Helen was sent away and educated in Minneapolis, and later in New York she went on to a school for the theater. She became an actress noted for her deep resonant voice. She gave performances in London, Paris, and Berlin, and once, it is said, acted with Sarah Bernhardt. Her most memorable role was Lady Macbeth!

But in 1875 she returned to Montana, taught school at Fort Benton and lived for a time in Helena with the family of Wilbur Fiske Sanders. From 1882 to 1890 she was school superintendent for Lewis and Clark County. She also spent some time in Oklahoma working on land allotments of various tribes, staying with the family Sherburne who eventually followed her back to Montana. From 1900 to 1902 she lived in California, but returned from San Francisco to reside at Midvale with her relatives the Clarkes and the Dawsons. There she died in 1923. Her Indian name was prophetic: *Paióta-apoahkaii* which I interpret as "Homing Bird."

She was the aunt of the mute sculptor John Clarke. (See *Who Was Who...* for more information.)

HELENA: The Montana state capital was named for a town in Minnesota, and both a mine and the Siyeh rock formation in Glacier carry the name of the capital. Perhaps because of the imposing neo-Gothic cathedral, this name is sometimes construed to mean Saint Helena, after the mother of the emperor Constantine. In any case, long before Saint Helena, the name was used for the Great Mother of the Gods, the Earth Mother and goddess of fertility of the ancient Mediterranean. Greece was called *Hellas* and its inhabitants *Hellenes*.

HELL ROARING CREEK is in Waterton Lakes Park, but the name is such a favorite that it pops up several times in the Whitefish Range just west of Glacier as well as in Kootenay National Park, British Columbia. It is applied even to a kind of limestone in the parks. It is probably also a mining name.

HENKEL*, MOUNT, is near Many Glacier. Joseph Henkel was a pioneer settler on Lower Saint Mary Lake, generally known to whites as Joe Butch and to the Blackfeet as "Red Sore Eyes," *Ikaipini(?)*.

HENRY*, MOUNT: this mountain which stands between Two Medicine and East Glacier was once noted for the railroad bell mounted on its heights. Hikers could pause there and clang away to their heart's content while the mountains echoed back. The mountain is said (without any certainty) to have been named for Alexander Henry, the younger, famous explorer of the Northwest. His journals of 1799–1814 have been edited by Elliott Coues. He covered the territory between Montreal and Lake Superior to Keewatin, Dakota, and Oregon. His adventures played a counterpoint to those of David Thompson, and Dr. Coues treats these two men together: Henry the profit-seeker and Thompson the scientist and the brother of everybody.

The Indian name assigned to Mount Henry by Schultz is "Chief Bear" or "Bear Chief," *Ninohkyaiyo*, often mentioned by Prince Maximilian, 1833 (not very favorably). Bear Chief had formerly been named Spotted Elk but assumed his new name for leading a small party that killed forty-five Salish and two French Canadians. (Was this the party that crossed via the Cut Bank in 1812? See MARIAS.) At Fort McKenzie he was honored by the factor ("factor" was the word for the boss at a trading post) for his partiality for Americans over British traders, but this ploy backfired into a chain-reaction of jealousy and blood feud. Bear Chief was put to shame and many Kaina people quit the post in high dudgeon, though Bodmer managed to paint portraits of the rivals. One leading rival was Iron Shirt.

The feud was suddenly interrupted by an attack of 600 Crees and Assiniboines. When all was over but the wails and groans, there was still bedlam. But Bear Chief found himself intact and rejoiced that he had been untouched by bullets simply because Bodmer had painted his picture. (See IRON SHIRT.)

HERBST* GLACIER, is named for Francis Herbst, a topographer in the U.S. Boundary Survey of 1861. Schultz, however, labels this glacier *Nitohkyaiyo* (Lone Bear) for a white friend from Chicago, Charles Phelan (an Indian name for a white man assigned by another white man! A strange kind of authenticity).

HERRIG CREEK: a Forest Service name. Fred Herrig was one of the earliest rangers in Glacier Country. (See THEODORE ROOSEVELT.)

HIDDEN FALLS is in the Swiftcurrent Pass country.

HIDDEN* LAKE, **CREEK**, and **MEADOW**: See BEARHAT, SILVERTIP.

HIGH LINE: From Logan Pass to Fifty Mountain Camp, this twenty-mile trail provides some of the most spectacular views in Glacier.

HOLE-IN-THE-WALL* FALLS: A descriptive name for a high spot near Bowman Creek where the water flows from a cave.

HOWE* CREEK, LAKE, and **RIDGE** are all named for Charlie Howe, one of the first homesteaders of Apgar around 1893. He and his wife Maggie hailed from Wisconsin and belonged to the Chippewa tribe. With Joe Cosley, Mrs. Brewster, the Sansevere family, and others, they formed a Chippewa-Cree community at Lake McDonald. Charlie had been a boatman on the Great Lakes and became one of the most expert boatmen on Lake McDonald and the Flathead River. He ran cruises on the North Fork and in Bad Rock Canyon, and one of his clients was novelist Mary Roberts Rinehart. In those days this water route to town may have been more convenient than the road through Bad Rock Canyon.

Maggie Howe was a fine cook and homemaker, and Joe Cosley often visited the Howes at Lake McDonald, probably for a square meal. Charlie built a log house with the logs vertical like palisades, a pointed roof and cupola or a lookout. Here he stored furs collected from Joe Cosley and other trappers, trading with Lewis at the head of the lake. Though he had been a partner of Milo Apgar at a store in Great Falls, they had a falling-out over the boundary of his homestead. In fact, Charlie and Dimon Apgar are said to have sawed a barge in two, dissolving the partnership. But their wives remained good friends (there must be a moral in this).

When Mrs. Howe was substituting for a Japanese cook at the Belton Hotel, she drank by mistake a cup of poisoned wine (or coffee) that had been prepared for someone else. She called for Charlie, who barely had time to get to her before she died.

Charlie had interests in local mining claims known as Honduras, Monte Cristo, and Lake View. Howe Creek is also called Spruce Creek. The Kootenai names are "Lost Rider Lake," *Kukiłnuk Kyawnqamik Akuq̓nuk,* and "Lost Rider Mountain," *Kukiłnuk Kyawnqamik Akwukłi'it.*

HUCKLEBERRY* MOUNTAIN is the northern terminus of the Apgar Range. It used to be called Eagle Peak. In Kootenai "huckleberry" is *ławiyał* .

HUDSON* GLACIER is probably named after Francis (or T.) Hudson, who was a member of the U.S. Boundary Survey of 1861. The Indian name is "Curly Bear," a name which has now been transferred. (See CURLY BEAR, TRIPLE DIVIDE.)

HUDSON BAY* CREEK and **DIVIDE**: The bay and the divide are usually spelled this way, but the fur company's name is written as Hudson's Bay Company. The divide carries at least two names in the Blackfoot language: *Niz'-Pawahkui* (Real or Only Ridge) and *Apakazoasko* (Wide Forest). The upper portion is also known as Saint Mary Ridge and is scarred by a bare spot locally known as The Beaver Slide.

HUMBOLDT is the name of one of Joe Kipp's mining claims, ultimately derived from the German-French naturalist Alexander von Humboldt. He is especially renowned for his studies and explorations in Latin America. Humboldt was an inspiration, perhaps a personal mentor, to both Louis Agassiz and Prince Maximilian. His brother Wilhelm was a noted linguist and philosopher. (See AGASSIZ, CARIBOU, HENRY.)

HUNGRY HORSE town and dam: There are at least two different stories about two different horses. One says that about 1895 one of a prospector's two horses died in the winter, while the other, a buckskin, survived. The other story claims that in 1900 a freighter had two lead horses, Tex and Jerry. Both were missing near where the town is today but were found a month later. Oats were packed in to them. One was eventually used on a delivery wagon, and the other on a fire wagon in Kalispell.

IBEX is the name of an old mining claim belonging to Dutch Louie Meyer. In the 1880s "ibex" was the term in popular usage for the Rocky Mountain goat, which has since become the logo for Glacier National Park, the Great Northern Railway, and the Glacier Natural History Association. James Willard Schultz (as usual) claims to have given the name "mountain goat" to the "ibex" during his hunt with Oliver Sandoval in 1883 around Saint Mary. Scientists may be reluctant to accept this story, and the term "goat" may not be much more accurate than the term "ibex." A second mining claim with the name Ibex occurs in the Josephine complex. (See JOSEPHINE.)

A curious side issue is the Cree name for the "Rocky Mountain Goat" which is *wápitik/wápitihk.* It derives from the ancient Proto-Algonquin *atik* (deer, caribou) and prefixing *wap-* for "white." See the item on *wapiti* in the entry ELK.

ICEBERG LAKE was named for its icebergs either by Hugh Monroe in the 1850s or by Grinnell in 1890—or both. In Blackfoot this is *Kokutói Omahxikimi* (Ice Lake). Behind it looms the Cathedral Wall with its descriptive name. (See ALLEN, WHITE ELEPHANT.)

INDIAN HEAD MOUNTAIN: Said to look down on the west side of Waterton Lake, this mountain has not been identified to everyone's satisfaction. Apparently, the name refers to a profile in the rock formation, but such a formation is attributed also to both Mount Blakiston and Mount Richards, formerly known as "Sleeping Indian" or "Dead Indian" Mountain. Does this try your imagination beyond a reasonable limit? Well, we shall leave it here as another name floating about looking for a mountain to alight upon. But we also find mountains peeping up looking for names (especially in the northwest corner of Glacier). Should we match them up?

The *Lethbridge Herald* for September 15, 1923, offers us "the legend of Indian Head," for which I give no guarantee of authenticity: Crow Chief of the Blackfoot tribe insists his daughter Bird Woman marry Weasel Moccasin, the son of the Blood Day Chief. Bird Woman, however, is in love with Running Antelope and threatens to run off to the land of devils(!) west of the mountains. So away she elopes with Running Antelope. As her father in pursuit with his warriors is about to overtake them, Running Antelope heroically offers himself as a sacrifice if the Sun will please save Bird Woman. So the sun sends a cloudburst that forms a lake to separate the lovers from the pursuers (Waterton Lake?). When Crow Chief almost catches up with the lovers the second time, Running Antelope grows tall enough to become a mountain that again isolates Bird Woman from Crow Chief.

Compare the story of Sahkumpi in the entry on WATERTON LAKES PARK.

IPASHÁ* FALLS, GLACIER, LAKE, and **PEAK** in the Fifty Mountain country: Ipashá was reported to be the mother of Joe Kipp and the daughter of Mandan chief Matótopa, who had been familiar with the greats and near-greats of the Upper Missouri from Sacajawea to the Culbertsons. Her name is translated as "Good Eagle Tail," and she may have also had the Blackfoot name of "Earth (Lodge) Woman," since her people the Mandans were known as the "Earth Lodge People" because of their earth-covered homes. Ipashá's name used to be applied to Pyramid Peak, while Mount Kipp or Ipasha Peak was then called the Lady Collins for the Cattle Queen of Montana. The Cattle Queen's claim lay adjacent to Kipp's.

But there is some discrepancy about Ipashá's relationship to Joe Kipp. By one account the woman who gave birth to Joe on Knife River in 1849 was Martha Garneaux, and Martha was the daughter of Pierre Garneaux and Eagle Tail Woman or *Ipashá*, the daughter of Matótopa. Joe may have had brothers and sisters, but if so, all were reported dead by the small pox.

ISABEL* LAKE was named by R. T. Evans for the wife of Thomas Dawson, guide and mountaineer. Isabel was a daughter of Malcolm Clark, born in 1861. Like her sister Helen, she was spared by her father's murderer. Her name is the Spanish form of the Biblical Elizabeth, though it seems she was the daughter of Kakokima, Malcolm's Piegan wife, rather than his Hispanic-Piegan wife. Isabel died in Great Falls in 1935. The Kootenai name for the lake is "Lone Woman Lake," *Ḱuki Paɫkiy Aknuq̇nuk.*

JACKSON* GLACIER and **MOUNT:** in 1891 Grinnell named the peak or something near it for William Jackson, grandson of Hugh Monroe and a scout with Reno on the occasion of Custer's downfall. Billy Jackson and his brother Robert were both scouts on that frontier. While Robert associated more with the Crows and especially the Bravo family, Billy served with Nelson Miles and the Royal Mounties during the Riel "rebellion." His Blackfeet name was "Blackfeet Man," *Sixikáikoan*, which in 1940 the Geographic Board flatly declared too difficult to pronounce. The members of the Board must have been tongue-tied because every syllable has its equivalent in English. It may be that the similarity between this name and that of the Sixika tribe of the Blackfeet caused an early confusion about this name. Grinnell called this area "the Crown of the Continent," perhaps referring to the peak now named Jackson in particular. McClintock, who had also been guided by Billy Jackson, agreed that Glacier would contain "an apex of the continent....the Blackfoot Mountain with the great Blackfoot Glacier." Such an appraisal seems a bit extravagant today, but it would have to refer to Mount Jackson, not the present Blackfeet Mountain. Besides, we easily forget how much the glacier has shrunk since these men first beheld it. My guess is that Grinnell intended to name the peak that he thought was the Crown of the Continent for the Blackfeet tribe, but a mix-up of some sort caused the switch of similar names. Regardless of the messed-up name, this peak is one of the most prominent, and you can get a magnificent view of it directly from the Kalispell airport.

JACKSTRAW* LAKE was named by Evans in 1910 for the piles of burned wood on its shores. This was the era of the most devastating of forest fires. This lake may be the former Lake Katherine, the headwaters of Ole Creek.

JAMES*, MOUNT: Grinnell named the present Mount Stimson after Dr. Walter R. James of New York and gave the name Stimson to the present Mount Logan. Somehow these names were switched around and unfortunately, this switch has confused the historical significance of their meaning. The Mount James of today juts up in front of the Mount Stimson of today as it is viewed from the eastern foothills (near where Highway 89 crosses Cut Bank Creek) and hence may have been confused with it. That is not a very convincing explanation, but how can you find a better in such toponomic chaos? The Blackfoot name for Mount James is *Nitáina* (Lone Chief) after one who signed the historic Judith treaty of 1855.

JANET* LAKE: The Board on Geographic Names approved the name Janet in 1929 but can no longer state why or for whom. But luckily, the lake has alternate names. One is Haunted Lake. Ranger Reynolds claimed that an Indian camp was attacked here and the women and children fled. A baby who cried was cast over a cliff with the result that its spirit still haunts the place. (Again the theme of throwing babies off cliffs. Believe it if you like.)

The third name is Natawista Lake, and Natawista is a lady of whose identity there is no doubt, the sister of Seen From Afar and the wife of Alexander Culbertson. (See NATAWISTA.)

JAVA CREEK, MOUNTAIN, and **STATION:** The station is now called Nimrod, but creek and mountain are still Java. One wonders if they were named for the island or for the delight of coffee addicts. But recently an Indonesian visitor was pleased to find the name here. Most of this area lies just south of Glacier and in the past has been a center of abortive mining activity. Claims near Java include Calumet, Nevada, and the Queen of the Rockies. Jack S. Stewart had a claim named for himself, while the Geifers had one named Coeur d'Alene (1908), a Salish tribal name meaning (in French) "needle-hearted" or "heart of awl." (See NIMROD.)

JEAN LAKE is now called Lake Elizabeth. Originally it was named by Lieutenant Ahern for his bride, Jean Gill. So we know who Jean was but no one knows Elizabeth. The West Butte of the Sweetgrass Buttes is called Mount Jean (perhaps in this case French for "John").

JEFFERSON* PASS was named for Thomas Jefferson, but not for the man you're thinking of and not much like him either. This one was "Uncle Jeff," a packer with a long white beard who lived near Lake McDonald. He was about six and a half feet tall, lanky and an excellent horseman. He had served as a pony express rider out of Saint Joseph, Missouri, and as a scout for General Miles. He came up the Missouri to Fort Benton and fell in with the wrong bunch (since in old Benton there was hardly any other kind to fall in with). His buddies were a gang of horse rustlers. When ranchers formed a vigilante offensive, Uncle Jeff escaped. About 1905 he came up the North Fork, a favorite resort for escapees, although he may have been in the park area as early as 1890. He became a packer for the surveyor (and superintendent) Chapman. "Thomas Jefferson" may have been his alias. His pass was known among the Piegans as "the place where the Stonies fled across the mountains under attack by the Gros Ventres."

JOHN F. STEVENS* CANYON is named for the engineer who reconnoitered Marias Pass for the railroad, and at a rather late date at that. He is not to be confused with Isaac I. Stevens. John F. had a distinguished career and it's too bad his reputation has to depend so much on this rather trivial double-check. He later became an executive for the Panama Canal and the Great Northern, Trans-Siberian, and Chinese railroads. Theodore Roosevelt agreed to share with Stevens the naming of the route across the mountains.

JOHNS LAKE is named for "Dutch" John Elsner, a homesteader who had a claim above Lake McDonald.

JOSEPHINE* LAKE, once called Lake Louise (which it does resemble a little), may have got its current name from the Josephine mine on Grinnell Point. Its Blackfoot name is listed by Schultz as *Nitáki* (Lone Woman) after a woman warrior. It may also be one of two or three waters that have borne the name "Jealous Woman's (or Women's) Lake" from a story attributed to both the Kootenai and the Blackfeet. This was the heart of the Swiftcurrent Mining District, where, for example, lodes patented as late as 1911 included Josephine, Ibex, Big Horn, Sunshine, and Silver Tip. Grinnell Point was formerly called Stark Peak, probably for the mining partners of Joe Kipp, Scott, and Parley Stark. Parley ran the hotel at Altyn, and his patented claims were named Snowshoe, Bullshead, and Mountaineer. Very few claims were actually patented within the present boundaries of Glacier. Josephine Lake and the Josephine mine may have been named for Josephine Doody or even for a miner's mule, but Dan Doody was also active around the Altyn area. (See Doody.)

KAINA* CREEK, LAKE, and **MOUNTAIN**: The name *Kaina* (formerly *Kainah* and today sometimes spelled *Kainaa*) is pronounced like *ky* in "sky" and *nah*. It refers to the Blood tribe of the Blackfoot confederation. Its meaning is disputed. It may derive from a root *kai* for "(dried) blood," or perhaps it is from an old form meaning "many chiefs," *akaina*. (The root *akai-*: many + *(n)ina*: man, chief.) A third possibility is a derivation from *akai-* (many) + *ini* (die) with the meaning "many dead," said to refer to the horrible epidemic of smallpox in 1837–8. This last name was sometimes used for Saint Mary River. The sign for Blood Indian is made by closing and crooking fingers across the mouth and imitating the motion of picking clotted blood from the teeth. There is a fourth possibility that the root *kai-* refers to anything stuck together or piled up and therefore to anything clotted like blood or to a pile of corpses, victims of an epidemic. In any case the imagery has nothing to offer the romanticist. Well, unless you are talking about the first wife of Charles Conrad, a Blood Lady named *Kaiyis*, whose name seems to come from this same root.

The Blood tribe has its agency at Cardston, Alberta, with a forest reserve enclosed in the bounds of Waterton Lakes Park. This branch of the Blackfoot alliance used to have an hereditary chieftainship or dynasty, which may have had some authority over the entire confederation. However, the authority of the chief, even if we call it dynastic or royal, was not the absolute abstract power understood by white people in their own history, but rather a kind of personal prestige, more persuasion than command.

KAKITOS MOUNTAIN: The Blackfoot word for "star" is *kak-(n)atós(i)*, a derivative from the root *nato-* for "holy, spiritual" with a prefix *kak-*. The mountain is supposed to look like a star though I confess I have never been able to see much similarity. The term is also a personal and family name. One of those who bore the name was a Piegan descended from the early Mexican *engagé* named Pablo, while another was Schultz's and Schaeffer's main informant or interpreter for Kootenai place names, John Star of Fort MacLeod and Elmo. (See PABLO, STARR.)

KALISPELL: The county seat of Flathead County and the site of the so-called Glacier Park International Airport. The name is probably a variation of a term for camas fields. Spelled with only one final *l*, it is also the name of the Kalispel tribe, sometimes called *Pend d'Oreille* (French for "earrings"). This is a Salish group that had some claim to the upper portion of Flathead Lake, while the Flatheads (also Salish people) centered in the Bitterroot Valley. So the Kalispels were the nearest Salish people to Glacier, though moved here in the late 1800s at government urging from north of Spokane. The name of the city is said to have derived from its founder Charles Conrad as appointed by Jim Hill to find a site and a name for a point on his "Manitoba" railroad. The story or legend is that Conrad was having supper served by ∞milie, a daughter of Louis Brun, who with his Indian wife and children was one of the earliest settlers of the upper Flathead valley. Conrad asked the young lady for advice about a name for the town he would establish and she suggested the name of her mother's tribe, Kalispel. Conrad then added the extra *l* to distinguish the town from the tribe. (See BROWN.)

KATOYA* LAKE: McClintock says *katoya* is Blackfoot for incense and balsam fir, *abies lasiocarpa*, also called sweet pine, alpine fir, and more recently subalpine fir. The name was applied to this lake by Dr. Ruhle and satisfied the preference for Indian language place names expressed by the Board on Geographic Names. Katoya is one of three lakes called the Morning Glory Lakes located in the high country north of Two Medicine, a fisherman's paradise—sometimes. (See SWEETGRASS, MORNING GLORY).

KELLY'S CAMP is an old resort on Lake McDonald, named for a local resident. Frank Kelly ran boats on the lake from 1906 to 1921 or even longer.

KENNEDY* CREEK and **LAKE** were named after John Kennedy, who built a post at the mouth of the creek entering Saint Mary River near Babb. This was in 1874 at the end of the whiskey era across the border. Whiskey posts formed a chain that ran between Fort Benton and southern Alberta and Saskatchewan. The road from Benton to Fort Whoop-Up near Lethbridge was known as the Whoop-Up Trail. Another post in the section northeast of Babb, but across the line, was at Whiskey Gap. Whiskey traders were very creative, lacing their brew with various goodies like tobacco, red ink, red pepper, tea, laudanum and (one suspects) maybe an occasional dash of arsenic. The concoction was called "rot-gut" and other appetizing names. In 1874 the North West Mounted Police put a halt to the whiskey traffic north of the border. Kennedy Creek is also said to have been named Joe's Creek after Joe Kipp.

KING EDWARD PEAK is near the border in British Columbia. (See KISHENEHN.)

KINNERLY* PEAK: This mitre peak is one of the most dramatic spectacles in Glacier Park. The Ivory Tower would be a good description, but it already has received more names than it needs. The Kootenai name is listed as "Deaf Mountain" with no explanation now available: *Kɫitkapaɫnitit Akwukɫi'it.*

Early maps show Kinnerly Peak (and/or Kintla Peak with which it is occasionally confused because these two peaks are almost identical twins; see KINTLA) as "Audubon." This may have been an attempt to honor the artist-naturalist Jean-Jacques Audubon, who was royally entertained by the Culbertsons at Fort Union in 1843 and did (or began) portraits of both Alex and Natawista. Or it may be in honor of Audubon's wife who was the boyhood teacher of George Bird Grinnell.

The origin of the name Kinnerly is not well attested, but it is probably a clumsy spelling for "Kennerly." In that event, it may refer to (1) Dr. C. B. R. Kennerly, surgeon and naturalist of the U.S. Boundary Survey from 1857 to 1861. In this last year he died on the trip back home and was buried at sea off Acapulco. Or (2) Henry Atkinson Kennerly (1835–1913), grandson of Pierre Ménard, one of the founders of the Missouri River fur trade. In 1855 this Kennerly came to Montana as an attaché for the expedition of Isaac Stevens and Alfred Cumming. He made an excursion to Saint Mary Lakes and eventually married a daughter of Mountain Chief, served in the Montana legislature and was treasurer of Chouteau County.

But the peak still has borne another name: Mount Thompson, presumably in honor of the old explorer David Thompson. This was the name current in Canada at the time Glacier National Park was established. In connection with the International Boundary Survey of 1910, Reginald A. Daly transmitted from M.I.T. in Boston to the commissioner in Ottawa a long report of a geological survey of the mountains along the border that he had just completed. In this book he refers to "Mount Thompson" with a photo clearly of Kinnerly Peak and remarks that it is composed of siyeh limestone and towers 5,500 feet above Upper Kintla Lake.

KINNIKINNICK (*Kinikinik*): A former resort area on Half Moon Lake near West Glacier, not in operation at the present time (2003). The name is that of a plant or plants used by Native Americans to mix with tobacco. More specifically, it refers to the larb or bearberry, a trailing evergreen plant with red leaves that were sometimes eaten as medicinal by the Indians who also smoked the leaves as tobacco. The word *kinuk-kinuk* derives from an eastern Algonquin dialect and means a "mixture."

In Alberta *Kinikinik* is the name of a post office, and the word is defined as a mixture of tobacco with red willow bark. With this spelling, *kinikinik* is the only known word of four syllables that is spelled the same way forward and backward.

KINTLA* CREEK, GLACIER, LAKES, and **PEAK**: The name *Kintla* is a Kootenai word meaning "sack." It seems to have been used for many features in this area, perhaps even the area itself in the sense of *cul de sac*. Upper Kintla Lake is called in Kootenai *Kinła Nana Akuɋnuk*. The main Kootenai trail bypassed most of it for a more convenient passage just north of the border.

It is said that Indians usually avoided the waters of Kintla and that when one of them drowned here, the body was never recovered. The Jesuit map of 1846 marks Kintla Lake and Creek as *Lac et Rivière de Joset* for one of the missionaries active in Idaho. There is still a relic of oil drilling on Lower Kintla Lake, and once there were several mineral claims named Kintla, evidently owned by Ed Dow of Belton and his partners (1904). There were also two claims here of Paul Schoenberger and one called Jumbo (1901). Natural gas is released in this area. The U.S. Survey of 1861 located the Kintla Mountains and Lakes at 114º15′ W. But one thing that surveyors and trekkers seem often to have overlooked is the fact that the peaks Kintla and Kinnerly form identical twins—or at least appear so viewed from the northwest. Kinnerly is a horn, eroded on four sides. Kintla looks that way from the northwest but hides some of its bulk on the opposite side. It is also a little taller than Kinnerly. Kintla is 10,101 feet; Kinnerly is 9,944 feet.

KIOWA KAMP (Camp) and Junction lie just east of Glacier where the Browning road joins Highway 89. The Kiowa are a tribe of Oklahoma, related to Shoshonis and emigrants from southern Montana.

However, the name here derives indirectly from the Souian tribe called Iowa. The proprietor of the camp once asked Mrs. Fisher what to call his resort. Mrs. Fisher was a long-time county superintendent of schools and was supposed to have all the answers. Her answer this time went like this: "You're from Iowa. So why not just put a *k* in front of that?"

KIPP* CREEK and **MOUNT:** Probably no one has been more closely associated with the Glacier/Waterton area, for better or worse, than Joseph Kipp, son of James Kipp, a Canadian executive of the Upper Missouri Outfit. James built Fort Union at the mouth of the Yellowstone and hosted Catlin, Maximilian, DeSmet, Audubon, and Palliser. His son Joe was born on the Knife River in 1849 by his father's Mandan or part-Mandan wife. (See IPASHA.) His name in Mandan was "Bear-Looking Back," *Mató-i-karup-tahe*, and his Blackfoot name was "Raven Quiver," *Maistóinopázis* and often just plain *Kipa*.

When his father went back east to his "French" wife in Missouri, Joe seems to have lived with the Culbertsons, perhaps first at Fort Benton, then at their estate near Peoria. He put in a couple of years at Bryant and Stratton College in Peoria, probably as a fellow student of Jack Culbertson. But the break-up of his own family seems to have turned Joe into a young cynic. Most of his later life was spent in his mother's country. In 1862, on one of his trips up the river, he was on the epic-making cruise of the *Spread Eagle* with the Culbertsons, Father DeSmet, and "the father of American anthropology," Lewis Henry Morgan. All these people became informants for Morgan.

At Fort Benton Joe was a clerk for Andrew Dawson and George Steele. When Steele's black stallion was stolen by a young warrior, Joe showed remarkable courage in recovering the prize horse. He is also reported to have penetrated the Saint Mary country as early as 1866 in a party of eighty prospectors and to have made another prospecting trip as far as Fort Edmonton with Charles Thomas and John Wrenn. On this trip they forgot a pair of pincers [*sic*] and so gave the name to Pincher Creek [*sic*].

Engaged by Colonel de Trobriand, Joe became a scout for the U.S. Army. Just at the wrong time, as it turned out, because he was assigned to accompany Eugene Baker's troops and volunteers in the tragic encounter on the Marias, January 1870. (See HEAVY RUNNER.) In remorse for the massacre, Joe took to wife the surviving daughter of

Heavy Runner, Martha Double Strike, and also adopted her (half?)-brother Dick. However, Dick nursed a grudge against Joe and is said to have given Joe a severe thrashing. Yet J. W. Schultz compared Joe to Kipling's Kim for his kindness to the needy and even idealized him as "Berry" in his book *My Life As an Indian.*

Joe, nevertheless, was a kingpin among the whiskey runners. He and his associates built whiskey posts north of the border, Stand Off and Whoop Up at the northern end of the Whoop-Up Trail. There Joe took part in the killing of the bully Calf Shirt or Calf Robe, though Joe's act may have been in self-defense. (See CALF ROBE.)

When the Mounted Police shut down the whiskey traffic in Alberta in 1874, Joe moved back into juicy-wet Montana and started up a post at Dupuyer. He joined the mining rush to West Flattop Mountain with the Cattle Queen, Joe Cosley, McPartland, O. S. Main, and the Stark brothers, all of whom are recalled in local place names. The sites named for Joe himself are in this same Fifty Mountain area. He also had a cabin near Mount Kipp. At Fort Conrad and "the notorious Robare," he was associated in business with Schultz. In later life he retired to his farm near Kipp Lake.

Frank Linderman tells us that he once proposed writing Joe Kipp's story, but Joe protested, "Nope, Frank, if I'd tell the truth, they'd hang me yet, sure's hell."

But is it really that sure? This writer has pleasant memories of Joe's son. (See AKAMINA, CARIBOU, MORGAN, MONTEREY.)

KISHENEHN* CREEK: This name is usually said to mean "no good" in Kootenai, but on the British Columbia side of the border, where the creek begins, it is spelled *Kishinena* and reported to mean "balsam" or "white fir." (See KATOYA.) Alternate Canadian spellings include *Kishenina, Kishenehn,* and *Kishnenehno.*

In Charles Wilson's diary of the British Boundary Survey he reports camping on the Kishenehu River, July 25th, 1861, and calls the "river" a tributary of the Flathead or Pend' Oreille (Pend d'Oreille). Nearby the surveyors came upon cairns of stone marking the international line just south of two peaks Wilson calls Kirby and Spence. He was again on the "Kishenehu" a few days later. The spelling *Kishinena* does appear on government maps of both Canada and the U.S. The less-than-phonetic spelling *Kishenehn* seems to date back at least to the

U.S. Northwestern Boundary Survey of 1861, which set up Camp Kis-e-nehn and used the name for a creek and a mountain at 114°20′W (by their calculations). However, these men also used the form *Kish-ne-néh-na* for mountains at 114°15′W, perhaps the Boundary Mountains and Long Knife. This suggests there may have been two names, cognate but not identical, with the Canadian term derived from one and the U.S. name from the other.

Kishenehn Creek flows by the ancient Indian trail from the North Fork across the southeastern corner of British Columbia to the Akamina Road. The story of this trail reported by Olga Johnson runs this way: the Kootenais adopted a Piegan boy and named him Kishenehn. But when the lad grew up he crossed the mountains to his own people. So several Kootenais decided to do away with him. Heading toward the pass, they ran into Kishenehn along this creek, but he only laughed that their arrows would bounce off him. Unknown Bear shot an arrow that proved otherwise. Kishenehn, the unwanted and unloved, lay dead in the forest.

KOOTENAI* PASSES, PEAK, and **CREEK**: The name is spelled many ways: *Kootenay, Cottonahaw,* and so on, but anthropologists generally use the spellings *Kutenai* and *K'tunaxa,* while some of the Kootenai people themselves prefer the form Kootenai. This, however, is a Blackfoot term, and the Kootenais' name for their own people is *Ksanka* or *Ks'ank'a,* said to mean "Standing Arrow." These people are called in French *Arcs-á-Plat* translated as Flat Bows in old writings. Some modern scholars have identified the *Tunaha* or *Kutenaha* with the branch of Kootenais who lived around present Fort MacLeod, Alberta. Of this group, some are said to have moved west across the Divide while others joined the Piegans. This colony is also regarded as belonging to the Tobacco Plains division of the Kootenais. These seem to be the people who came down into Montana from time to time and camped on Saint Mary Lakes, where they were met by Schultz and Grinnell. When Schultz camped with the Kootenais at Saint Mary in 1887, he named the present Curly Bear Mountain (or a peak near it) as Kootenai Mountain and also named the Kootenai Lick for his guides.

The Kootenai people are divided generally into Lower and Upper (and sometimes Middle) groups and are divided again by the international border. Most of them live in British Columbia. The Lower Kootenai lived around Lake Pend d'Oreille in Idaho and Kootenay Lake, British

Columbia, while the Upper Kootenai were grouped around the Tobacco Plains as their culture center, and extending to the Columbia
Lakes and the headwaters of the Columbia River. There were at least
seven bands altogether, of which the Akanahonek and Akiniyik were
important to the Waterton and Glacier area. A small group lives today at Elmo, Montana. The isolation of these various divisions has
not redounded to the political advantage of the people.

Of all the Indians who lived in and around Waterton/Glacier the
Kootenais were probably the most frequent and regular visitors, so
Kootenai place names (or at least geographical descriptions) are the
principal native names in the area. (The Blackfoot names were mostly
applied by white people.)

The Kootenai Pass that connects Waterton Lake southward with the
McDonald drainage is called Flathead Pass on Canadian maps, perhaps because Blakiston claimed it was used by the Flathead Indians to
reach "the Saskatchewan Plains" for hunting buffalo. The Kootenais
used this pass in winter, and Stonies used it too. At 5,700 feet, it's the
lowest transcontinental pass in this area.

The Waterton Lakes are fed by the Kootenai River flowing through
the Kootenai Valley in Glacier, where also lie the tiny Kootenia Lakes.
This strange form *Kootenia* is the name of a mining claim (Kootenia
Chief) and probably goes back to an 1895 map of British Columbia
that marked the Kotenie River. As if all this were not confusing enough,
this river and/or Olson Creek seem to be the *Kin-nook-kleht-nán-na*
of the U.S. Boundary Survey of 1861.

The Blackfoot name for Kootenai Pass is *Kutenai-ozitámiso-(iaw)*
(where the Kootenais go up or west), and for the valley, *Izitáwakozihp
Kutenai* (?) (where we fought the Kootenais). This is a reference to a
skirmish there about 1810. Kootenai Peak is said to be called in
Blackfoot *ozínipizistaki* (the mountain where someone froze); Kaina
hunters there discovered a frozen corpse.

There is also a Kootenai Creek just south of Glacier flowing into the
Middle Fork, and of course there is the great Kootenay River that
heads near the headwaters of the Columbia in British Columbia and
twists as the glaciers once forced it to do into Montana, back into
British Columbia and into Idaho. Kootenay National Park in British Columbia protects the headwaters of the Kootenay River. And

north of the border there are another three Kootenai Passes: South, Middle, and North.

South Kootenai Pass was probably the most frequented and was known as the Buffalo Trail, open all year round without much snow, not so steep, good for horseback and negotiable in nine days. It was used by Stoneys as well as Kootenais. As Reeves assures us, archaeological sites in the Blakiston valley indicate that this route has been used for over eight thousand years. It comes from the Tobacco Plains, up Grave Creek to Yakinikak Creek, over to Trail Creek, across the North Fork, up Kiskinena Creek and branches to South Kootenai Pass and Akamina Pass.

So the geographic picture is as complicated as the ethnographic one. Well north of the Kootenai Passes the Kootenay National Park in British Columbia looms over the headwaters of both the Kootenay River and the Columbia River together in Canal Flats. The Columbia heads north while the Kootenay heads south, then each does a radical about-face to join each other and the Flathead. The ancient glaciers were responsible for shoving the scenery around, a rare and remarkable feat to which tourists hardly give a nod.

KITCHEN HILL is on the edge of East Glacier near the golf course and the trail to Two Medicine Falls. The name probably should be Kittson Hill for one or both of the Kittson brothers, railroad workers who married into the Blackfoot tribe. One of them settled here near the son and grandson of Malcolm Clarke.

KUPUNKAMINT* MOUNTAIN: *Kupumqamik* in Kootenai means "shakes himself." It normally refers to an animal but here it is said to be the name of a man. The Kootenais applied the name to Double Mountain, but the name has been relocated to this other peak. (See YELLOW.)

LAKE* CREEK: Descriptive; it is near Kiowa Junction.

LAKEVIEW RIDGE in Waterton Park looks down on Waterton Lake.

LANGERMAN LAKE: A forgotten body of water north of Lake McDonald, probably a part of the system of Camas Creek. (See CAMAS, BIG CEDARS.)

LEE* CREEK and **RIDGE**: Lee Kaiser was a bullwhacker whose last name has rested on both Chief Mountain and Mount Cleveland as well as the creek and ridge here mentioned. While he was on this creek with two companions (from Choteau) he shot himself by accident. A Piegan woman with a married name Kaiser is on the Blackfeet rolls of 1907–8. The Blackfoot name of the creek is "Rope Across" or "Rope Stretched Across," *Apamístapisetan,* and of the ridge, "Middle Ridge" or *Tazik(i)-pawahkui.* Gable Pass is on this ridge. Another way of transcribing the name of the creek is *sakemahpeneu,* but I do not know what to make of that. In Kootenai Lee Creek is *Akatánku'* (standing lodge pole).

LENA* LAKE was probably named by surveyor Evans for his wife. The Blackfoot name is "Buffalo Stone Woman" or *Iniskim-aki,* after the wife of Bull's Back Fat. Portraits of both husband and wife were painted by George Catlin. Buffalo stones are certain plant fossils, highly prized by the Blackfeet.

LEWIS OVERTHRUST: This special type of fault helped to make Glacier and Waterton parks what they are. That is, the land on one side of the fault overrides the land on the other side so that mountains sit on top of prairies. The classic example is Chief Mountain, and the effects of the fault are clearly seen in Marias Pass on the sides of the mountains to the north. This overthrust was discovered and named by geologist Bailey Willis in 1901–2. (See LEWIS RANGE.)

LEWIS RANGE: This is the range that includes the eastern portion of the International Peace Park and the place where the Lewis Overthrust is most easily noticeable. Though officially the name Lewis Range is confined to the park area, the range itself is regarded as running southeast from the park to a point near Helena and including the escarpment called the Chinese Wall. Evidently, someone thought that escarpment resembled the Great Wall of China. (The resemblance is not striking.) Both the range and the overthrust were named by Bailey Willis at the same time in honor of Meriwether Lewis, Jefferson's man from Virginia. Willis defined the range as extending from about 46°45' to 49°10' in Alberta. There does not, however, seem to be a clear-cut consensus about the identity of the Lewis Range. Sometimes it is called the Lewis and Clark Range, sometimes the Sawtooth, and yet again the Front Range. The name Sawtooth Ridge has been used also for a portion of the Clark Range in the Kintla area. Sawtooth is the name once applied to the Boundary Mountains. (See LIVINGSTON, BOUNDARY.)

LIME CREEK is the first creek beyond Rubideau Creek on Apgar Mountain. The reason for the name is not evident.

LINCOLN* CREEK, LAKE, and **PEAK**: These features were named for Mrs. Anna T. Lincoln of Minnesota, who came to this area in 1899. The Kootenai names are "Greedy Mountain," *Kwiłxasik Akwukłi'it*; "Equal Lake," *Kxaɛqakǫnuk*; and "Crane Collar Lake," *Qaspiłu'k'ana Akinmituk*. At one time the lake and creek were called Little Saint Mary in the move to use east-side place names along the railroad. (See ELLEN WILSON.)

LINEHAM PEAK, LAKE, and **BROOK** in Waterton: the brook used to be called Seepage Creek. John Lineham of Calgary and Okotoks was an old-time prospector for oil in the border country. Born in Ontario, he came west in 1878, became a rancher, and ten years later went to the legislature.

LINNET LAKE is in Waterton Lakes Park, a tiny lake just under the Prince of Wales Hotel and a good place to swim. The linnet is the small red-breasted songbird of the finch family. Its name has the same root as "linen" because it likes to eat flax seeds. It is a species belonging to Europe and Asia, and there are no true linnets native to the Americas. However, the name is loosely applied to a few related American birds like the house finch.

LITTLE CHIEF* MOUNTAIN: This magnificent peak may have been named by Grinnell for the head of the Pawnee Scouts, Major Frank North, whose Pawnee name is said to have been Little Chief. But the Blackfoot form, *Kinax-ina* or *Inax-ina*, was the name of Tom Dawson, and that would certainly be more meaningful to Glacier. It is absurd how many of the "Indian" names in Glacier, mostly applied by Schultz are really the "Indian names" of white people.

Little Chief is also the name of a mining claim, and a portion of the mountain is called North Gendarme while the mountain itself has also been called Red Eagle. Adolf Hungry Wolf says the peak was named for a warrior who was killed in 1865 in a fall during a buffalo hunt. (See RED EAGLE, DAWSON.) This may be the same man called Little Chief by Father DeSmet in his *Travels*, pp. 597–9. His story is well worth re-telling:

In September of 1846 DeSmet and other Jesuits were approaching Fort Lewis (the predecessor of Fort Benton), or as DeSmet and the French called it, Fort Maragnon (after the River Marias or *Maragnon* in French). Among their companions was a Piegan named Little Chief who paused and drew DeSmet aside for a smoke and a talk. Bluntly, he told DeSmet that he had an old quarrel with a chief of *Gens de Sang* (the Bloods or Kaina) who was now waiting inside the fort to kill him. One has to wonder if this Blood chief was the notorious Calf Robe. DeSmet does not say, but whoever he was, he once killed a Nez Perce who was a guest of Little Chief.

In return for this smirch on his honor, Little Chief then shot the Blood chief but failed to kill him. So now the Blood was waiting inside the fort for the ultimate showdown.

Father DeSmet tells us the outcome of this critical challenge to the Christian message: As Little Chief and his followers prepared their weapons, two messengers emerged from the fort and warned them not to enter. But the French and Spanish "defenders of the fort" welcomed the Jesuits by ringing the bell and throwing wide the gates.

The Jesuits and the principal chiefs were gathered onto an isle in the Missouri River where some Bloods were encamped. Big Lake was at hand with Sata, Little Chief, and various other dignitaries of the Piegans and the Bloods. DeSmet addressed them on peace and forgiveness, and Little Chief gave his enemy a horse and a robe embroidered with porcupine quills and pearls(!). Then the pipe of peace wafted the smoke upward in the prayer of reconciliation.

LITTLE DOG* MOUNTAIN: The name Little Dog has skipped from peak to peak until it has now alighted on a mountain that has been named for three different chiefs. This mountain, overlooking Marias Pass, used to be called "Wolf Tail," which can be either a Kootenai or a Blackfoot name. But the Kootenai name for the same mountain is "Big Knife." This must be the chief whose Christian name, "Aeneas," also appears in the Swan or Columbia Range and has even been used for Marias Pass, which Aeneas used. There have been several members of the Kootenai and/or Salish nations by this name, all of them partly of Iroquois ancestry. Somewhere along the line some missionary must have admired Virgil's hero, but the name seems to be a misconstruction of the French name Ignace (Ignatius).

Now for the present name "Little Dog," which in Blackfoot is *Imitáikoan* or "puppy." The man of this name was head chief of the Piegans but apparently also of Kaina descent and perhaps a cousin of Natawista. In his younger days he led a raid on a covered wagon train along the Oregon Trail but later became a man of peace, probably because he realized peace was better for his people than a suicidal war against whites. However, among his own people he was regarded as something of a tyrant. Because he is supposed to have given some information about Marias Pass to Isaac Stevens, his name was transferred from the mountain now called Brave Dog to the peak overlooking the pass.

Little Dog and his son "The Fringe" or "Never Tires" rode together. In 1866 Little Dog was still struggling to keep the peace (or co-existence) against all odds, and in token of this cause returned a dozen stolen horses to the agency at Fort Benton. On their way home, while The Fringe paused for a swim, his father was set upon by a (drunken?) group of his own people. As The Fringe rushed out of the water unarmed, he was shot down with his father.

LITTLE MATTERHORN: Some—not this author—see a resemblance between this peak and the famous Monte Cervino (also called the Matterhorn) on the Italian-Swiss border. It is visible from the foot of Lake McDonald with a more remote peak rising just to the left of it, probably Mount Reynolds. S. M. Logan suggested this peak be named Mount Kalispell. An older name for the Little Matterhorn is Comeau's Horn.

LITTLE PRAIRIE is in Waterton Lakes Park.

LITTLE RAKIOT is a peak east of Mount Merritt. My serious attempt to find a reason or meaning has failed.

LIVINGSTON* RANGE: Except for minor ranges like the Belton Hills and the Apgar Mountains, the International Peace Park is made up of two ranges: the Lewis and Clark Range and the Livingston(e) or

Clark(e) Range. The identity of these mountains has become a complicated subject, on which U.S. and Canadian authorities have not always agreed.

Geologist Reginald Daly (about 1910) wrote about the chaotic nomenenclature of the mountains along the forty-ninth parallel. The entire system from the Great Plains to the Pacific has borne a variety of names: The Shining Mountains (1743–1802, etc.), Mountains of the Bright Stones (late 1700s), Stoney/Stony Mountains, the Cordillera of the Andes, the Northern Andes, and so on. Daly settles for the Pacific or North American Cordillera, restricting the Andes to South America.

The local nomenclature is equally confusing. Some say the Canadian Rockies begin at Lake McDonald and go north, others object. And there are problems with the Livingston(e) and Lewis Ranges. There is a range in southern Alberta named Livingstone by Blakiston himself for the famous medical missionary of Africa, Dr. David Livingstone, but it is not identical with the range in Glacier. In Canada the Livingston Range of Glacier was described by Daly in 1910–12 under the name Clarke, selected to pair off with name Lewis on the range parallel to it. (There has always been a question about the spelling of William Clark(e)'s name.) When Daly and Bailey Willis conferred on this nomenclature, Willis happily agreed to the name "Clarke" instead of his earlier suggestion of "Livingston," because between the Livingston Range of Montana and the Livingstone Range of Alberta there occurs "a complete structural and topographic break." So Daly proposed the name Clarke for the range south of that break as far as McDonald Creek. Willis saw his point, but on the Canadian side of the line the range is called Clarke but on the U.S. side Livingston.

LOGAN* PASS CREEK, GLACIER, MOUNT, and **PASS** were all named for the first superintendent of Glacier, William Richard Logan (1856–1912). Born at Fort Belknap, Texas, to an Army captain who made a career of fighting Indians, William became a scout for the Army against the Sioux under Gibbon and Terry and also against the Nez Perces (1875–77). After his father was killed at the battle of the Big Hole, William settled in Helena and became involved in mining, ranching, and family life. He was the brother-in-law of Lieutenant Van Orsdale, whom he joined in 1883 in the exploration of southern Glacier conducted by Raphael Pumpelly. He was also the brother of Sydney M. Logan, the Kalispell attorney.

Though certainly no friend of Indians, whom he stereotyped as "natural beggars and bummers," William was selected by Senator Carter as Indian agent to the Blackfeet (1899–1900). Soon wearied of his job, he resigned but was nevertheless re-appointed as agent to the Assiniboines and Gros Ventres of Fort Belknap, Montana. Then again, no champion of conservationists, he was made supervisor of the brand-new Glacier National Park. After the terrible fires of 1910, he introduced a program in the new park that accorded with the Hills of Great Northern and proved developmental rather than environmental.

At the Belknap Reservation he had known the cattle kings of the Circle C, the Coburns, and their foreman Horace Brewster. Logan summoned Brewster to serve in Glacier as a ranger. This may explain how a peak in the new park was named Mount Coburn, the same mountain that later would be called Mount Logan and had previously been known as Wolf Gun and also as Bull Head (for a Blackfoot warrior and chief) and even as Stimson.

The Coburns were friends of people as varied as Granville Stuart, Charlie Russell, Theodore Roosevelt, Chief Joseph, and probably Butch Cassidy and the Curry gang, but they were not friends of Jim Hill. They introduced sheep onto their own cattle range, employing crews of Hispanic shepherds that circulated from California and the low border to the high. One son of the family, Walt, became a well-known Western writer, while another, Wallace, turned out to be a poet, movie actor, and director. In 1905–6 an older son, Will, took a neighboring Spanish-speaking rancher descended from Ponce de Leon on a remarkable trip through the pampas to the Andes of Argentina.

Logan Pass and Creek used to be called Trapper Pass and Creek, and according to Schultz, the pass was named *Misam-ohsokoi* (Ancient Road) by the Blackfeet. It was used, he adds, by the Kootenais, Salish, and Shoshonis. For Logan Glacier Schultz uses the name of his artist son by Natahki, Hart Merriam Schultz or *Nit-óhkuyi*, the Blackfeet translation of Hart's Navajo name "Lone Wolf." (Navajos say *ma'i-asahá*: wolf alone.) Hart spent much of his time in Arizona.

Just why the name Logan is used so often in Glacier remains a mystery, but the name seems most firmly fixed to the pass (with which Superintendent Logan had little or nothing to do). The Kootenais, especially the band called *Akiyinik*, used this pass in wintertime on showshoes going west to east. They referred to it as the trail "where packs are pulled up in a line," *Yakił yuxaxalkiakulum*. The great cliff near the summit on the west side made this route impractical for horses, and even people had to climb hand over hand while their baggage was pulled up by ropes. Then from the skirt of Mount Reynolds, they would slide their packs down to the lake below and cross Upper Saint Mary on the ice. Chief Paul David recalled using this route in the 1860s. Brian Reeves reports finding "a number of archaeological sites" at the summit that indicate "Precontact" use of this trail in summer. The Kootenais who used it in winter west-to-east, however, returned east-to-west with their buffalo meat by a more southerly route.

LOGGING* LAKE, CREEK, MOUNTAIN, and **RIDGE**: In 1891 or so there was a lot of logging activity in this area. Though acres of ponderosa pines were destroyed, majestic stands of these trees luckily still survive. Some have regarded the name "Logging" as inappropriate for a national park, and Dr. Ruhle urged the use of the Kootenai name, "Big Beaver" or *Yakił Wił qa'ki Sina* (where there's a big beaver) adding *Akuq̓nuk* for the creek and *Akwukłi'it* for the mountain. This name refers to a story that a beaver twenty feet long was found there. The map of 1846 shows a lake and a stream marked *Lac et Rivière Mengarini*, after Gregorio Mengarini, an Italian Jesuit who authored a Salish grammar in Latin and a Salish-English dictionary. Both he and DeVos were transferred to Mission Santa Clara in California where he helped establish the oldest university in the West. Still another name was applied to Logging Lake by the local Democrats: Lake Cleveland. That name did not take hold for the lake but made a comeback for the mountain.

There was also a Logging Pass used by Kootenais who ascended Logging Creek, camped at a place they called Camas Prairie, then moved up to another campsite on Logging Lake, then along the northern shore to still another campsite at the head of the lake, then to another place to camp just before reaching the summit. They could sustain themselves during this long trip by hunting goats and sheep along the way. Another campsite was at the headwaters of McDonald Creek from which they crossed Flattop Mountain and descended via Kootenai Pass to Waterton River and Lake. (See KOOTENAI PASS.)

LONE LAKE and **LONESOME LAKE** lie in Waterton Lakes Park. So is Lone Brook. Lone Lake is on Mount Festurbert, which marks the boundary between Alberta and British Columbia.

LONE PINE* PRAIRIE: Descriptive.

LONE WALKER MOUNTAIN: Lone Walker was a tall handsome man of great dignity, probably a leader of the Small Robes band in the early part of the nineteenth century. His name in Blackfoot can be expressed in different ways, but the most common form seems to be *Nitawahka*. He is said to have been called *Kionama*. Schultz claims he was a friend of the Mandan chief Matótopa. If so, Lone Walker must have been a far traveler. He had sixteen wives occupying five tipis. One of his wives was Bird Woman. He would walk about his camp carrying his lance, followed by his two pet bears. When Hugh Monroe first went to live among Lone Walker's people, he was afraid to pass through the tipi doorway with the bears lying at the door, So Lone Walker spat into Hugh's hands and rubbed his hands over the heads and mouths of the bears. Presto! Bear problem solved! (This technique is not recommended for park visitors.)

LONEMAN* MOUNTAIN: The Blackfoot term is *Nitáina*. The mountain was named in 1885 or perhaps in 1902 by Schultz and his companions Billy Jackson and Emerson Hough, the author of the novel *The Covered Wagon*. The three of them were on a winter hunt, camping on Nyack Creek with the weather thirty-three degrees below zero. The man for whom they named the mountain is not known. The Kootenai name is "Wolf Gun," *Ka·kin Tawu*.

LONG BOW* CREEK and **LAKE**: See Harris, Red Medicine.

LONG KNIFE* CREEK and **PEAK**: The Blackfoot form is *Ino-ístoan* in reference to U.S. soldiers and their swords, but Dr. Ruhle traces the name back to the Powhattans of Virginia. Long Knife Peak, close to 10,000 feet high, is the loftiest point on the entire U.S.-Canadian border and the climax of the Boundary (Sawtooth) Range. Omer Raup of the U.S. Geologic Survey isolated the highest point on a shoulder of Long Knife Peak, a third of a mile northwest of the summit at an elevation of 9,600 feet.

LONGFELLOW* CREEK and **PEAK**: For the poet, of course. The name was given by R. H. Sargent, the surveyor. The square rock on the peak is called Paul Bunyan's Cabin. The Kootenai name for both creek and peak is listed as "Coyote Woman," *Skinkut Pałkiy*.

LOOKING GLASS HILL is the grade on the south side of Two Medicine Ridge. Take your choice of reasons for the name: (1) From the ridge the Two Medicine Lakes are seen to resemble a map of the two

Americas; (2) From the ridge Rising Wolf Mountain presents the appearance of a black mirror; (3) From the lakes a flat rock on the ridge (now removed by road construction) used to resemble a black mirror; (4) As some wag has it, the road is so crooked that when you travel it you see yourself coming and going.

LOOKOUT BUTTE is in Waterton Lakes Park, partly in the Blood Timber Reserve.

LOOP: A switchback on the western slope of Going-to-the-Sun Road.

LOST* BASIN: The Kootenai name is Sacred Ground Basin: *Nupika Amak Akikqłała'mi*. The term *nupika* has a meaning similar to that of *sumésh* in Salish and *manito* in Algonquin: spirit, spiritual energy, or medicine (in the jargon of the frontier; in French, *médecin* refers to a person while *médecine* refers to a medicine). The name Lost Basin was conferred by Evans.

LOST LAKES and **MOUNTAIN**: Lost Mountain is a lonely peak in Waterton Lakes Park. There is one Lost Lake in Glacier and others in Waterton. Dr. Ruhle notes the ecological damage caused by the Logan Pass road near Glacier's Lost Lake.

LOST CABIN PLACER: About the turn of the twentieth century a lady from Dakota paid one or two visits by stage to the remote boom-town of Altyn (Many Glacier) and made a stir by claiming her two brothers had been slain by Indians over the Lost Cabin Placer. Perhaps instigated by such rumors, a local journalist for the *Acantha* of Dupuyer (!) began to pursue the story. He signed himself only as "A.B.C." Where professional journalism leaves off and A.B.C.'s imagination takes over is difficult to decide. At least some of his story is verifiable.

About the same time "a quaint old man" of eighty years known along the border country and in Lethbridge as Mexican Pete, passed to a life where there are no borders and no gold placers. According to A.B.C. he had come to Montana with Lt. John Mullan in 1856. (The date could be a bit awry but Mullan did make trips up from California in the late 1850s and the 1860s.) The Mexican married Bird Widow of the Blackfeet tribe and had two or three children. The surname assigned to him, "Larb," and later variations of it are impossible in Spanish but not altogether unlike the Spanish Basque name Larrabe. (But the plant called "larb" probably gets its name from the French *l'herbe*.) I suppose that "Mexican Pete" was one of the many *arrieros* (muleteers or packers) who came up to Oregon Country from Los Angeles, some of whom could have been associated with Mullan. A.B.C. claimed he had interviewed Mexican Pete ten years before and at that time the Mexican said he had lived among the Blackfeet forty-five years "off and on." Once, when he was wintering in a Blackfeet camp near Chief Mountain, he heard gossip that white men were back in the mountains taking money out of the ground. And a party of Kootenais appeared in camp with three scalps of white men, a quantity of gold and two horses. They had left behind a spooky animal that made a frightening noise.

Mexican Pete and his companions zigzagged into the mountains, found the cabin and buried the three corpses under a cross. The scary beast turned out to be a burro or mule, which they brought back to camp. He also brought back some nuggets that he showed to a visiting priest, who advised him to keep the matter under his hat. A.B.C. also claimed that one or two Kootenais had corroborated some of the story of the Lost Cabin Placer. But the cabin is still lost, and lost too is the trail.

Well, the story would be no fun if it had a solution. So while there is a little more to it, I shall follow the advice the priest gave to Mexican Pete and keep the rest under my *sombrero*.

LUBEC STATION, **LAKE**, **CREEK,** and **RIDGE** are near Marias Pass on the east side. The name of the railroad station has been changed to "Rising Wolf." Lubec was a part Indian or *Métis* trapper. The old ranger station, which had been built in 1907 and used by both the U.S. Forest Service and the National Park Service, was burned down, but the barn as an historic relic was moved to Saint Mary.

LUNCH CREEK flows between Pollock and Piegan Mountains. It was a lunch stop for early tourist parties, now grizzly country.

LUPFER GLACIER: Alexander M. Lupfer was a construction engineer for the railroad. A station on the railroad and a street in Whitefish also carry this name. The Kootenai name for the glacier is "Thirsty Woman Ice," *Kuknuq̓ɫuma Paɫkiy Akwiswitxu.*

MACKINAW BAY is in Upper Saint Mary Lake, probably named for the mackinaw trout or *namaycush*. The term derives from the French Canadian *mackinac*, the name of the island and the strait between Lake Huron and Lake Michigan. This name in turn comes from the Chippewa *machi-makinak*: Big Turtle. Mackinaw is also the term for a kind of boat and a kind of shirt.

MAD WOLF* MOUNTAIN: Mad Wolf is *saiyi* in Blackfoot, meaning a rabid or crazy wolf or other animal. It was the name of the Piegan warrior who recovered the sacred albino bow case from the Crees or Assiniboines. This recovery was one was the exploits most frequently discussed in Blackfoot war records. Schultz says of Mad Wolf: "He had more bitter hatred of white men than any other Indian that I ever knew. A tourist once asked the old man to give him a Blackfeet name." Then Schultz goes on to describe in detail Mad Wolf's "grim" reply and his prayer to the sun that "this dog-white-man" may be "utterly destroyed and soon." So the tourist gave him a little gifts "and ever afterward and at every opportunity" told people he was an adopted member of the tribe.

Walter McClintock has an opposite view. One day when he was riding with Billy Jackson, they met Mad Wolf, who signaled for a talk, "warmly" shook McClintock by the hand and proposed adopting him. When the young white man agreed, Mad Wolf arranged an elaborate naming ceremony. Was McClintock "the tourist"? As described by McClintock, Mad Wolf was key figure in his life and researches among the Blackfeet. The old man could look far back to the visit of DeSmet to the Blackfeet (1846). Members of the Mad Wolf family whom I have known match McClintock's story, not Schultz's.

For reasons unknown, there are two mountains in Glacier named for Mad Wolf, one in English, the other in Blackfoot but strangely spelled *Siyeh*. Perhaps the true meaning of the term was not known to the topographers. The mountain now called Mad Wolf in English seems to be the one Schultz labels *Kyaiyistoan* (Bear Knife) for a warrior he says was killed by the Crows in 1853. (See MEDICINE GRIZZLY.)

MAHTOTOPA* MOUNTAIN is one of the peaks on the southeastern side of Upper Saint Mary Lake that form "the grand march of mountains." *Matótopa* (Four Bears) was a Mandan chief painted by George Catlin in 1832, and in the terms of Bernard DeVoto, comes near to being the hero of Catlin's book. He was indeed a great warrior-hero to the Mandans, whose deeds are recorded at some length. He welcomed Lewis and Clark and was a favorite too of Prince Maximilian, a sort of living model of the "Noble Savage." Always and ever he was a friend and helper of the white man, even to the controversial factor Chardon. He was also, says Schultz, a friend to the Piegan chief Lone Walker, and is especially well known as the father of Ipasha. It is reported that Joe Kipp, his grandson or great-grandson, suggested this name for the mountain on Saint Mary Lake while he was guiding Grinnell. (See KIPP.)

During the devastating smallpox epidemic in 1837, as Matotopa witnessed his people being exterminated by the awesome disease, he took a second look at the white man – a dying look. Arraying himself in his finest attire, he rode about his village of earth lodges urging his people to rise up and strike the pale-faced invader. No one arose. Probably no one could. So he rode to the fort alone and challenged Chardon, again without response. Then he rode home to die, and with his dying breath uttered an imprecation upon the white men, that set of "black-hearted dogs." The Mandans, indeed, came to the very brink of extinction.

According to L. O. Vaught, the names "Red Eagle," "Little Chief," "Almost a Dog," and "Four Bears" were applied in 1887 by Grinnell and his party, which included Gould and Jack Monroe, but the name Four Bears (which could also have referred to Malcolm Clarke) was turned into its Mandan form in 1932. The person who made the switch was identified by Vaught only as "a petty park official." This remark typifies the resentment local "sage-brushers" felt toward the National Park Service.

MANITOBA: A Great Northern station near Glacier with the name of a lake, province, and railway of Canada. James Jerome Hill, born in Ontario, 1838, became one of the giant railway moguls of Canada and the U.S. The many railways in which he played some role include the Canadian Pacific, Burlington, and "the Manitoba," which ultimately became the Great Northern. In 1907 he turned over the presidency of Great Northern to his son Louis Warren Hill.

The name "Manitoba" is a compound of *manito* + *wapa*, and *manito* is a Chippewa-Cree term for "spirit" or "transcendental factor," while *wapa* means "narrows." The wind through the Narrows or Pass seemed to be the voice of the Great Spirit. One must not construe the concept of spirit in American Indian animism as something sharply distinguished from matter or the physical as it is in the classic Gnosticism and ancient Stoicism and more recent Cartesianism commonly taken for granted in Euro-American culture. In other words, to indigenous peoples matter and spirit do not form a dichotomy but rather a complementarity, somewhat analogous to matter and energy in Einstein's famous equation $E=mc^2$ and even in sacramental religions. (Note, for instance, the idea expressed in the March 2000 issue of *Theological Studies*, p. 80, that "all matter, including all human matter, has something spiritual about it." It specifies "all the atomic material in our universe." More inclusive than that I cannot imagine.)

I am stressing this point because it is crucial to understanding many place names of indigenous origin. In sum, original native peoples did not drive a wedge or build a "wall of separation" between the physical and the metaphysical, the "natural" and the "supernatural," the empirical and the transcendental.

MANY FALLS TRAIL: A trail around a portion of Upper Saint Mary Lake.

MANY GLACIER CAMPGROUND, DISTRICT and **HOTEL.** The Blackfoot name for the area is *Ohpskunakáxi* (waterfalls). However, a Blackfoot translation of "many glaciers" is *akokokutói*, which is not plural because it really means "lots of ice." So the irony is that the name in English is a clumsy ungrammatical attempt to imitate the Blackfoot language, evidently on the theory that the simple "primitive" language does not have a plural. The truth is that Blackfoot does have plurals (though their use is sometimes optional) and also has a richer grammar than English.

MANY SWANS LAKE is on the map as Nooney Lake. Many Swans, *Ak-ómahk-kaiyi*, was a chief who was tempted to break a tribal taboo – the taboo which forbade communication with one's mother-in-law or even prying into her private affairs. Finally he could resist the temptation no longer and stole a look at the poor woman. With that, he was so stricken with shame that he and his wife withdrew from their people and went to live with their traditional enemies the Crows. But as it turned out, at least in Schultz's story, he was able to establish peace between the Crows and the Blackfeet. I wonder how long it lasted! (See NOONEY, NORTH.)

MARGARET* LAKE: No one seems to know who Margaret was. But the Blackfoot name is "Bird Woman": *Siszáki*. *Siszi-* means a small bird as opposed to *pixi-*, a large bird. The Sioux language also makes such a distinction, and *zitkala* is a little bird too. (See BIRD WOMAN.)

MARIAN LAKE. This is north of Grace Lake but the reason for its name is not known. Who were Grace and Marian?

MARIAS* RIVER and **PASS**: Probably the most historical place in the area, the pass is named after Marias River, which traces its headwaters here – and elsewhere and in other passes. In 1805 Captain Meriwether Lewis named the river for his cousin and perhaps fiancÈ, Maria Wood. The final *s* is what remains of the possessive form. The river is one of the principal tributaries of the Upper Missouri. The Blackfeet called it *Kyaiyaisisahtai* (Bear River), the Nez Perces *Comawinnim*, while other tribes knew it as "Grizzly River" and called the pass "the Big Gap," "the Low Gap," or "the Pass of Aeneas." The name of Chief Aeneas was also once attached to the present Little Dog Mountain overlooking the pass. Schultz gives two or three Blackfoot names for the pass: *Pitamakan*, (more adequately spelled *Pitawmahkan*) meaning "Running Eagle" or "the running of the eagle" or "the way the eagle runs," and *Natokiókasi* (Two Medicine) because the south fork of the Two Medicine flows from the pass. Since the Rockies were sometimes thought of as the Backbone (of the world?), the pass can also be referred to by the word for "backbone": *mokakíni*.

Chief Paul David said that the Tobacco Plains Kootenais got red paint from somewhere near the source of the Marias River and therefore referred to the river (the Marias or the Missouri) as the "Red Paint River". Brian Reeves proposes that this story may refer to Cut Bank Creek or Birch Creek which furnished paint to the Piegans. Bullrobe of the Elmo Kootenais, however, claimed that his people got red paint from the Missouri near Helena.

French Canadians or Métis called the Marias *le Maragnon*, a name used in French and in Spanish (spelled *Marañón*) for other important rivers – like the Amazon!

Some Indians (and a multitude of non-Indians) have preferred to avoid Marias Pass because of blizzards, zero visibility, exposure, high winds, tribal hostilities, and some would add, because it is haunted. Governor Stevens evidently heard this last theory from Little Dog.

The National Park Service once printed a chronology of Glacier's history in which it is indicated that a nameless Spaniard may have been the first European through Marias Pass. This story was suggested by J. Neilson Barry's theory of Konapee, a castaway marooned at the mouth of the Columbia River. The story was later brushed aside but re-emerged in the legend of Shining Shirt. (See FLATHEAD RIVER.) The pass must have been visible to Meriwether Lewis and his companion Drouillard who approached the present park in 1806. In 1810 some 150 Kootenai and Kalispel Indians set out from Saleesh House near Thompson Falls armed by David Thompson and accompanied by Finan McDonald, Michel Bordeaux and Baptiste Bucher (Buch, Buchard). As they crossed Marias Pass, they did battle with a large force of Blackfeet near Bear Creek and the modern Skyline Siding. Though the Blackfeet were defeated this time, two years later Bordeaux, Michel Kinville and some Flatheads tried another crossing by way of Cut Bank Pass. The Blackfeet killed many of them. (See HENRY.)

In 1833 Prince Maximilian witnessed the start of a little expedition setting out to the Kootenais, led by Doucette and Isidoro Sandoval. They may have approached or entered Marias Pass but had to cut their trip short when Doucette was wounded. Hugh Monroe probably knew the pass but showed himself quite wary of it. His companion in 1854 James Doty, with or without Monroe, did enter the pass and probably reached about the same point that John Stevens did years later. In the 1860s Aeneas led some Kootenais on snowshoes to clear the way into the pass, and in 1873 Duncan McDonald and several Kalispels guided by Charles Shushave came over the pass on snowshoes. Duncan made other trips through the pass after that. About 1879 Andrew Garcia fled though here or near here (perhaps a little south) and had to bury his beloved Nez Perce wife, fatally wounded by Blackfeet, in the "wild Marias Mountains." (See Holterman: *Who Was Who...* for more information.)

So what becomes of the Great Northern hoopla about the "discovery" of Marias Pass in 1889? See COONSA, BEAR, JOHN F. STEVENS and for the story of McCartyville, see DOODY.

MARTHA'S* BASIN: Martha, alas, is unknown but the Kootenai name makes up for the vacuum: *K̓uɛmiki Akikqɫaɫa mi* (Tickling Basin). "Tickling" may be someone's name as is the word *kuɛkuɛ.* (See AURICE.)

MARY BAKER LAKE: Though it is said this lake was named for a tourist from Pennsylvania in 1934, it was probably named in 1897 for a young lady from Fort Benton. At least that's the story of L. O. Vaught who was in a position to know such details.

At that time Charles Conrad paid a visit to Sperry Glacier with his wife Alicia, his son Charles Jr., his sister Mrs. Adams, and a niece named Mary Baker. Mary was of the family of I. G. Baker, the merchant prince of Fort Benton and an old partner of Conrad. The ladies in the party were eager to prove they could reach the glacier just as well as the men and were probably the first to get there. So it was on that excursion that the little lake was named for Mary Baker. But evidence cited from Vaught says the name was Myra rather than Mary. And another puzzle in the story is the fact that Charles Conrad Jr. was the son of Charles Sr. by his Kaina wife Kaiyis and was usually living in Quebec Province, whereas Charles' son by Alicia was named Charles Davenport, not Charles Jr.

MATAHPI* PEAK: See GOING-TO-THE-SUN.

MCCLINTOCK* PEAK: Walter McClintock bore the Indian name "White Weasel Moccasin" (perhaps *Apa-izikin*). He came to the region with a government party headed by Gifford Pinchot in 1896 and guided by Billy Jackson and Jack Monroe. During that trip and subsequent visits McClintock gathered material for his writings on the Blackfeet, especially his book *The Old North Trail*, arguably the most scholarly general work on the Blackfeet people. His Indian name was given him because of his blond hair and blue eyes. The Blackfoot name for the mountain is *Stamik-ohsokoi* (Bull's Road or Bull Trail) after a warrior who fought the Crows.

MCDONALD LAKE, CREEK and **FALLS**: The map of 1846 marks Lake McDonald as *Lac de Poissons* (Fish Lake) and Dr. Ruhle offers an alternate that I cannot accept unless it is revised to *Lac de la Peche*. These names may be a vestige of an Indian tradition preserved today in the names of Fish Lake and Fish Creek. But a portion of McDonald Creek is labeled *Rivière de Ravalli* after the medical missionary Antonio Ravalli, S.J., who brought smallpox vaccine from Italy in 1845 to save Indian lives. He spent most of his life among the Indians of Montana and a little while at the Jesuit college in the old Mission Santa Clara in California.

The first recorded visit to Lake McDonald occurred in 1873: two U.S. Army officers, Charles Woodruff and John Van Orsdale reached the lake and named it Terry's Lake after their general, Alfred Terry. From Lake McDonald and the Middle Fork they followed Nyack Creek to Cut Bank Pass.

McDonald Creek has also carried the names Goat Creek and perhaps Gibbon's River. (See NYACK, FLATHEAD.) But the prize-winning name for McDonald Creek must be the Blackfoot name *Kyaiyo-Ahtiwapixi* which I would readjust to *Kyáiyo-awawatuyi-apixiw* (The bear wags its tail). Too bad! I do not know the origin of this little gem, nor can I explain why McDonald Creek would get a Blackfoot name.

There are several theories about the name McDonald, but the most probable and popularly accepted story derives the name from Duncan McDonald. Duncan was the son of the well-known Angus MacDonald [*sic*] of the Hudson's Bay Company, and of Catherine Baptiste, a lady of Nez Perce, Mohawk, and French ancestry. Her Indian name was "Eagle in the Wind." As a young girl, in 1841, she had the remarkable experience of traveling with Manuel Martin and a motley caravan to Arizona and the Gulf of California. Duncan's Indian name was "Crooked Heels." He was sent by the Deer Lodge newspaper to consult with the Nez Perces who fled to Saskatchewan when Chief Joseph surrendered and probably made the trip through or around Glacier.

In November of 1878, he made a trip to Canada camping at the foot of the lake that now bears his name with Chief Aeneas and two packers. By his own account, he idly carved his name and the date on a nearby tree. In time, people who saw this tree applied the name to the lake. On his way up the North Fork to Canada, Duncan ran into a party of Nez Perces. Since he was related to them, as he says, he urged them not to continue trying to get home to Idaho lest they be arrested or killed. So they turned back into Canada, helping Duncan and his party through the snows.

An older Kootenai name for the lake and the general area is translated by Schultz as "Sacred Dancing." It has now been preserved by Francis Elmore who attached it to the cascades above the lake. It is believed to refer to ceremonial dances old-timers say were performed at the foot of the lake. The name in Kootenai is given by Thain White as *Yakił Haqwiłnamki*: "a good place to dance" or "where (people) dance." For the lake add *-akuq̓nuk*, and for the creek *-akinmituk*. Though the authenticity of this name has recently been questioned, I must say that I consider it basically genuine. Brian Reeves suggests that it refers to the area of Hungry Horse near the mouth of South Fork. Upstream on the South Fork were the Kootenai tobacco gardens.

L. O. Vaught rejects the idea of the lake being named for Duncan McDonald – rejects it with some hostility – and opts instead for the theory that it was named for John McDonald. Some have taken this to be Sir John MacDonald [sic], the Canadian statesman, but the John indicated by Vaught was a trapper who had a cabin on the lake and was well known around the upper Flathead valley in the early 1880s. But in 1885 he was lynched by a mob at Birch Creek along with another poor fellow named Felix Constant. Though the charge leveled against these victims was horse stealing, it was locally suspected to be a frame-up concocted to steal John's money or secret cache. Both stories, John's and Duncan's, were reported to Vaught by George Stannard of Demersville.

Upper McDonald Creek was known to the Kootenais as "Barrier Creek" above the mouth of Logan Creek and "Avalance Creek" from there to the lake. (Actually the name translated by "avalanche" is much longer and descriptive.) This information was obtained by Schaeffer from Chief Paul David of the Akanahonek band at Roosville, British Columbia, just across the border from Eureka, Montana.

Schultz in *Red Crow's Brother* (cited by Reeves) mentions an attack by Sixika (North Blackfeet) on some Kalispels camped at the foot of Lake McDonald.

MCGEE* CREEK, LAKE, and **MEADOW** were named for an old settler. The most probable is Thomas N. Magee, who married a daughter of the Blackfeet man Buffalo Run. Their son Thomas B. Magee married Julia Grant, daughter of James Grant and Mary Cadotte. If James was James Cuthbert (as I think he was), he was the son the famous old Hudson Bay Company trader at Fort Hall, Idaho, half brother to the equally famous Johnny Grant of Deer Lodge, full brother to Julia the wife of Christopher Higgins (founder of Missoula). Both James and Julia were the grandchildren of Finan MacDonald and his Indian wife Peggy Ponderay. (See MARIAS.)

MCPARTLAND* MOUNTAIN: Frank McPartland was a prospecting associate of Joe Kipp and a resident of Lake McDonald, where he came to look for copper. He also searched for gold in the Sweetgrass Buttes and there perhaps had killed a man in a fight. In 1893(?), he was cruising Lake McDonald with the Cattle Queen, Mrs. Elizabeth (Libby) Collins, and also with Chan (who was a brother of the Cattle Queen or perhaps a Chinese cook). They were enjoying the contents of a jug. That is, until the boat rocked and pitched them all into the lake. McPartland is said to have clutched desperately at Libby but when she broke loose, he drowned. Needless to say, this is only one of varying accounts of this episode.

Ironic, therefore, is the Kootenai name for the mountain: "Crossing Over Victory" or *Kałqanałłama'ka Akwukłi'it*. For Frank McParltand's mining claims, see AKAMINA, CARIBOU, MONTEREY.

MEDICINE GRIZZLY* LAKE and **PEAK**: The Blackfoot term *Natúyi-apohkyaiyio* or "holy white bear" refers to at least two different grizzlies ("white bears"), one hostile, one friendly, or perhaps to one grizzly with a dual personality. Mad Wolf's war party got into a fight with Gros Ventres in Cut Bank Valley. When the last of the Gros Ventres was killed, the Blackfeet discovered he had grizzly power. So when a huge grizzly appeared and killed some of the Blackfeet, the survivors believed the bear was the Gros Ventre warrior come back to life. This Cut Bank grizzly is said to have been killed by a government hunter from Columbia Falls. How do you kill a mythological creature?

The other story is supposed to have occurred around the 1870s or earlier and deals with Onistaiyi or Sacred Robe. Because of its homonymy, *onista-* can be translated as either "sacred" or "calf", but I cannot identify the root *-yi*. Anyway, the name is usually called "Calf Robe" and under that translation has been assigned to two peaks in Glacier, Cathedral Peaks in the north section and the mountain still named Calf Robe in the south. The details of Onistaiyi's story vary from one account to another, but the general theme runs something like this: Onistaiyi and three comrades go south and steal horses from the Shoshonis who overtake them and kill all but Onistaiyi. Wounded, he takes shelter in the woods but is soon too weak even to crawl to water. A coyote comes and looks him over. Then a grizzly comes to stare. "Which part of me will he eat first?" Onistaiyi asks himself. But instead of chewing on him, the grizzly licks his wounds. Soon both the bear and the coyote bring him meat. Finally he manages to crawl onto the grizzly's back and the two animals take him home, either to the Marias River or to Fort Benton. At the fort, Alexander Culbertson rejects his story, but Natawista believes it. One version of this story as told by Albert and Joe Calf Robe occurs in Eli Guardipee's oral interview and is said to date back to about 1840. The story is used to explain the taboo against killing bears in hibernation. Dr. Ruhle reported a son of Calf Robe living at Heart Butte adding that a story something like this was told him by Dick Sandoval (Sanderville), who had it from Calf Robe's son, and also that another version recalls the story of Eagle Plume. Grinnell gives a similar tale about Mikapi or Red Old Man, and there is still another about a "medicine wolf" who aids a woman captured by Crows to make good her escape back home to the Blackfeet. This woman is identified historically as Sits-by-the-Door, the mother of Calf Looking, and the Calf-Looking involved here may be the one who tangled in a skirmish with Meriwether Lewis in 1806. After one of the Crow women helped her escape, she wandered till food was gone and moccasins worn. When a curious wolf ventured close, she begged him, "Brother, help me!" He brought her a fresh kill to roast and then allowed her to ride him. In time he brought her home. She took him into her tipi, but the dogs drove him out. He still lingered near in hopes she would come out to him, but she lay too sick to move. (May I add that my own experience suggests that a wolf can be this loyal.) The wolf leaves her with the admonition: "the gun that shoots at the wolf-kind will never shoot straight again." (See EAGLE PLUME.)

The name assigned to this mountain by Schultz seems to be "Elk Tongue," *Ponoká()-úzini*, after a man who traveled to the Spanish land and received the Dreaming Pipe from the South People, perhaps the same man who caught the attention of Maximilian and Bodmer. Schultz tells another story about Spaiyu (Spaniard) who wandered helpless into Blackfeet country and later led a raid south to capture his own brother.

MEDICINE LINE: An Indian term for the Canada-U.S. boundary, especially along the forty-ninth parallel. (See AKAMINA.) Even after the survey of 1874, the line zigzagged so much that surveys had to be undertaken again in 1902. The older expeditions had left cairns at intervals and the straight lines were drawn between the points indicated by the cairns or on the maps. But the curvature of the earth prevents the forty-ninth parallel from ever being a straight line (contrary to Euclid's axiom).

The term "medicine" is a crude English translation of the French *médecine* which is a crude French translation of the Chippewa-Cree word *manito*. (See MANITOBA.) The Medicine Line, fiction as it is, has had a pervasive effect on the history of the Waterton/Glacier country peopled by smugglers, refugees, bootleggers, and people persecuted on one side of the line or the other.

MEDICINE OWL* CREEK, LAKE, and **PEAK**: This name, *Natúyi-spisto* is a personal Blackfoot name applied here by Dr. Ruhle. The word *natúyi-* means "sacred, holy," but it has traditionally pleased white people to translate it as "medicine" and make it an adjective! It seems that almost any animal can be a medicine animal, and long ago men and animals could talk to each other. McClintock quotes Bring Down the Sun's explanation: "We can still talk to the animals, just as we do to people, but they now seldom reply, except in dreams." The owl, however, was a special object of awe, and the way to appease an owl, the portent of death, was to assure it that you were its relative.

MEDICINE PEAK is a point on Mount Henry.

MERRITT*, MOUNT, is named for Gen. Wesley Merritt (1834–1910). Graduating from West point in 1860, he served throughout the Civil War and then mostly on the frontier until 1879. For several years in the 1880s he was superintendent at his alma mater. In 1898 he was commander-in-chief of the U.S. forces in the Philippines. Schultz calls this mountain Old Sun, which is still the name of its glacier. The Lithoid Cusp is a pinnacle between Merritt and Ipasha. (*Lithoid* is Greek for stone-like.) Merritt is also a claim name. (See CARIBOU.) But Vaught maintains that the name "Merritt" was conferred in 1891.

In September of 1891 Troop C and the lst Cavalry came to Fort Assiniboine and to Saint Mary. These were probably African American troopers commanded by white officers, W. C. Browne (later General), Lieutenant F. S. Foltz with his brother C. F. Foltz, Lieutenant J. F. Morrison of the 20th Infantry and Dr. Allen Smith, post physician. They named the mountain for General Merritt, commandant of the Department of Dakota, and named Shaffer Creek for Sergeant Shaffer of Troop C – and perhaps Boulder Creek as well. They passed or encountered the expedition of Grinnell and Stimson described in the entry ALLEN. Forest fires were raging around them. (See OLD SUN, SHAFFER.)

MICHE WABUN* FALLS, GLACIER, LAKE, and **PEAK**: Crees were among the Indian nations that used to visit the region of Glacier and Waterton Parks. When this neglected phase of regional history was brought to the attention of General Hugh Scott, he decided to do something about it. During a visit he and his party made to a Cree reserve in Canada, they looked for Cree names they could add to the scene in Glacier. They found a few elders of the reserve who could recall trips to Glacier Country and one man of about seventy-five who described the area around Mount Cleveland and Belly River. Unfortunately, the good intentions got sidetracked by mistaken linguistics.

The name Miche Wabun was selected as a proper name to apply to some feature of this northeastern sector of Glacier. The problem is that this is a Chippewa (Ojibwa) term for Great Coming Day or Great Dawn. The question is further complicated by the similarity between the Cree and Chippewa languages and also by the similarity of the words for "dawn," "white," and "rabbit," all of which include the root *wap-* (or perhaps two homonyms). As a result, the term "Miche Wabun" has been thought to mean "The Great White Rabbit" and even "The Great Spirit," and apparently white people who were typically confused about both animism and blasphemy failed to detect the problem.

MIDGET CREEK: Near McDonald Lodge.

MIDVALE* CREEK: Midvale was the old name of East Glacier. Midvale Basin used to be called "the Slaughter House" because game was killed there.

MILK RIVER: This name was conferred by Lewis and Clark because the river (in its lower reaches) had the color of tea with milk. The Blackfoot name is "Little River": *Kinaksisáhtai*. The river interested Lewis and Clark particularly because it indicated the northernmost limit of the Louisiana Purchase, even though it crosses the present international border twice. The explorers called it by its Minnetaree (Hidatsa) name in their unscientific transcription: *Ah-mah-tah Rushush-sher* (The River That Scolds All Others).

MINERAL* CREEK: Associated with the mining claims of the Cattle Queen. (See MONTEZUMA.)

MIRROR* POND: In Blackfoot this is *Sapiázis Omahxikimi.*

MISSOULA COUNTY is older than the state of Montana, originally a part of Washington Territory. It included the western portion of present Glacier National Park. Flathead County was cut off from Missoula County in 1893. The word *missoula* may mean something like "awesome river" in Salish, though there is no consensus on this point. The "Missoula group" is a formation of red, brown, and greenish rock.

MOCCASIN CREEK: Just south of Glacier. By metathesis, the Chippewa *makitsin* (which is the form the English word is believed to come from) is *maskisin* in Cree and *mazikin* in Blackfoot.

MOKOWANIS* CASCADE, LAKE, and **RIVER:** The lake is also called Lois Lake. (See Belly River.)

MONTANA: The word is Spanish: *montaña* for mountain, mountainous region. It can also be Latin without the tilde.

MONTE CRISTO is a mining claim near Belton Station (1893), named after the Italian island. (See Belton.)

MONTEREY is a mining claim on the headwaters of McDonald Creek. The name refers to both a city in Mexico (usually spelled with double *r*) and the old Spanish and Mexican capital of California (usually spelled with a single *r*). The claim is one of a parcel all belonging to Joe Kipp, Frank McPartland, Louie Meyer, et al., and also including claims named Montana, Mastodon, Buena Vista (good view), Diogenes, Se–orita, Mariposa (butterfly), Anthracite, and Copper Crown (1894).

MONTEZUMA is a mining claim of the Cattle Queen, et al., lying on the Divide between the headwaters of McDonald Creek and those of Belly Creek (1894). The name is Aztec (Nahuatl): *motecuzuma*: "your lord is angry." The companion claim is Reindeer, which seems to have been adjacent to the claims of Joe Kipp and his partners. (See Caribou.)

MONUMENT FALLS is near Avalanche Lake. The name is probably descriptive.

MOOSE LAKE lies at the head of Swiftcurrent River. A moose jumped into the water here and got away from the hunters. There is also a Moose Creek just west of Glacier. *Moos* is the Chippewa word for this animal, and *môswa* is the Cree term. The moose habitat most easily available to tourists is near McDonald Creek.

MORAN'S BATHTUB is Swiftcurrent Ridge Lake, maybe named for miners Pat or Tom Moran.

MORGAN*, MOUNT: The Kootenai name is "Otter Mountain": *Aqawxaɬ Akwukɬi'it.* But who was Morgan? No one knows, perhaps a miner. Another possibility is Lewis Henry Morgan, "the father of American anthropology" (1818–1881). He came up the Missouri on the famous voyage of the *Spread Eagle* in 1862, along with skipper Charles Chouteau, Father DeSmet, the Culbertsons, Malcolm Clarke, and the Dawson's, father and son. From these people and especially from Natawista and Joe Kipp, he obtained much information for his scientific theories which he communicated to various scholars of his time: Darwin, Huxley, Spencer, Longfellow, Marx, Engels, etc. (See RAINBOW.)

MORNING EAGLE* FALLS: *Apinákui-Pita* was a famous old warrior who had manito energy that gave him the strength to crack skulls and control ghosts. But about 1847 he must have lost it all. When Assiniboines captured the sacred albino otter hide from the Blackfeet, two parties set out to recover it. One was led by Mad Wolf with Morning Eagle as its elder. While Morning Eagle paused to drink at a creek, he was shot dead. But Mad Wolf brought home the sacred hide.

Morning Eagle Falls is the bottom portion of Feather Plume Falls and the climax of a little vale called by Elrod "The Garden of Heaven." There is also a Morning Eagle Lake near East Glacier, and the name persists among living persons, thank God, since I'm one.

The name Morning Eagle has many similarities among American Indian names: e.g. Dawn Eagle, Eagle from the Light (the Rising Sun), Red Eagle, Eagle Speaker. Such names are widely scattered in origin, not only in the Plains and the Northwest but in the Southwest, Mexico etc. The reference may be to an idea that the eagle from the sunrise speaks the word of the Great Spirit and must therefore be heeded.

MORNING GLORY CREEK and **LAKES**: These little lakes include Pitamakan, Katoya and Solomon's Bowl. They seem to be the three lakes sighted by Lieutenants Woodruff and Van Orsdale in the fall of 1873 and named by them when they camped nearby. But the names they gave were Viva, Mamie, and Lillie for three (little?) girls who lived around Fort Shaw in the Sun River country.

MORNING STAR* LAKE: the origin of the name is unknown, but Morning Star was a prominent figure in Plains Indian mythology, possibly referring at different times to the planets Venus, Mercury, and Jupiter.

MOSS ROCK Spring is above Avalanche Gorge.

MOTHER DUCK TRAIL: Anyone who has ever watched a mother duck will know at once what a beautiful name this is. The trail runs from Cameron Lake to the international border and becomes the North Boundary Trail in Glacier.

MOUNTAIN CHIEF MINE: *Ninaistako* is the old and respected name of Mountain Chief. But there is a bit of confusion about this name. It may be an alternate form for the name of Chief Mountain, *Nináistaki*, or it may also be an alternate for *manístokos* as is suggested by older forms on record: *ni-na-sta-koi* and *mena-es-to-ka*. Perhaps there was an archaic shift from *m* to *n*. *Nina* is the root for "man, chief," deceptively similar to the root for "father" *ninna*. Add *s* to the *ko* and you get *-kos*, a root for "child." So mystery lingers about this name, long before it was conferred on Dr. Ruhle and the Duke of Windsor.

Then why has it been restricted to a mere mining claim and not given more prominence among the place names of the parks? Perhaps the negativism attached to it by the U.S. Army has something to do with that. Yet the identity of the historical figures the name usually refers to is not always easy to establish. The first Mountain Chief on record was the companion of Eagle Ribs once known as Woman's Moccasin. He may have been a member of the Blackfoot party that encountered Berger's trappers on Badger Creek when they came making overtures for the fur trade with Chouteau's American Fur Company. His portrait was painted by George Catlin at Fort Union is 1832. Soon after that he was involved in the fight that cost the life of trader Henry Vanderburgh. This same chief appears to be a leader second in prestige among the Piegans who signed Stevens's treaty of 1855 at the Judith River (which was ratified) and also the treaties of 1865 and 1868 (which were not ratified). He had five wives and twenty children. He must have been the Mountain Chief related by common law marriage to Malcolm Clarke and so blacklisted by the Army. In 1872 he was killed by one of his own people. A son of his was also called Mountain Chief and was on the records at least in 1892. This man was probably the one who died about 1941, deeply mourned by his people. I used to go ice-skating with his grandson – ah, so long ago!

MUD* CREEK and **LAKE**: See Camas, Winona, Nyack.

MUIR* CREEK is named for the naturalist John Muir. More commonly associated with Yosemite Park and Alaska, he also came to Glacier with his message of conservation and transcendentalism at a time when most people could think of little else but exploitation. Transcendentalism has always been one feature of U.S. culture that remains a conundrum to most U.S. American people. Muir Creek is also called by the Kootenai name of "Two Owls", *Ki'as Kupi*, which originally was the name of some unidentified stream in this part of Glacier.

MYERS GLACIER: South of Quartz Creek and probably named for Louie Meyer. His name has various forms with no consensus as to which is correct: Myer, Meyer, Myers, or Meyers. (See DUTCH.)

NAHSUKIN* LAKE and **MOUNTAIN**: *Nasu'kin* was the Kootenai name of Vulture Peak but was transferred to the feature now so labeled on the maps. The word means "chief" but can also be a personal name. It may have been used by the Kootenais for Chief Mountain.

NAPI* ROCK: *Nápi(w)* (Old Man) is a Blackfoot arranger and trickster, the typical dualistic figure of Algonquin tales. "Napi stories" tend to be earthy as distinguished from "star legends," which are more poetic, perhaps even mystical. The word *napi* seems to derive from two distinct Algonquin roots, one for "white" and one for "person." It was applied to this point of rock, also known as "The Stone Head" by General Hugh Scott. The Kootenai name for this rock seems to be *Natanik* (sun or moon), a reminder that the Kootenais frequented the Saint Mary country. *Natanik-amak* means moon dust and was the name of a son of Joseph Black Bear. To make it clear whether you mean "moon" rather than "sun," you can also say *keilmitil natanik.* Some have suggested that the face in this rock (?) is the reason for the name Saint Mary on the lakes beneath it. Who knows?

NARROWS: The straits in Upper Saint Mary Lake caused by the Altyn formation in the rocks. Sun Point is here opposite to Silver Dollar Beach, and though sadly demoted by modern "improvements," it was once one of the glories of world travel.

NATAHKI* LAKE: *Natahki* is the name by which James Willard Schultz usually refers to his Piegan wife, also known as "Fine Shield Woman." She is the heroine of his autobiographical *My Life As an Indian* and of *Floating on the Missouri.* She was the mother of his son, Hart Merriam Schultz or "Lone Wolf," and the daughter of Black Eagle and Carrier Woman as well as the niece of both Red Eagle and Little Dog. She was caught with her parents in the camp of Heavy Runner when it was massacred by Baker's men in 1870. Her father escaped to warn Mountain Chief. Her mother was not hurt, but Natahki was crippled in the hand for life. (The Blackfeet census of 1907 tells a different story, but I think in this instance it is less reliable than Schultz.) Her husband describes Natahki as a person who saw beauty in everything. In *Floating* he calls her by the name *Sah-né-to.*

147

The tribal census reports for 1891 and 1892 named her Susan Schultz, mother of Hart M. Schultz and an adopted daughter, and gives her age as twenty-six in 1891 and as twenty-two in 1892. (If only we could all be like that!) The tribal reports variously name her father as Pulling Lodge Down and Bull Road and her mother as Kills in Sight or Potato (Potatoes). Schultz calls her mother Pataki or Carrier Woman, but the discrepancy is resolved when we note that pataki does derive from the words for "carry" and "woman" but is also a loan word for "potato" – a homonym. One report lists Yellow Wolf as her brother, rather than her uncle.

NATAWISTA LAKE: Also known as Janet Lake, The daughter of the Kaina chief Man'stokos and the sister of the elegant traveling chief Seen Afar, she well suited the role Audubon assigned her as an "Indian Princess." The Man'stokos was perhaps the man known as Bad Head or Two Suns. (See Two Suns.) Her name in the Blackfoot tongue is given variously as *Natoapxíxina* or *Natúyizixina*, but in either case translatable as "Sacred Serpent" or "Medicine Snake". One has to wonder if it refers to the Plumed Serpent of the Aztecs and if so, has it some reference to Seen Afar's travels to the Spanish Lands. She was only about fifteen when she was given in marriage to the aspiring leader of the Upper Missouri fur trade, Alex Culbertson, and she was brought to him in procession, probably to Fort Union. It is not likely that she had anything to say about it. The *engagés* humorously labeled this arrangement *le mariage á la façon du pays* – a "country marriage," and it was regarded as satisfactory until some wandering priest would come by and make it canonical. So the Sacred Serpent must have wondered when wandering priests came and went and her husband made no move for their good offices. She must have wondered too when her husband, reputed to be a linguistic expert, could not even pronounce her name and settled instead for "Natawista" or sometimes "Natawista Iksana" (neither of which means anything in Blackfoot). In social life she was also called "Madame" and "the Major's Lady" since head traders received the honorary title "Major" or even "Colonel." (Alex aspired to Colonel.) She, on the other hand, did not like to speak her husband's tongue.

But at the numerous balls held at the trading posts, she was well gowned and performed as the model hostess. While her taste for raw liver and calf brains appalled some guests, her beauty and magnificent skill at swimming charmed everyone. All the notable visitors on the frontier fell into the orbit of her charm: men like Audubon, DeSmet, Lewis Henry Morgan, the La Barges, and the Chouteaus. But alas, her daughters were taken from her by her husband and sent east to be raised like fine ladies of the white man's world and so were mostly lost to her. This maneuver of her husband tends to sabotage any romantic view of her marriage.

Still, she put up with it, and when Alex retired they went to live on a large estate near Peoria, Illinois. There her oldest son Jack went to school with Joe Kipp. Jack was about fifteen and her latest, Joe, still in his nanny's arms when Natawista was baptized as "Nellie" and married to Alex by a priest (though Alex was a Calvinist). It was an ornate wedding that hit the social column in the Peoria news. She did enjoy rubies and fast blue-ribbon horses and the private paddock of buffalos and other western wildlife, and she laughed when her frisky team smashed her carriage. But she pitched a tipi on the front lawn of her magnificent mansion and sat there staring back when the noble neighbors rode by to gawk in amazement. She may even have secretly enjoyed it when Jack rode his horse up the front steps or brought his pet goat into the stately chambers to smash the priceless hall mirror.

With such lavish living, the money dwindled and the Civil War wiped out the fortune. So back to Fort Benton, Montana, moved the Culbertsons, striving just to make ends meet in the roisterous town Alex had founded.

Jack could speak both Blackfoot and Sioux, was a friend of artist William Cary and a favorite of Sitting Bull. He evidently wandered to New York and California but eventually home to the high Missouri.

But the high Missouri was as luckless for Natawista as Illinois. Her son Jack was beaten to death in a bar, while in Fort Benton nothing could keep the peace. After the Baker massacre when most Blackfeet sought sanctuary in Canada, Natawista fled too, north to her Blood people on Belly River. There she died in 1893 and was buried at the Catholic church in Stand Off.

The story of Natawista thrusts upon us a view of women on the frontier, and Indian women in particular, that most historians avoid. It challenges the myths of Manifest Destiny and the American Dream. Were these women really wives or were they slave-wives? And of course a slave-wife is a slave or a concubine, not a wife. What about the Sacred Serpent? (See Holterman: *Who Was Who...* for more information.)

NATOAS* PEAK: The *mas* or *(m)as(i)* is an edible bulb or root and the *natoasi* is a sacred one which was dug by the earthling wife of Morning Star. When she peered down through the hole in the sky that she opened up by digging the bulb, she got homesick. Her heavenly husband had to allow her to return to earth. The *natoasi* is a sacred ceremonial object in the Medicine Lodge, but in common language usage the term seems to have become confused with those for Sun Chief and Old Sun. The name was applied here by Dr. Ruhle. A version of this story appears in Longfellow's' *Hiawatha.*

NEVER LAUGHS* MOUNTAIN: *Kat-áiyimi,* the name of a Piegan band.

NEWMAN PEAK is in Waterton Lakes Park, named in 1858 by Thomas Blakiston for the English naturalist, Edward Newman (1810–1875).

NIMROD: A railway station at the southern point of Glacier, not operating, named for the Biblical hunter and warlord of Babylon. The station was once called Java.

NINAKI is the Blackfoot term for "chief woman" or "chief's wife." Dr. Ruhle explains that two pinnacles between Gable and Chief Mountains were called by the Indians *Ninaki* and *Nináipoka* or "chief's child." With Chief as papa, this makes a family circle. *Ninaki* is also used for a woman of prestige and is the term for "queen" applied to both Victoria and Elizabeth II.

NIRVANA PASS lies between Evangeline and Dutch Ridge. The term *nirvana* is Sanskrit for "blowing out" (as a candle) and in both Buddhism and Hinduism refers to the extinction of selfishness and suffering as the soul enters the beatific state (which is not usually nor necessarily regarded as annihilation or loss of consciousness as some Westerners claim.) Maybe there is something beatific in the view from the pass.

NO NAME LAKE: No comment.

NOONEY* LAKE is one of the North Lakes, just south of the border. James Nooney was with the U.S. Boundary Survey in 1861. The Blackfoot name is Many Swans.

NORRIS* MOUNTAIN is named for Hank Norris, who had property at Saint Mary. This peak has also been called Morris Mountain and, perhaps with Split Mountain, the Monroe Twins.

NORTH FORK: The Kootenai name for the North Fork of the Flathead River is "Wolf Tail": *Ka·kin Aqat Akinmitk*. The Boundary Commission of 1860–61 (probably represented by George Gibbs) wrote this name or something like it as *Akinisuhtl*.

NORTH LAKES: Wurdeman, Nooney, Waseeja, Shaheeja, and Carcajou.

NORTH STAR: A mining claim of Dutch Louie and Charles Aubrey near the headwaters of Belly River but across the Divide. The term *Keewatin*, used as a place name in Canada and also the name of an ancient ice sheet, has this meaning. (See COPPER.)

NOT A GRIZZLY MOUNTAIN: I must confess I do not know where this mountain is. I can tell you this, however: it must be named for one of the most famous of Kootenai chiefs, the father of Back-in-Sight and the counterpoint to the warlike chief Numa. See the next entry. "Not a grizzly" in Kootenai is *Ka'in Kławła*.

NUMA* CREEK, LAKE, and **RIDGE**: In Kootenai *numa* means "thunder." It was the name of a tribal elder and also of Trapper Peak. Numa Ridge has an alternate name of Iridium Ridge. Iridium is a chemical element, and its name derives from the Greek for "rainbow."

The chief named Numa was sketched by the German artist Sohon who accompanied Governor Isaac Stevens. According to Schaeffer's informant Gravelle, he was "aggressive and hard-boiled". His son was killed by Piegans in a fierce battle. Numa was captured along with Not a Grizzly and burned up alive. Numa was the grandfather of Pascal, one of the four Kootenais tried and hanged for murder in Missoula, 1890. (I suspect this story needs to be re-examined by historians.)

NYACK CREEK and **LAKES:** The creek was called *Ka·kin Akiœqahiy* (Wolf Finger) by the Kootenais. It marked a favorite old trail across the Divide which loops about Mount Stimson in a valley shaped like the waning moon. It leads to Cut Bank and Red Eagle Passes. This trail was followed in 1873 by Lieutenants Van Orsdale and Woodruff, who called the creek Gibbon's River after their Colonel. Always best to remember the Colonel especially when he gives his famous lecture "Other Worlds Than Ours." The loyal lieutenants left their own names on points along Nyack Creek: Van Orsdale's Flume and Woodruff's Falls, as well as the name of "our regiment's commanding officer" on Gilbert's Cascades, just above the mouth of

Nyack Creek. And yet in 1883 the creek itself was called Mud Creek.

But the name *Nyack* is an old one too, in use here before 1910, and it is applied to the "flats" across the river from the park as well as to a prominent peak in the Flathead Range of the Great Bear Wilderness. The word is a Delaware Indian term meaning "point" or "corner" (perhaps "in the corner") and has variations *Naiag*, *Neiak*, etc. It was the name of Delaware (*Lenne Lenape*) villages on Long Island and on the Hudson River at present Nyack, New York. Many Delaware Indians, transplanted to Missouri and Kansas, accompanied early explorers, like Fr mont's aide Tom Hill and Governor Stevens guide Delaware Jim. Both of them ranged from California to Montana and have descendents today on the Salish-Kootenai Reservation. It is possible such men knew this Nyack trail across the Divide.

Many others have used Nyack valley to reach Marias Pass. In 1898, Louis Hill conducted on his railroad through here the young Crown Prince of the Belgians (later King Albert of World War I).

The railroad calls its station here Red Eagle, where the village of Nyack used to lie, and reserves the name Nyack for its other station two miles northwest, opposite Red Eagle. Glacier used to operate a ranger station with a basket on a wire to cross the river ("the rope stretched across"). The Nyack valley is especially lush and in the springtime fairly bursts with creeks and waterfalls: Deerlick, Great Bear, Beaver, Skiumah, Cascade, Ramona, etc.

The Nyack Fault, probably originating in British Columbia, runs the length of Glacier National Park in a southeasterly or northwesterly direction. It forms a huge crease in the topography. The North Fork of the Flathead flows southeasterly down the northern sector, while the Middle Fork flows up northwesterly through the southern sector. West Glacier lies somewhere in the middle, but the two forks of the Flathead meet farther on near Blankenship Bridge. While the Nyack Fault appears to slip into Glacier near the Camas Creek Entrance cutting across the lower end of Lake McDonald, the parallel Flathead Fault is believed to bisect all the major West Lakes (including the upper end of Lake McDonald). A linking fault seems to join the Flathead and Nyack Faults near Essex. The Flathead Fault and Nyack Fault then continue on southward.

OASTLER PEAK and **SHELTER**: Dr. Frank Richard Oastler was a surgeon, gynecologist, and a devoted conservationist who held the chair for surgery at Columbia University for twenty years. Yet, with his wife, he tramped over the Great Divide from the southern Rockies to the Yukon. He died at Many Glacier Hotel in 1936 at age sixty-five. The story of Waterton and Glacier is not just what people do to or for these parks, but what these parks do for people. Another great physician who drew inspiration from Glacier National Park was Dr. Walter Alvarez.

OBERLIN* FALLS and **MOUNT** were named by Dr. Sperry for Oberlin College in Ohio. Lulu Wheeler, wife of Senator Wheeler and frequent resident of Lake McDonald, attended Oberlin.

OLD MAN* LAKE: See Napi.

OLD MAN'S PLAYGROUND: An area along Old Man River north of Waterton Park and sacred to members of the Blackfoot confederacy. It was here that Napi or Old Man played games with his children the animals, notably the hoop and dart game. (See Napi.) Nearby is the archaeological site of Heads-Smashed-In.

OLD NORTH TRAIL: *Apatohs-ohsokoi* (North Trail) in Blackfoot and *Kiwetin Meskanaw* in Cree. This is the ancient, even prehistoric travois trail that skirts the eastern edge of the Rockies and leads from the Arctic to Mexico – or Peru. Traces of the travois may still be visible just east of Glacier, for example, on the Two Medicine Ridge. Another Blackfoot name is reported: *Mísmoyai-móhsokoi-aistóhzim-istakisz-awáhka(w)*: "Old Trail Passing Near the Mountains." The Old North Trail is the principal migration route of the American Indians and is mentioned in the *Delaware Walam Olum*. In late historic times, during the era of whiskey smuggling and later, this route was paralled or extended by the Whoop-Up and other whiskey trails. The lower road ran from Fort Benton across the Marias at Abbott's post, north of Rocky Springs to Fort Hamilton and Fort Kipp (whiskey posts, both of them), and to Fort MacLeod (a Mountie post). The upper road ran fifty miles west from Fort Shaw to the old Agency on the Teton, Fort Maginnis on the Badger apparently via Riplinger's post, then on to the Saint Mary River north of the border to Stand Off and Fort

MacLeod. One of these may have coincided with the old "Red River Cart Road" of the Métis.

OLD SQUAW* ROCK: this pejorative probably refers to a rock on Squaw Mountain near East Glacier. Today this name is regarded as offensive and should be removed.

OLD SUN* GLACIER: Old Sun is *Api-natosi*, a Blackfoot personal name which can also be translated as "white sun." Dr. Ruhle wanted to avoid confusion between "Old Sun" and "Olson." Ahern and Old Sun Glaciers together are called the Hanging Glaciers.

OLE* CREEK and **LAKE:** Ole was an old trapper whose Scandinavian name replaced the Kootenai name which was "Buckskin (Horse) Creek": *Kanukyukxu Aknuxu'nuk*. But buckskin leather is *Aknuɋiła*.

OLSON* CREEK and **MOUNTAIN** were named for Charlie Olson, a camp cook. Well, maybe. There were no doubt other Olsons, Olesons, and Olsens in this part of the country who were just as likely to get something named after them. One such family closely associated with the railway lived in Whitefish, the division point. The father was a fireman, then an engineer. His daughter Myrtle married a young man named Salcido descended from the most distinguished Spanish families of California, Covarrubias, Carrillo and so on. He was well liked in Whitefish but moved with Myrtle to Ventura.

Schultz lists this mountain as named for a horse, the famous war horse of the Blackfeet, *Sikap-azaps* (Crazy Gray). (*sik*: black + *api*: white + *(m)azaps*: crazy). The Board on Geographic Names thought this name was too long. This horse belonged to Black Eagle and was slaughtered at Black Eagle's funeral so that they might go together to the Great Sand Hills. However, for a much different story of Crazy Gray see PTARMIGAN.

Olson Creek may be the stream called *Kin-nook-kleht-nán-na* by the U.S. Boundary Survey of 1861, corrected now to *Aknuɋli'itnana*.

OTATSO* CREEK and **LAKE:** See KENNEDY. John Kennedy was called by the Blackfeet "Walking Stooped." The Board evidently preferred the Indian term.

OTOKOMI* LAKE and **MOUNTAIN:** The Blackfoot *Otah-komi* means "Yellow Fish," the name of Charles Rose, the son of an American Fur Company *engagé* said to be from Quebec and his Piegan wife who raised the boy in Piegan ways. The father was employed at Fort

Benton and Astoria near the mouth of the Columbia. Rose Creek at Rising Sun was also named for Otahkomi (though often misspelled Roes). Vaught claims Grinnell assigned the names "Rose Creek" and "Yellow Fish Mountain" on his first trip (1885).

OUSEL PEAK and **CREEK** are just south of Glacier National Park in the narrow canyon of the Middle Fork (Seven Mile Canyon). The ouzel or dipper is a gray wren-like bird that hovers near waterfalls and lingers in the spray. The dictionary prefers the spelling "ouzel", defines the term to include "various European thrushes," and as its first choice for pronunciation cites the *u* in "rule."

PABLO, MOUNT: Just southeast of Glacier National Park, this guardian of Marias Pass commemorates Michel Pablo, born near modern Fort Benton of Blackfoot and Mexican ancestry. An orphan, he was raised in the Flathead country where he eventually married and settled down to ranching. About 1878, a Kalispel(?) named Walking Coyote and his wife drove a few buffalos across the Divide and with the encouragement of Agent Peter Ronan, Pablo and his partner Charles Allard used a few of these buffalos to establish a herd in the Flathead country. This enterprise helped to save the species from extinction. The herd grew rapidly and part of it was sold and scattered abroad. The famous round-up of these animals attracted cowboys, artists and journalists from far and wide, among them Hart Schultz, Duncan McDonald, and Charlie Russell. Remnants of this herd formed a basis for the one now roaming the National Bison Range at Moiese. For a branch of the Pablo family on the Blackfeet Reservation, see STARR.

PACIFIC* CREEK: See TRIPLE DIVIDE.

PACKERS ROOST, at the Loop on the Going-to-the-Sun Road, used to be a place for rearranging the packs of horses near the present Loop. Bill Yenne, in his autobiographical *Switchback* relates many incidents of packers' life in Glacier and elsewhere. A number of packers in the Waterton/Glacier area have been named in these pages. Another Yenne tells about is the Mexican Taylor Velverde (Valverde) during the fires of about 1929.

PAINTED TEPEE* PARK is in the Two Medicine District. It used to be called Wigwam Peak (*wigwam/wigwam* in eastern Algonquin), and indeed it does resemble this type of dwelling. There is also a Wigwam River west of Glacier and in British Columbia, a base camp of boundary surveyors. *Tipi* is a Siouan word.

PAIOTA* FALLS: This is a Blackfoot word from the root "to fly." It can mean "bird" and can also be used as a personal female name.

PAOLA CREEK and **STATION** are just south of Glacier. The name is the Italian form for "Paula" but here is the surname of a settler and/or railroad contractor. There used to be a post office here.

PAPOOSE CREEK and **RIDGE:** A common Algonquin word is *papoos* for "baby" or "suckling." The English probably comes from the Narragansett, but the root also occurs in Blackfoot. This creek is behind Chief Mountain near the pinnacle called *Papoose* or *Ninâipoka.*

PARADISE* CREEK, CANYON, POINT, and **PARK:** The name was applied in the Two Medicine area by Evans, probably to the creek and the park. The canyon, however, is on the opposite side of the Divide, on McDonald Creek above the falls.

PARK* CREEK: Descriptive. The Kootenai name is Far Buffalo: *K̇iłqakiykam Kamquǧukuł Iyamu Aknuxu'nuk.* Efforts to avoid the confusion with "Parke" have been unavailing, though Park Creek is in the south and Parke Creek is in the north.

PARKE* CREEK, PEAK, and **RIDGE:** Lt. John C. Parke was chief astronomer of the Northwest Boundary Survey of 1860–61. The Kootenai name for the ridge is "Green/Blue Mountain": *Kaqłuyitqa Akwukłi'it,* but it is also called Kintla Ridge. The creek is alternately known as *Aqukała Nana* (Red Medicine Creek).

PASS* CREEK: Descriptive. There is one Pass Creek in northern Glacier National Park and another in Waterton Lakes Park.

PAUL BUNYAN'S CABIN: See Longfellow. Paul Bunyan is a mythological hero, probably of Métis origin derived from the Algonquian legend of Kwasind, the Strong Man of *Hiawatha.*

PEABODY*, MOUNT: R. V. Peabody was a guide to the U.S. Boundary Survey 1857–61. There were also men named Peabody with the mining interests: George, James, and E. L. The Kootenai name is "Coming On Top Victor Mountain": *Kyuwakałłama'ka Akwukłi'it.* (See McPartland.)

PENROSE, MOUNT: is one of the outstanding peaks just south of Glacier and next to Nyack Mountain. It was named for Senator Boies Penrose (1860–1921), who backed the project to establish Glacier National Park (1907–1910), or perhaps for all the brothers Penrose together. One of them, Richard, was a prominent geologist, another, Charles B., was a physician who is said to have been connected to the famous Johnson County colonization scheme but quit the project when alerted to its ulterior motives.

On September 1, 1907, the brothers Boies, Charles, and Spencer made camp about the 7,000-foot level on the range southwest of Nyack. Nearby was the camp of A. A. Stiles, the cartographer for the U.S. Geologic Survey. When Dr. Charles Penrose went out deer hunting with Stiles, he killed a young grizzly, only to be attacked and severely mauled by its mother on the thigh, breast, head, and arm, with thirty tooth wounds in all. He managed to shoot the sow, and a second cub escaped. With the aid of Stiles, he got back to camp and spent three hours sterilizing and dressing his own wounds. The next day he and his companions descended the 4,000 feet with no trail to the station at Nyack, where they received the hospitality of the stationmaster and his wife, then flagged the 9:00 P.M. train for the east.

The sow that mauled the doctor was estimated to weigh three hundred pounds, and all three bears were uncommonly white. The doctor carefully recorded his adventure for the "Boone and Crockett Club" of Roosevelt and Grinnell, pointing out that he had felt no pain, suffered no infection and endured no impairment. He compared his experience with that of David Livingstone who reported no pain when chewed on by a lion, adding, "Every surgeon knows that acute traumatism is usually painless." (It is not clear whether this quote is from Penrose or Livingstone.)

Another version of this episode is in circulation claiming that the doctor realized he needed more care than he could give himself and that therefore a rescue crew was called to get him down off the mountain by way on one of the many creeks that tumble pell-mell onto Nyack flats. This episode is regarded as the origin of the place names Mount Penrose, Rescue Creek, and the Great Bear Creek, Falls, and Wilderness Area. However, the doctor's own account does not include all these details.

Senator Boies Penrose died in Washington, D.C., and immediately acquired a reputation as the ghost of the capital. The ghost story is told by Mary Roberts Rinehart in her autobiography. She not only believed in ghosts but was personally involved with this one. Needless to say, she did not flatter the Senator.

PERIL* CREEK and **PEAK**: The Kootenai names are *Kwiłqłi Akinmituk* (Big Horn River), and *Kwiłqwat Akwukłi'it* (Big Ear Peak). Evans called the mountain "Peril" because of the hardship he endured in climbing it.

PHILLIPS*, MOUNT: has also been called "Ram Mountain" for the many rams seen there, and the Kootenai name is "Long Arm":

Kwułaí. No one seems to know who Phillips was. There was a mine claimant named George Phillips. Or was the peak, like the county of eastern Montana, named for rancher Benjamin D. Phillips? He and his neighbors the Coburns were cattle and sheep barons who spent their winters and golden years in California and Arizona. "B.D." had a mansion at Oakland on the old Spanish land grant of Peralta, and whether by design or coincidence, employed a Peralta and his sheep-shearing crew on his vast Montana spread.

PIEGAN* FALLS, MOUNTAIN and **PASS**: The pass has also been called Flower Pass. The Piegans are one of the three main branches of the Blackfeet confederacy, the branch which now lives mostly in the U.S. and which has the closest association with Glacier National Park. They are also called the South Piegans by anthropologists because there is a group of North Piegans (or as they spell their name: Peigans) living at Brockett, Alberta. The name in Blackfoot is *Pikáni* with the *a* short as in "above." It may mean "Far Robes" or may be a shortened form of *Apikáni*. (See APIKUNI.) The sign for "Piegan" or *Pikani* is to rub the cheek with a closed fist. By some at least this sign is interpreted to mean "poorly dressed (buffalo) robes," and if so, the sign suggests the meaning for the tribal name "scabby or spotted robes." These people occupy the Blackfeet Reservation just east of the park in Glacier and Pondera counties. The agency is at Browning, where it was established to be on the railroad in 1894–5 – in the path of eternal winds. The first agency was Old Agency on Badger Creek, established in 1875. Before that and since 1868, the agency had been on Teton River. The demands of stockmen gradually reduced the reservation to its present limits, shifting the agencies northward.

PINE LAKE: See AHERN.

PINCHOT* CREEK and **MOUNT** overlooking Nyack valley were named for Gifford Pinchot (1865–1946), first head of the U.S. Forest Service and a leading conservationist of his age. He is called "the dean of American foresters." For his trip in the Glacier area, see MCCLINTOCK, AHERN. The Kootenai name is *Wuqti Akwukłi'it* (Fisher Mountain).

PITAMAKAN* FALLS, LAKE, and **PASS**: The Blackfeet name *Pitawmáhkn* means "Running Eagle" or "the running of the eagle" or "the way the eagle runs." It is typical of Indian names that focus on the verbal element rather than the noun and are therefore awkward to translate into noun-oriented English. It is composed of *pita* +

omahka + *n* (eagle + run + a gerund-forming suffix). It is a personal name and in this case, that of a woman warrior whose story is the basis of a book by J. W. Schultz. Occasionally a male name may be given to a female warrior. Since the falls of Two Medicine Creek that issue from a cave, once known as Trick Falls, have been associated with this girl's vision quest, the name has been changed to Running Eagle Falls. Marias Pass has also been called by her name since she used it to cross the Divide, notably on her last raid when she was killed on Flathead Lake. But there are different versions of her story, one by Adolf Hungry Wolf.

Since Mary Roberts Rinehart was also a "warrior woman," that is, she was a war correspondent during World War I, she was also given the name *Pitamakan*. Her experiences during the war include her interview with King Albert of the Belgians (the one who came to Glacier Country as the Crown Prince) and her terrifying venture at night to an old church in the middle of no-man's-land, where a lone monk kept his cats.

Pitamakan Lake is also called East Lake and the Lake of the Seven Winds, and is one of the Morning Glory Lakes. (See RUNNING EAGLE.)

POCKET* LAKE and **CREEK**: Descriptive. The Kootenai name is *Kaƚxu Akuq̓nuk* (Broad Body).

POIA LAKE and **CAVE:** The Blackfoot word *páiye* means "scar" and is the name of the legendary hero Scarface. The form *poia*, which Ruhle applied here, must have been taken from McClintock and was also used as the title of an opera composed on the same theme by Arthur Nevin. There is a Scarface Point on the trail of the Garden Wall. According to the story, Scarface is a poor boy, the laughingstock of his people because of an ugly scar on his cheek. Yet he dares to love the chief's daughter, "a child of plenty." But she tells him that before she can marry him he must get rid of his scar. So off he goes wandering first in one direction then in another till he tries all four directions (the sacred number), always in quest of a cure. At last he crosses a great water (to the west?) on the back of swans. He is going to the sun. (It is altogether possible that this story suggested the place name.) In the land of the sun, he saves the life of Morning Star by fighting off some vicious cranes. So the parents of Morning Star, the sun and the moon, befriend Scarface. The sun cures his scar and sends him back home with new "medicine." This story may be a version of the world-wide "ascension myth." (See GOING-TO-THE-SUN.)

The opera based on material from McClintock, varies this plot, romanticizes it and uses the name Natoya for its heroine – to my own amazement, because I had previously invented this very name for a different protagonist but based on the root *natuyi-*. I suppose that both my invention and the opera's sprang at least subliminally from McClintock's term *katoya* (sweet pine).

This grand opera *Poia* was composed by Arthur Nevin with a libretto by Randolph Hartley. Nevin, from Pennsylvania and later Virginia, and of Scotch descent, visited the Blackfeet with Walter McClintock in the summer of 1903, collecting native music and folklore. Joined by Hartley, Nevin returned to the Blackfeet in 1904. The opera they produced in three acts makes Poia a suitor for the chief's daughter Natoya in rivalry with the wicked Sumatsi. But Poia must first remove the taboo of his face scar. So he finds his way to the Court of the Sun-god, rescues Morning Star from "foes," and is rewarded by the sun who removes his scar. Back he goes to earth, where Sumatsi tries to kill him but kills Natoya instead. Poia carries her into the sky. Selections from the score were performed by the Pittsburg Symphony, and a grand reception was given by President and Mrs. Theodore Roosevelt. In 1910 the opera was played in Berlin before the royal family but received vigorous opposition from some Germans who resented American intrusion into the world of opera.

Nevin himself was much confused by "the strange mixture of friendliness and enmity" he encountered in Germany. Explicitly grateful for favors he had received from various persons, among them Engelbert Humperdinck, he also had to recognize "the strong anti-foreign sentiment" current among the German people.

POLEBRIDGE VILLAGE and **RANGER STATION** are named for the old bridge of poles that crossed the North Fork into the park. The bridge was badly damaged during the floods of 1964.

POLLOCK* MOUNTAIN was named for W. C. Pollock who headed the team of Grinnell and Clements in negotiating the Agreement (not treaty) of 1885–6 to buy or lease the eastern portion of what is now Glacier National Park. The intention was not to establish a national park but to release this area for prospectors, miners and hunters. So many were already illegally active on reservation land that they had become a nuisance to the government (though they included government employees). This problem exacerbated the other problem of trespass by cattlemen and settlers who were demanding that reservation land be opened to settlers. Grinnell was intent upon promoting the cattle industry for the Blackfeet only and thought this Agreement was a way to forestall or prevent the allotment system. He also expected the Agreement to terminate. Therefore, the Agreement must have been a lease, not a purchase. Though Congress ratified it, Congress also set it aside in a few years and re-arranged everything to suit itself.

PONDERA COUNTY: Pronounced "ponder-ay," this name must be derived from the tribal name *Pend d'Oreille* (earring) or *pain doré* (golden bread, toast). Both are French terms.

PORCUPINE* RIDGE and **LOOKOUT** are near Cathedral Peaks. The Blackfoot name for the ridge is *Kaiskahp Pawahkui.*

PRAY LAKE: For Charles N. Pray, a judge and congressman who helped push the bill to establish Glacier National Park.

PRESTON* PARK: We do not know who Preston was.

PRINCE OF WALES HOTEL: One of the outstanding examples of hotel and chalet architecture in the Waterton Glacier International Peace Park, this was the last of the big hotels to be constructed (1926–1927) by the Glacier Hotel Company. It is believed, however, that the idea of the hotel was conceived by Louis Hill at a much earlier date. Louis Hill's admiration for the architectural style of the French and Swiss chalets climaxed in gigantic proportions at "The Prince." Part of it was to be seven stories tall. But the fierce winds, fire and floods all took their toll before the new hotel became popular. Some of the wooden giant was pegged together without nails. The site of the structure on the bleak rocky moraine did at least offer refuge for local residents of the town site in times of flood.

Though the name of the hotel may refer to the title rather than to any particular person holding the title, it was probably an allusion to Edward VIII, later the Duke of Windsor. He owned a ranch on the Highwood River. There is no public record, however, of any member of the British royal family visiting Waterton Lakes Park, but Prince Charles has come to the Blood Reserve, was received by the tribe and was given the title of their traditional head chief, "Red Crow."

"The Prince" served a purpose that perhaps had never been intended. South of the border prohibition was in effect. North of the border prohibition was only a "provincial option," and the Province of Alberta opted out. So The Prince offered a refuge for thirsty Montanans who sprang from the long tradition of rum or rotgut started by the fur trade. The vice-president (and later president) of Great Northern, William P. Kenny, did not fully share Louis' enthusiasm for The Prince and did not enjoy its reputation as a last hope for heavy drinkers. Moreover, Alberta had its own blue law: No dancing on Sunday. So a strange symbiosis soon developed via the launch *International* that plied the waters of Waterton Lake. Boozers from Montana would catch the launch from Goathaunt up to The Prince while dance fans with their own band sailed down to Goathaunt in Glacier to dance away the Saturday nights or Sundays.

PTARMIGAN* CREEK, FALLS, LAKE, TUNNEL and **WALL:** The word "ptarmigan" is of Scottish origin and applied to various kinds of northern grouse that change plumage in the winter for camouflage. The local name is supposed to have started because the ptarmigans showed no fear of the first humans they saw, even walking about the feet of one of the earliest. The Ptarmigan Wall has also been called Castle Mountain, Pinnacle Wall, and Amphitheater Wall, and the highest point on the wall behind Iceberg Lake was named Crazy Gray Horse Mountain by Superintendent E. T. Scoyen (1931–1938).

Scoyen was much impressed by the Blackfoot story of their famous war horse (Crazy Gray) that would plunge fearlessly into chase or battle, perhaps uncontrollable by the rider but sure to bring the rider fame for his exploits. (It was whispered that the rider might have been scared to the toes of his moccasins.) But about 1857 Crazy Gray was with seven Blackfeet in the Sweet Grass Buttes country when they were overwhelmed by a huge war party of Sioux. Crazy Gray was among the dead. It is obvious that this story preserved by Scoyen (Glacier Drift, VIII, 10–11) is at variance with the story told by Schultz. (See OLSON.) Perhaps there were two or more horses by this name. Perhaps Schultz was a better novelist than historian.

PUMPELLY* GLACIER and **PILLAR** are named for Raphael Pumpelly of Harvard University (1837–1923). He was a distinguished geologist and mining engineer whose research carried him across the world. Born in Oswego, New York, he pursued his quest of science from Lake Superior to Arizona, from Mexico to Japan, China and Central Asia, and over much of Europe and the Middle East. He pioneered in the exploration of the Gobi Desert. His adventures involved him with many famous persons you would not expect – Geronimo and Cochise, for example.

In 1882–3 he was exploring in Montana as part of the Northern Transcontinental Survey for the Northern Pacific Railway. He was making a study of the potentials of this area for agriculture and mining in the classical alliance of science and business so easily taken for granted at that time but in the long run destined for the doing and undoing of the U.S.A. Among scientists associated with Pumpelly in this operation were Bailey Willas and Charles S. Sargent, both from Harvard. As guide and packer Pumpelly hired William Logan, one day to become the park's first superintendent. Lt. John Van Orsdale, who had been in the area ten years before, joined Pumpelly's group (perhaps not altogether welcome).

Pumpelly Pillar has also been known as "Pinnacle Peak" and "Sacred Shield Mountain": *Natowap-áwotani-istáki* in Blackfoot, this last after an Indian who knew Prince Maximilian in 1833. The Kootenai name for the pillar seems to be the tribal name that Kootenais use for themselves: *Ksanka Akwukłi'it. Ksanka* means "standing arrow" or "arrow in the ground." The Kootenai names for the glacier are said to be "Daughter's Ice" and "No Bear Ice." This last is *Kqa'in Kławła Akwiswitxu.*

Somebody has confused Pumpelly's Pillar with Pompey's Pillar in southern Montana, the rock probably named for Pomp, the son of Sacajawea.

PYRAMID CREEK and **PEAK**: It was almost inevitable that somewhere in Glacier there should be a mountain named with this ancient Egyptian root, and here is was applied by Chaney or perhaps Joe Cosley. The mountain was once called "Fraternity Peak" and also *Ipashá.* There is another Pyramid Peak just south of Glacier, which sheds Pyramid Creek and waterfalls into Nyack valley. And there is still another Pyramid on the northern edge of Glacier where Boundary Pass crosses into Waterton Lakes Park. The party of Lord Lathom and Stavely-Hill named this one "Pyramid Hill" in 1883. The word "pyramid" is of course of Egyptian origin.

QUARTER CIRCLE BRIDGE is a curved bridge that spans lower McDonald Creek.

QUARTER CIRCLE M R Ranch is in the North Fork country.

QUARTZ* CREEK, LAKE, and **RIDGE:** The Kootenai names are "Head of Rhubarb Lake": *A·kɫam Wuṁaɫ Akuɋnuk* and "the Lake Where the Rhubarb is Long": *Yakiɫ Wuqa'ki Wuṁaɫ Akuɋnuk* . The first name is for Upper Quartz Lake, the second, Lower Quartz. The map of 1846 shows these features as the *Lac et Rivière Hoeken* after one or both brothers Adrian and Christian Hoecken, both of them Jesuits. Christian died of cholera on board a Missouri steamer in 1851.

In 1876 William Veach is reported to have come up from Texas with a small party of companions finding a thirty-ounce gold nugget near the lake. About 1889 Louie Meyer discovered a quartz vein at the head of the creek. But these ventures proved ephemeral as always.

QUILLOUX, MOUNTAIN OF: This term appears in DeSmet's journals as a landmark of the border country. The question is: to which mountain did DeSmet refer? Perhaps to Chief Mountain. Perhaps to Crowsnest Mountain. And to what does the name refer? Perhaps to the area of the Old Man River, a holy place in Blackfeet lore as the land of their tribal origin. Hugh Dempsey has proposed that the term may be a misprint for French Canadian *quilleur*, a bowler, one who bowls, derived from *quille* for "ninepin." This sacred area was marked by three stone cairns because here Old Man (Napi) played with the animals at a game somewhat resembling ninepins. There is another possible explanation: the word *quilloux* may be a French spelling of a Cree word for "eagle": *kiyiw*. French was the language of DeSmet and his guide at this point was a Cree. (See SAINT MARY.)

RAILROAD* CREEK crosses under the GN tracks west of East Glacier. In southern Alberta Railway Creek or River was named by Blakiston because it seemed to be a promising place to build a railroad.

RAIN SHADOW PEAK: So named by climbers because clouds sidetracked by Mount Cleveland leave this peak in the sunshine or else draw it into the shadow of the rain clouds. It is close to Goathaunt.

RAINBOW* CREEK, GLACIER, and **PEAK**: The Kootenai name is "Otter Woman Glacier and Mountain": *Aqawxał Pałkiy Akwiswitxu* and *Akwukłi'it.*

But there is some question whether "Otter Woman" is the name for Rainbow Peak or Mount Morgan or both. The mountain, by another account, was named Rainbow because of strata of rock near the summit that suggested the name. Still another report has it that Ranger Frank Liebig remarked to surveyor Sargent, "The glacier shines like a rainbow."

RAINBOW FALLS is near Waterton Lake. Probably a descriptive name.

RAINBOW SLIDE is on the western face of Mount Seward and shows red, yellow and gray.

RAMPAGE* MOUNTAIN: Named for the forest fire there in 1910, perhaps by Evans. The Kootenai name is "Small Weasel": *Mayuknana.*

RAVEN QUIVER: See Kipp.

RAZOREDGE* MOUNTAIN: Descriptive. The Kootenai name is "Running Fox": *Kanłukpqa Nakyu.*

RED MOUNTAIN: In Blackfoot *Ikuz'-istaki.* If you are confused about the word for "red" which seems different every time we come to it, you are not alone. All or most of the forms of the word for "red" stem from the same root: *mahk-, mik-, mek-,mikuzi-, ikuzi-, mikap-, ikap-* and *amahk-.* Note that the initial *m* tends to drop out as often happens with both *m* and *n* in Blackfoot.

RED BLANKET BUTTE (Hill) is a high point on Cut Bank Ridge where Highway 89 crosses it east of Glacier. It is the burial site of Red Blanket, *Mahk-áipiszi*, originally in a "tree burial." The story of Red Blanket Hill is hardly a bedtime story and certainly not a part of Louis Hill's Myth of Glacier.

The terrible epidemics that swept away so much of the American Indian population devastated the Blackfeet and their neighbors at least in the 1730s, 1837–38, 1870 and 1900. During one of these disasters, a band under Red Blanket was fleeing the ravages of the disease farther north, and when they realized they were already infested and spreading the plague far and wide, they camped here in despair. On this hilltop they would face death, and from its height you could almost see the Great Sand Hill (land of the dead) or *Omahk-spaziko*. Here, one by one, they all dropped dead on the rocks. Red Blanket himself, one of the first to fall, was deposited in a tree. While white tourists whiz by on Highway 89, Blackfeet (those who dare pass this way) may pause here in meditation.

Eventually, a younger man, one of those who greeted tourists at East Glacier, approached the remains of old Red Blanket seeking spirit power. The reply he got: "I am lonesome here. Go kill a woman for me." The young man withdrew in frustration. No, he could not kill a woman. Better to go without that kind of spirit power.

RED BOX CANYON: No information.

RED CROW* MOUNTAIN: Evans conferred this name, but whom did he have in mind? Apparently the name was originally applied to the mountain now called Curly Bear or perhaps to Kupunkamint, whereas the present Red Crow Mountain (which overlooks East Glacier) was listed by Schultz under the name of "Bull's Back Fat." If Schultz had given the name "Red Crow," I would think it referred to the son of Lone Walker. But since Evans gave the name, it seems more likely the Red Crow he had in mind was the head chief of the Bloods in whose honor a cairn has been erected near Stand Off, Alberta. This chief was a nephew of Natawista and a brother-in-law of Crowfoot. He remained neutral during the Riel Rebellion of 1885 and accompanied Father Lacombe and Crowfoot to Qu bec. Red Crow in Blackfoot is *Meki-aisto/Mekaisto* (since *(m)aistó(wa)* is crow or raven).

RED EAGLE: There are several Blackfoot forms for the name "Red Eagle" because there are so many variations on the root for "red". And the word for "eagle" is normally *píta* with the *i* short in value but prolonged in emphasis, so that some people write it with a double *i*. It has another form *pítan*, which may be archaic. One theory is that since the Blackfoot word for "eagle" is altogether different from the term in other Algonquin languages, it must originate from some descriptive term, perhaps from the root for "white": *api-* + an ancient root for "tail": *-otani* (found in Virginia in the seventeenth century!). Oh well, it's a guess. No wonder then that we get various ways to say "Red Eagle": *MáhxiPíta, Mikuz'-Pítan, Ikúzi-Píta,* etc.

And then there is the old word for "eagle" that Pocahontas must have used: *opatenaiok,* more like the Blackfoot term and suggestive of the Blackfoot roots for "feather", *-anik-* and *awanoki*. Then one has to wonder if the ancient Proto-Algonquin term *kili-wa* for "eagle" has evolved by metathesis and the usual shift of *l* to *n* into something like these modern roots in Blackfoot. See MORNING EAGLE (and RISING SUN for a real miss).

The Kootenai name for the glacier is said to be Old Woman Ice, corresponding to the Kootenai name for Saint Mary Lake and forming a cluster of kinship names for neighboring glaciers: Blackfeet Glacier is Old Man Ice, and Harrison Glacier is Old Man's Daughter's Ice. Does this occur by design or by coincidence? The main Red Eagle Lake lies at the eastern foot of the Divide, but the lake on the west side now called Halfmoon has also gone by the name of Red Eagle Lake.

There is also a Red Eagle Campground on Lower Two Medicine Lake and Red Eagle Motel at Saint Mary.

Red Eagle Pass was used by Kootenais and was reached in 1891 by Schultz and Grinnell. The pass is called *Mikuzí-Pítan ozitamisohpi* (where Red Eagle went up) and used to be one of the main Indian routes across the Continental Divide in this sector of the mountains, leading to and from Nyack Creek and the Middle Fork on the western slopes. Whether Red Eagle the Piegan medicine man ever used this pass is doubtful, but it was used by William T. Hamilton and a camp of Kootenais escaping from the Bloods over Red Eagle Pass – that is, if you can believe Hamilton's braggadocio.

The majestic, photogenic peak over Upper Saint Mary called Little Chief has also been called Red Eagle. The U.S. Geological Survey, in its Bulletin 600 of 1914 on "The Glacier National Park," designated this peak as Red Eagle and illustrated it with one of the earliest of many photos. On the other hand the summit of the peak now called Red Eagle on the topographical map occasionally displays a reddish color from the Grinnell argillite, but whether this fact has influenced the name seems doubtful. It is possible that the two mountains, close together as they are, were confused in the beginning. We have only the word of Schultz as to the naming of the mountain by his wife Natahki for her uncle – and that as they were seen from Thunder Bird Island in Lower Saint Mary where Schultz and his family had taken refuge.

The Kootenai term for "Red Eagle" is *Kanuhus Kyaq̇nuka't* and the word for the pass is *Yakił Ałqanamki Kanuhus Kyaq̇nuka't*.

Great Northern Railway has complicated the story of this wandering name by assigning it to a station at Nyack, now called "Red Eagle," and this writer has contributed another complication by naming his residence at this station "Red Eagle Ranch". The station still goes by this name and indeed at the very point where Mount Stimson dominates the scene so completely that many a train passenger must assume that the name refers to the peak. (Perhaps it should.) The name is not inappropriate for the west side as well as the east side since it also occurs among west side tribes. There was a Salish leader Red Eagle: *Kúlkuls-keim'*. He may have been the man otherwise known as "Little Michel" who took part in the treaty of 1855. When whites first contacted the Kalispels, one of their chiefs had this name, and another Kalispel chief, related to the earlier one, bore the name "Red Eagle" and died sometime after 1900. One of these three chiefs could have been the man Dan Whetstone had in mind when he suggested that the railway station had been named after a Salish chief. The name may have come to the Salish from the Nez Perces through intermarriage or other cultural contact.

Vaught claims that Red Eagle Mountain, Lake, and Creek, as well as Gould, Little Chief, Almost a Dog, Kootenay Mountain, Show Mountain (no longer identified), Monroe Peak and Basin, and Cataract Creek were all named by Grinnell during his second visit to the area in 1887. Could Grinnell, like Schultz, have bungled?

RED MEDICINE BOW CREEK and **PEAK** are in the northwest corner of Glacier. The name evidently refers to the same Kootenai story that occasioned the name Long Bow. It is one of the frequent stories of giants among the Kootenais and Salish. The giant Red Medicine once found a long bow with *nupika* energy, either on this peak or on

Harris Glacier. One has to wonder about *nupika* energy as well as *manito* energy and similar forms, whether it is benign or malign. Does it depend on the person using it? Kindly solve this question, oh you anthropologists!

REDGAP CREEK and **PASS** were named for the red rocks of the area. In Blackfoot "red earth" is *Ikuzi-xahkum.*

REDHORN LAKE and **PEAK**: Red Horn was a Piegan sub-chief described by Prince Maximilian, blacklisted by the U.S. Army, and killed in the Baker massacre. Whether all these things happened to the same person, it is hard to tell. The name is *Ikuz-ózkina.* "Red Horn" was also a Kootenai name for Bighorn Peak.

REDROCK* FALLS, **LAKE**, and **POINT**: Named for the red cliffs nearby. There is also a well-known Red Rock Canyon in Waterton Lakes Park.

REUTER PEAK: The Kootenai name is Took Many Guns: *Kyunoł wakwu'tił.* The name on the map derives from "Black Jack" Reuter, also known as "Dutch Wannigan." John D. Reuter was an early settler at Big Prairie, a good-looking man if not always well behaved. Perhaps a German by birth, he was locally known as expert at building log cabins. But he had a checkered career as a roughneck in the Bad Lands of North Dakota in the 1880s. He rode the range for Theodore Roosevelt and may have been a cook for the Marquis de Mor s. After one or more shoot-outs, Reuter became especially hostile to the French-Spanish nobleman. The Marquis is said to have offered Reuter a grubstake if he would just go west. The story may be phony, but Reuter did move west – as far as Lake McDonald and the North Fork.

REYNOLDS* CREEK and **MOUNTAIN**: This magnificent matterhorn was named by Grinnell for Charles E. Reynolds, an editor of *Field and Stream.* People acquainted with Glacier history may assume that the name refers to the pioneer ranger Al Reynolds ("Death on the Trail"), and perhaps it should have been. Or they may be thinking of the scout Charlie Reynolds. The Blackfoot name for the creek is Beaver Creek, in reference to Three Sun's wife, a holy woman. And for the matterhorn, the Blackfoot name is that of a prominent old fur trader, hard as nails, Kenneth McKenzie, *Kinúk-suyapi-koan* (Little Water Whiteman). McKenzie ran his business in high style and was one of the most successful of traders. However, I doubt Indians named this or any other mountain for him, unless prodded by Schultz. The term *napikoan* means "white man" (with the initial *n-* weak and removable); *suyápikoan* means "water white man," that is, a white man from across the water (or as the Crees say, "comes ashore") and refers especially to the English or Scots. (McKenzie was a Scot.) Even today *suyapi* is a common term for "white man" in the Pacific Northwest, but whether it derives from this source, I do not know.

Mount Reynolds is probably visible on clear days from the foot of Lake McDonald – just to the left of the Little Matterhorn.

RICHARDS, MOUNT: is in Waterton Lakes National Park, close to the border and even overlapping it at Boundary Creek. It is also called Sleeping Indian Mountain because of the reclining figure it forms on its eastern side. It was named after Admiral G. H. Richards of the Boundary Commission, 1858–1862. At that time, however, Richards was not admiral but captain of the British survey ship, the *Plumper*.

RIMROCKS: These are rocks just below Logan Pass at the cut.

RISING BULL* MOUNTAIN or **RIDGE** was named for the likeness it has to a buffalo bull getting onto its feet. The name may be of Indian origin. (See ROCKWELL.)

RISING SUN: This is the visitor service center on Rose Creek and Upper Saint Mary Lake, formerly Rose (or Roes) Creek Campground and even East Glacier. Someone got the bright notion that it would be nice to have a corresponding Setting Sun on the west side at Lake McDonald, but luckily the name did not catch on.

A Kootenai chief of Tobacco Plains was named Rising Sun or *Kiwakam Natanik.*

RISING WOLF* MOUNTAIN is one of the most famous peaks in Glacier, dominating the Two Medicine area. In Blackfoot this name is *Mahkúyi-opuáhsin*, literally meaning (according to Frank Guardipee) "the way the wolf gets up." The problem with translating many Blackfoot names into English is that the emphasis in Blackfoot may be on the verb and in English on the noun, so that the meaning is distorted in translation. Frank's suggestion is his way of getting around this problem.

This was the name of Hugh Monroe, perhaps for his manner of getting up in the morning. He was born at L'Assomption, Quebec, August 15, 1799, the son of Hugh Monroe Sr., and the former Mrs. Anqélique

LaRocque. A widow née Leroux, Angélique was the mother of François Antoine LaRocque, an early explorer of Montana who met Lewis and Clark. He was a clerk in the XY Company, then after consolidation in 1804, in the North West Company. Angélique was also the mother of Joseph Félix LaRoque, also a clerk in the XY and North West Companies and a very early trader in British Columbia. It is hard, therefore to explain how Hugh, the young half-brother of these Larocques came to serve in the bitterly hostile rival company Hudson's Bay. Hugh seems to have been apprenticed to Hudson Bay Company shortly after the War of 1812 in which he and his family took some part in the British ranks.

When he went out to live with the Blackfeet, his first host was Rising Head, but after falling out with Rising Head, he was adopted by Lone Walker. Baptismal records show that on September 6, 1838, three children of Hugh Monroe and Sinopáki were baptised at a fort along the North Saskatchewan: William (age seven), Marguerite (age three or five) and Emilien (age 4). So apparently Hugh had married Sinopáki around 1831. Other sons of Hugh were Félix, Piscan and Olivier who were all members of the Palliser expedition. (See Blakiston.). The name *Sinopáki* is Blackfoot, and it is commonly believed that Hugh's wife was a daughter of Lone Walker. The names of Hugh's wife and father-in-law are assigned to peaks in Glacier near the mountain Rising Wolf named for Hugh himself in a sort of family gathering. But Hugh seems to have spent a good deal of time also with the Kootenais, Crees and Métis.

In 1832 Hugh and his family were at the AFC post Fort Union. He claimed to have seen Saint Mary Lakes in 1836, perhaps in company with the Kootenais who used to camp there. When Governor Stevens came to Fort Benton in 1853, he engaged Hugh as guide and interpreter, with Pete Martínez as hunter. Hugh explored with James Doty around present Glacier but was reluctant to enter Marias Pass. He may have accompanied Isaac Stevens to Walla Walla. From a fight with a Sioux, Hugh was blinded in one eye, but he survived until the age of ninety-three in 1892 and lies buried near Holy Family Mission.

RIVERVIEW* MOUNTAIN was so named by Evans. The Kootenai name is "Patches of Hair Mountain": *Haƚiƚɂanuqƚuk Akwukƚi'it*. Compare this with Scalplock Mountain.

ROBBERS ROOST: A mysterious name used for Hidden Valley Ranch, where allegedly some outlaws once had a refuge. There are local traditions about smuggling operations through the Waterton-Glacier trench and along the North Fork. Mary Roberts Rinehart specifically mentions the smuggling of opium. Old-timers speak of smuggling Chinese. The name may be a vestige of those times.

ROBERTSON MOUNTAIN is now called Yellow Mountain, but its earlier name recalls a man that need not be forgotten. Samuel Robertson was admitted to West Point at age eighteen in 1875 and on graduation received an appointment as second lieutenant in the First Cavalry. He spent two years in Idaho at Fort Lapwai and environs, in and out of terrific snowstorms. Then he was sent to France to attend the famous cavalry academy at Saumur for his expertise as a horseman. Returning to the U.S., he was assigned to Forts Walla Walla and Spokane, to Lake Chelan and Vancouver Barracks. In 1886 he came to Fort Assiniboine in Montana. It was at this period that he made his explorations of what is now Glacier National Park, the two years that he himself declared the happiest of his Army life. His assignment as instructor in equitation at Fort Leavenworth was more disillusioning and he returned to Montana at Fort Custer. According to his hunting companion Dr. William T. Hornaday, he hunted in almost every range of Idaho, Oregon, Washington, Wyoming, and Montana. He was also a photographer and a writer with a graceful style. He wrote on "Saunterings in Mexico," cavalry life and his project of training Indians as cavalrymen, probably the work for which he is best remembered. He founded a group of Crow scouts and in 1892 the Crow troop of the First Cavalry. Among his scouts was the well-known Curley, who also assisted Lt. James Bradley. About 1890 Lieutenant Robertson began to form a similar group of Cheyennes.

It was at that time that the enthusiasm for the Ghost Dance was being spread among the Cheyennes by Porcupine, a delegate from the Prophet Wavoka. The Ghost Dance was basically pacifist, but the Army is not very tolerant of pacifists. When two young men about eighteen, Head Chief and Young Mule, killed a rancher, Robertson was assigned to bring them in. The young braves called upon their people to gather on the hills and watch them die. The whole tribe assembled to watch, even their mothers and fathers. The two young men appeared riding in war regalia, Young Mule in an especially magnificent war bonnet. Head Chief rode directly toward the troops and was shot several times. Young Mule circled about but after an hour his body was found amid his war garb and his blood splattered over the yellow leaves of autumn. (I think this dramatic story has been used for a movie.)

Many of the Army old guard denounced the project of training Indian scouts and in spite of the support given to it by General Hugh Scott, the program was terminated in 1897. Robertson, already sick at the time of the Cheyenne showdown, died in Texas in 1893.

ROCKBILL LAKE is near Harrison Lake but now has no official name.

ROCKWELL* FALLS and **MOUNT** were named after a pioneer. The old name was Rising Bull Mountain after a chief who was honored by both Blackfeet and Flatheads. His wife was Salish. The north spur of this peak is still called by this name. (See RISING BULL, SHEPHERD, SAINT NICHOLAS.)

ROCO CREEK: This name may be a mistake for Rose Creek.

ROGERS* LAKE, MEADOW, PEAK, and **RANCH**: Josiah Rogers was an early homesteader of the Lake McDonald area. He ran a saddle horse concession. The Kootenai name is "Traders Lake and Peak": *Ḳaquⱡiyawi Aquqnuk* and *Akwukⱡi'it.*

ROSE* CREEK and **BASIN**: Probably named in 1885 by Schultz or Grinnell for Otahkomi. (See OTOKOMI.)

ROTUNDA* CIRQUE: This descriptive name was conferred by Evans. *Rotunda* is the feminine form of "round" in Latin, while *cirque* is French for "circus," and also a geological term. The name is a stupid redundancy.

ROUND* PRAIRIE is on the North Fork.

ROWE LAKES and **BROOK** are in Waterton Lakes Park. Rowe Brook was once called Canon Creek. They are named after Lieutenant Rowe, an engineer and surveyor with the British Boundary Commission.

RUBIDEAU CREEK and **SPRING** rise on Apgar Mountain and have long provided much of the water supply for park headquarters. The spelling of the name is variable but, however spelled, is said to refer to some loggers on the North Fork and also to a homesteader. The county records are obscure on this point, though they do account for a John A. Robideau, a resident of Columbia Falls about 1905.

There was a much extended family of fur traders by this surname, again variously spelled, though historians of the fur trade have settled on "Robidoux." This family spread itself at an early date from Quebec to Saint Louis, Santa Fe, and Los Angeles. One brother is regarded as the founder of Saint Joseph, Missouri, another as a founder of River-side, California. Western branches intermarried with Spanish families of New Mexico and California, and three persons of this family on their maternal lines had some impact in the Northwest. Louis Rivet (1803–1902) came up the Missouri with McKenzie and James Kipp and married into the Blackfoot tribe. Someone from the California branch settled in Butte. Another, Senator Miguel Estudillo, helped establish Yosemite National Park and promoted the Pinchot-Roosevelt doctrine of conservation in Idaho.

RUBY RIDGE is in Waterton Lakes Park. It changes color with the changing light, carmine to violet – say those who know colors. (Some of us do not.)

RUGER* LAKE is a pond at the head of Camas Creek, locally thought to have been named for a young man who worked on the trail crew that built the trail to this lake about 1935. He went swimming here and drowned. Or the lake may have been named for General Thomas H. Ruger, who served in the Civil War and about 1890 held a command in Dakota and Montana. Lieutenant Ahern in 1890 named a mountain near the head of Camas Creek for General Ruger, but (according to Vaught) the surveyor Sargent, in 1902, changed the name to Longfellow. Maybe the name Ruger was settled on the pond instead.

RUNNING CRANE* LAKE: In Blackfoot this name is *Sikami-omahkan* (the way the crane runs). Running Crane was a chief of the Piegans about 1880 during some of the last buffalo hunts. His other name, *Apikuni*, he gave to James Willard Schultz. One of the most distinguished of Piegan chiefs, he was the mentor of a southern band of the tribe, and McClintock recorded one of his speeches. A daughter married Otahkomi (Charles Rose), a son married into the family of Spotted Eagle, and a descendent is one of the mentors of the writer of these lines.

RUNNING EAGLE FALLS: This is the Blackfoot name of the falls that flow from the Two Medicine Lakes through a cave. The wonder of the spot made it an ideal retreat for the vision quest and, according to Schultz, this was the place where "warrior girl" Pitamahkan came to seek her vision. The name of the falls used to be "Trick Falls," ceremoniously changed to "Running Eagle" in July, 1981. (See PITAMAHKAN.)

RUNNING RABBIT* MOUNTAIN: *Aazist-omahkan,* "the way the rabbit runs." Running Rabbit was a chief of the Kaina or Bloods, though the name also occurs among the Piegans. The Kootenai name is White Crow: *Kamnuqłu Qukin.*

SACRED DANCING CASCADE: An old Kootenai name for Lake McDonald, Lower (not Upper) McDonald Creek and the general area around them is translated by Schultz as Sacred Dancing. Francis Elmore preserved this name by applying it to the cascades on the creek above the lake. The name in Kootenai is given by Thain White as *Yakił Haqwiłnamki*, "a good place to dance," or "where people dance." For the lake, add *-akuq̓nuk* and for the creek add *-akinmituk*.

Though the authenticity of the name "Sacred Dancing" has been questioned as a bit of the imagination of novelist Schultz, more recent research into Kootenai lore and language generally corroborates it.

Besides Thain White already cited, Claude Schaeffer did extensive research into Kootenai place names, and this one "place of dancing" was the only name of the Akiyinik band of Kootenais in this region. A. Bullrobe of Elmo stated that "It was a traditional akiyinik campsite located a few miles from Belton (West Glacier) on the trail across the Rockies." (I quote from Brian Reeves report.) Bullrobe added that it took seven days from Kalispell to reach this spot, and here the Akiyinik band often celebrated their Blacktail Deer Dance (not performed by other Upper Kootenai bands). Schaeffer also found that "the dancing place" was the only campsite known to Bullrobe that the Akiyinik band used when they crossed the Divide to hunt buffalo. This route "to buffalo" was used after the Kootenais got horses even before they moved from Jennings to the Flathead valley, and more so thereafter.

Brian Reeves suggests that the name was also applicable to the Hungry Horse area at the junction of the South and Middle Forks of the Flathead. (See McDonald.)

SAGE CREEK flows from under Sage Pass, British Columbia, into Glacier National Park. It may be the stream labeled *At-tlak-a (Aknuqł uqna'qa)* by the U.S. Boundary Survey of 1861 at 114 degrees, 25 minutes. Sage grows with fair abundance on the plains of this country.

SAINT MARY* LAKES, RIVER, FALLS, RIDGE, and **VILLAGE**: No name in this entire book has probably aroused more speculation if not controversy than "Saint Mary." Schultz, with his anti-church premise, initiated the protest. Yet a firm conclusion to the speculation about the origin of the name still escapes us. The old Blackfoot "name" for the lakes is *Paht-omahxíkimi*: "inside big water." (Big water = lake.) This of course is not really a name but a description. A modern Blackfoot name is *Nato-aki omahxikimi* "Holy Lady Big Water," no doubt a translation.

Other Blackfoot names have been recorded, especially for the river on the Canadian side of the line: "Green or Blue Banks" (which I have never found except in translation but which I would tentatively reconstruct as *Ozkui-akixi* – a little bit like Henry Kennerly's transcription *Ats-ski-kix*.) Other names: "Banks that Dam the River," "Many Chiefs Gathered," and "Many Chiefs Dead" (in the epidemic of 1837–8). The name about damming the river is given in a source I cannot vouch for as *pa-toxiapiskun*, but since it contains the element *piskan* (corral of buffalo pound), I suspect it may refer to a place where the cliffs provided a buffalo jump. Schultz is the source for "Many Chiefs Gathered," which he says refers to intertribal counseling along the river.

A common story, cheerfully endorsed by some historians, is that the lakes were named by the famous Father DeSmet. But it is difficult – to say the least – to reconcile this theory with DeSmet's own letters and maps. True, in 1841 and 1842, DeSmet did visit the area of Flathead Lake and in 1845, also the Tobacco Plains. From there he crossed the Rockies, perhaps in the vicinity of Lake Louise, to the Bow River and Rocky Mountain House. Though warned by the traders, he then turned south in quest of the Blackfeet and Hugh Monroe for a go-between, accompanied by a young Cree Métis for a wrangler and the famous James Bird for interpreter. This man was the very one Prince Maximilian had regarded with suspicion and whom the traders cautioned DeSmet to "beware of." During ten days Bird grew ever more grouchy and finally abandoned his companions after they contacted a "Canadian and his Indian family." (To DeSmet "Canadian" must have meant "French Canadian" or *canadien*.) With these people DeSmet continued in his quest for Hugh Monroe for another eight days through a "labyrinth of valleys." But with war parties ranging the country and the snow beginning to fall, the Jesuit at last turned back north to the hospitable traders. From a letter he wrote Hugh Monroe five years later it is clear that he had never met Hugh in person, though (says he), "I followed your traces to your campground at the foot of the mountain of Quilloux, where I found the signs that you had left, evidently for my benefit." Further pursuit proved unsuccessful. Note on his map that he turned back near the present border.

The question of whether he ever got as far as Saint Mary might be solved if we could identify "the mountain of Quilloux." But that too remains something of a mystery. (See QUILLOUX.)

Other stories abound, derived supposedly from Hugh Monroe or his children via Schultz, Grinnell and the Fort Benton Press of 1890, stories of a *robe noire* and a wooden cross planted on the lake shore There is also a document neglected by almost everybody, "Recollections of Henry Kennerly of the year 1855..." (The name is spelled Kinnerly on the copy I saw.) It is all that is left of the memoirs of Henry A. Kennerly, the rest of which was destroyed by fire. Kennerly came to Montana as an attachÈ for commissioners Stevens and Cumming to make the treaty of 1855, and with Baptiste Champagne was sent on an errand to invite Blackfeet to the council. According to Kennerly, they advanced to the Sweetgrass Buttes and the camp of Lame Bull, perhaps near modern Lethbridge. From there messengers relayed the call to council while Henry and Baptiste turned back to Fort Benton by way of Chief Mountain. There they encountered a caravan of Métis accompanied by Father "LaCom," and that night they all camped together on the shores of a "beautiful lake" full of trout but as yet known only by its Indian name. The river flowing from the lake was called "Blue (Green) Banks" by the Indians. While they were in camp the "priest" had a cross set up on shore, one made of great pine logs, and then he named the lakes and the river "Saint Mary." Henry assures us that the priest thought that since this was the drainage of the Saskatchewan, it must still be British America. From there Henry and Baptiste returned to Fort Benton. There is no mention of Hugh Monroe in Kennerly's account but of course Hugh could have been a member of the caravan. And the "priest" could not have been Father Lacombe because he did not reach western Canada till a later date.

But whether the name "Saint Mary" was bestowed by DeSmet, Monroe, Lacombe, or perhaps the genial imposter Jean L'Heureux, it would have been conferred in the mother tongue of all these people: *les Lacs et la Riviére de Sainte-Marie*.

One Kootenai name is "Old Woman Lakes," perhaps for the feminine form and face in the cliffs above the lower lake, perhaps for the frequent white caps on this turbulent tarn. Brian Reeves cites from Schaeffer the Kootenai names for Lower (and perhaps Upper) Saint

Mary Lakes as Island Lake in reference to Thunderbird Island and Wild Goose Island: *Tɛa Kaukomi*. For Saint Mary River he gives the descriptive name "where rawhide was stretched across the river (to pull tipi bundles across)" *Yakił ałkó ɛikaxaki*. One has to wonder if this is a repetition or confusion with the name for Lee's Creek.

Why has everyone assumed that the name was imposed by a priest? Why could it not have been given by the Indians themselves? Perhaps it was a Christian interpretation for the Kootenai name of Old Woman's Lake: *Tiłnamu Akuq̇nuk* , especially as elderly people were regarded with great respect among native peoples. And we have noted how periodically Kootenai chiefs, Black Bear Hat and Back-in-Sight, would bring their band to camp at Saint Mary and ring a bell for prayers.

The village of Saint Mary used to be called Old Town. It was the center of the Saint Mary Mining District and also a recreational camp for African-American troopers, presumably from Fort Assiniboine. The oldest structure still standing there is probably the one-time Tribal Craft Shop, once an inn and reportedly built about 1887. Mary Roberts Rinehart is supposed to have stayed there. There's plenty of rumor but not much documentation, but the interview of Frank Harrison in the Glacier National Park library gives more reliable details.

SAINT NICHOLAS*, MOUNT: This splendid mitre peak or matterhorn is intermittently sighted along the railroad from Nyack to Essex and is said to have acquired its name from the famous old magazine "for young folk" Saint Nicholas. Letters to the editor began: "Dear Saint Nicholas..." Published from 1873 to 1940, it was edited in its heyday by Mary Mapes Dodge and featured prose and poetry from writers like Longfellow, Louisa Alcott, Helen Hunt Jackson, Frank R. Stockton, James Willard Schultz, and even had a section for primary readers. The Board on Geographic Names approved the name on 6 March 1929 but cannot state its origin.

Yet it does seem strange that a mountain should be named for a magazine. The name on the mountain has been cut to "Saint Nick" and secularized to mere "Nicholas," but nonetheless has proved more durable than many other park names. Saint Nicholas is a semi-legendary figure long esteemed in both the Greek and Latin Churches. According to the tradition, he was the abbot of Zion and bishop of Myra in Asia Minor, was imprisoned and put to torture under the Emperor Diocletian but managed to attend the Council of Nicaea in 325 A.D.

The protest over the name "Saint Mary" has been echoed in objections to the name "Saint Nicholas," but the simple name "Nicholas" seemed too bland .

The Kootenai name for the peak is *K̓lasinquwa* (Two Feathers). With the thought that it might have been named for someone among the Kootenais who may have had the missionary name of Nicholas, much as the city of Saint Louis carried the name of both Louis IX (who was canonized) and Louis XV (who was not), I did find one: a Kootenai chief and his family named "Nicola" or "Nukala" and a Blackfoot chief "Nicholas" married to a Salish wife. (See SHEPHARD.) But that does not seem to explain the name on the mountain.

The peak has another name: "Teakettle," one that it shares with the long low mountain behind Columbia Falls. The western Teakettle is supposed to have been named for a grove of firs, now obliterated, that resembled a Chinese teapot – if you can imagine anything like that! The first syllable is dialectal Chinese *t'e* (for "tea") and the second syllable evidently dialectal Gaelic. So it should make everyone happy.

SALAMANDER GLACIER and **FALLS** were once connected to Grinnell Glacier. The name is descriptive and comes from nothing more exotic than Greek.

SALVAGE* MOUNTAIN was so named by Evans because it was "saved" in the forest fires of 1910. The Kootenai name is Broken Leg," *Kyaqak*. Louis Broken Leg was a son-in-law of Aeneas Paul.

SARCEE* MOUNTAIN: *Sarci* (Sarsi, Sarcee) is the tribal name of a small Athabascan group residing near Calgary and the only Athabascans traditionally associated with the Waterton/Glacier region. The Blackfeet called the Sarcees *Sa-ahsi* (no good), but in spite of this pejorative sometimes treated them as allies or protégés.

The Athabascans, for whom the Athabasca River is named, are one of the three (?) great linguistic stocks native to the Americas, especially inhabiting Alaska and northern Canada but including the Apaches and Navajos of the Southwest. The other two great linguistic stocks are Eskimo-Aleutian (Inuit) and Amerind reaching from Hudson Bay to the tip of South America. (At least this summary seems to represent current opinion.)

SATA: See SHEPARD.

SCALPLOCK* MOUNTAIN: So called by Evans for a bunch of trees that were left standing after the forest fire swept through. The Kootenai name is "One Dog Lodge Mountain": *Kuktla Akwukłi'it.*

SCARFACE POINT is on the Garden Wall trail. (See POIA.)

SCENIC*: Descriptive. The point is on Mount Henry. You are supposed to see as far as Great Falls and in the old days even the gigantic tower of the Anaconda smelter.

SCHOENBERGER RANCH: Paul Schoenberger had mining interests at Kintla.

SENTINEL MOUNTAIN: In Blackfoot, *Nitái-istaki* (Lone Mountain).

SENTINEL, THE: Descriptive.

SEVEN MILE CANYON: A narrow canyon on the Middle Fork of the Flathead just southeast of West Glacier on the highway to Nyack.

SEWARD* MOUNTAIN was named by George Bird Grinnell for William Henry Seward III, grandson of Lincoln's Secretary of State. He visited the Glacier country in 1883 and again in 1902, when he climbed Chief Mountain with Grinnell. He was the brother of Cornelia Seward Allen. The entire ridge that connects to Chief Mountain was once called Seward's Ridge. The Blackfoot name for the mountain commemorates Long Lodge Pole: *In-anistam* (short *a*s), a chief supposed to have killed the Assiniboine White Dog.

SEXTON GLACIER: For Lawrence E. Sexton of New York. The Blackfoot name is *Nitái-kokutui* (Lone Ice).

SHAFFER CREEK: For Sergeant Shaffer of Troop C, lst Cavalry. (See SOLDIER, MERRITT.)

SHAHEEYA* LAKE AND PEAK: *Sha-i-yé,* etc. is the Assiniboine and Stoney word for the Crees, their sometime allies. Compare *Asina(w),* a Cree word used in Blackfoot for the Crees, Stonies and Assiniboines. Cree and Blackfoot are Algonquin; Assiniboine and Stoney are Souian. If the Board wanted a name for the Cree people, why did they chose one that other people call them? Why not the name a Cree calls himself, *Nehiyaw?* Simple and musical and can be pluralized: *Nehiyawak.*

SHANGRI-LA LAKE is on the slopes of Mount Wilbur. The name comes from James Hilton's novel *Lost Horizon* but does follow the pattern of Himalayan place names: e.g. *Kang-La, Tingri-La, Singri-La*. The *la* means a col or pass.

SHEEP* MOUNTAIN is in the southeast corner of Glacier near Nimrod and probably the scene of old mining activity. There is an old dam on the mountainside. The "sheep" must be bighorns, but the Kootenai name is "Has Gloves": *Kaqatin*.

SHEPARD* GLACIER: E. R. Shepard was a photographer with Dr. Sperry. But the glacier has also borne the name of Sata, a guide to DeSmet and Larpenteur. He was the son of the Blackfoot chief Nicholas and his Salish wife. DeSmet spoke very highly of this family and was especially delighted with Sata's three children.

SHERBURNE* LAKES and **PEAK:** The Sherburne family of Browning held oil and mining interests in the Swiftcurrent District. Right on the lakeshore were two placers, Lakeside and New Era. Hugh Monroe and his Piegan comrades once had watched two grizzlies fighting here and called the lakes: *Kyaiyoix ozitaizkahpi* (the bears, where they fought.) So Schultz's Sherburne Peak was named after Seed Woman or Grain Woman: *Insímaki*, the wife of Yellow Wolf and perhaps later of Yellow Kidney. She seems to be the same person who was a close friend of the Count and Countess Bernadotte and also the aunt or stepmother of Schultz's wife Natahki.

At one point in the early history of the two parks the faction supportive of the Hills and the Great Northern wanted to raise the height of the dam on Sherburne Lake so that the waters would rise high enough to cover the Swiftcurrent Falls and form one long lake from Swiftcurrent or Josephine out onto the Reservation. Luckily, Superintendent Logan put a stop to this project. Later on, Superintendent Kraebel had bitter comments to make about the destruction of the environment caused by the damming of Sherburne Lake.

SHIELDS* CREEK and **MOUNT** are said to have been named by Evans for a Virginian resident at Essex. The Kootenai name is "Marten Mountain": *Naqsaq Akwukłi'it*.

But from Don Spooner and Francis June, researchers in Essex history, comes a more detailed story: Tom Shields from Louisiana was a telegraph operator on the Great Northern who enjoyed exploring the woods for hunting and fishing. About 1909 he opened a mercantile south of Deer Creek —now Essex Creek, where his wife Almeda also was in charge of the post office. During the fires of 1910 both the store and the new schoolhouse survived. By 1914 Essex had a population of almost four hundred. Tom named Almeda Lake after his wife and Marion Lake after their daughter.

Along with a ranger named Arvin E. Havens and a forester from Michigan, Tom was caught poaching in the park. But about 1916 Tom and Almeda moved to Kalispell and eventually to California.

See ESSEX for further mention of Almeda.

SHINING MOUNTAINS: The Blackfoot translates the English rather than the other way round for a change: *Mistakisz-Ikanaz(iaw)* and *Sakókotuyístaki* (thanks to Frank Guardipee). But the name is one of the oldest in this region and on the continent, dating back to Jonathan Carver who in the 1760s cited Indian reports of mountains of crystal in the far west. It may be an Indian name that is even older as suggested by the text of the

Walam Olum, the Delaware book of pictographs. The Spanish scientific expedition of Malaspina sailing up the Pacific Coast and destined to discover the great Malaspina Glacier in Alaska, recorded the existence inland at about the latitude we are concerned with, of the *montañas brillantes*. In 1802 it was recorded in Morse Universal Geography. In 1804, at the transfer of New Orleans to U.S. jurisdiction, Captain Amos Stoddard, the man appointed to receive the transfer, referred to the western boundary of the Louisiana Purchase as both the Andes and the Shining Mountains. The first person on record to use the name specifically for the Glacier/Waterton area was Meriwether Lewis.

The Cree term for the "Shining Mountains" is *Wasiwapiskak*. Whether this is the ultimate source of the name I cannot say.

SIKOKINI SPRINGS drain Lake Five into Flathead River. *Sikokini* means "birch" in Blackfoot.

SIKSIKA* FALLS: *Sixika* is the name of the North Blackfoot people. The sign is to pass the hand down the leg and point to something black. The term does mean "black foot, feet."

SIKSIKAIKWAN GLACIER has broken off the Blackfoot Glacier. (See BLACKFOOT, JACKSON.)

SILVER DOLLAR BEACH lies at the narrows of Upper Saint Mary Lake, named for the islets just off shore. "Silver Dollar" is also the name of a mining claim. (See NARROWS.)

SILVERTIP: Popular name for the grizzly, also applied to a railroad siding opposite the mouth of Harrison Creek, and also applied to mining claims. Near here are railroad points Garry and Hidden Lake as well as old mining claims named Red Eagle, Black Tail, and Del Oro.

SINGLESHOT MOUNTAIN: Schultz named this mountain when Grinnell killed a bighorn here with one shot. The name has also been attached to the Highgate Siding on the railroad. Napi Rock is part of Singleshot Mountain.

SINOPAH* MOUNTAIN: *Sinopá* is the Blackfoot word for the kit or prairie fox. The name was applied here by Ruhle for *Sinopaki* (Fox Woman), the wife of Hugh Monroe and daughter of Lone Walker. There is also a Fox Woman Lake between Mount Helen and Mount Rockwell, named perhaps for the same person. And Sinopaki was also the name of the wife of Loreto, whose story is outlined in the entry SPOTTED EAGLE. Another person to bear the name *Sinopaki* is Estelle Manville, the Countess Bernadotte, who was adopted by the tribe when she was only a child in 1917.

SIYEH* CREEK, GLACIER, PASS, and **MOUNT**: *Sáiyi* meaning "mad, wild, rabid," can be a Blackfoot personal name but generally refers to a rabid wolf or other animal. (See MAD WOLF.) The Siyeh rock formation, so frequently surfacing in this area, is made of dolomite and limestone, sometimes split into layers that sandwich between them the greenish diorite of igneous origin that appears as a prominent band at various places in the parks. Some of the Siyeh formation, of Proterozoic ("first or dawn life") origin, contains rosettes of fossil algae that can be observed along the Logan Pass road, according to Ruhle, at 23.7 miles from West Glacier. The Siyeh formation is now often called the Helena formation.

SKELETON* MOUNTAIN: So called because the forest fire of 1910 destroyed the humus and burned the mountain white as bone. This sounds like one of Evans' names.

The Kootenai name is "Gambler": *Kalwaȼ,* which is a family name as well as a personal name, perhaps derived from John Kelwaȼ. He was nicknamed "Kilowatt" or "Kilowatts." Hallawat Creek on the Whitefish Range may have the same origin. John Kelwa¢ was the brother-in-law of Chief Kustata II, who, in turn, was the son of old Chief Aeneas. By his wife Kathleen, John had at least one son and a grandson who used Kelwa¢ as their surname. One person of this name accompanied Chief Baptiste of the Kootenai band that lived around northern Flathead Lake. In the region of present Hungry Horse, but on the South Fork of the Flathead River, their party ran into a group of Blackfeet – just a few of them, it seemed at first. But when one of the Blackfeet was killed, fourteen more of them rose up out of the woods. During the ensuing battle, both Chief Baptiste and Kelwa¢ were slain. After the Blackfeet had gone, survivors of the Kootenai party came back to the battlefield and buried the bodies at the site. This fight is dated at some time prior to 1876, after which date the Aeneas mentioned above became the chief of the local band. No one is certain whether this is the battle for which Bad Rock Canyon is supposed to have been named.

SKIUMAH CREEK flows into Nyack valley. *Squmu* is the Kootenai word for serviceberry, of which an abundance grows on the old flood plain. Skiumah Lake appears to have no surface outlet. It must sink into the mountain, and it bursts forth below on the steep mountainside. The falls are spectacular.

SKY LAKE in on the shoulder of Rising Wolf, perhaps the source of the waterfall sometimes referred to as Sacajawea Falls.

SKYLINE: A station on the railroad near Lubec and also some camps in the opposite corner of Glacier. The Skyline Camps were boys' camps on Bowman Lake, Lower Kintla and Upper Kintla and apparently involved the Rainbow Lodge on Bowman, which was also open to tourists. Skyline is not to be confused with Skyland, the name of a creek near Marias Pass.

SLIDE LAKE is on Otatso Creek, said to have been formed when The Tooth broke off, a story attributed to Kootenai Brown. (See VAN PELT.)

SLIPPERY BILL MOUNTAIN is south of Glacier but refers to a man involved in the history of the Summit. Morrison Creek was also named for this man. Slippery Bill was William Morrison, said to have been an Englishman educated at Oxford. (I doubt that anyone has seriously checked this report.) He was fond of classical literature and gambling, won brilliantly at poker in McCartyville, and kept a still and saloon at Summit. He was an admirer of Theodore Roosevelt and ceded the land for the obelisk at the top of Marias Pass.

SNOW MOON* LAKE: Snow Moon was supposed to be the Blackfoot name for February. The Blackfeet do have names for the four seasons: winter, *stuyi*; spring, *motó*; summer, *nepú*; autumn, *mokó*. But ethnologist Clark Wissler reports that the Blackfeet divide the year into two major seasons: summer and winter, with seven months allotted to each one. Obviously, with fourteen months the Blackfoot system will not coincide with the Euro-American system. Each month for the Blackfeet begins with the dark of the moon and each year begins with the white man's October.

The moons have numbers but may also have names, though every medicine man who keeps a winter-count (calendar) may vary the names and even the system itself. Roughly, the winter moons include "Beginning Winter Moon," "Wind Moon," "Cold Moon," "the Moon of Two Big Holy Days" (Christmas and New Year), "Changeable Moon," "Uncertain Moon," and "Geese Moon." The moons of summer are "Beginning Summer Moon," "Frog Moon," "Thunder Moon," "Big Holiday Moon" (Fourth of July), "Berry Moon," "Chokecherry Moon," and "Number Seven" (?). The number of days in each moon is considered to be twenty-six, but some people count thirty. Would that dispose of number seven? (Don't worry too much about the arithmetic!)

McClintock (pp. 486–7) gives a calendar that differs somewhat from Wissler's, but includes some fascinating descriptive names which can be applied only haphazardly to the Euro-American system: There is no Snow Moon, however, but there is an allusion to falling leaves. Snow Moon Lake may be identical with the Silver Moon Lake referred to by Dr. Ruhle.

SNOWSLIDE GULCH is near Sheep Creek.

SNOWSLIP* MOUNTAIN was named by Evans. Avalanches often occur here. The Kootenai name is "Red Grizzly": *Kanuhus Kławła*. It seems also to be one of the mountains that share the popular name of Three Tops. Geologists sometimes use "Snowslip" for the name of a rock formation.

SNYDER* CREEK, LAKES and **RIDGE:** George Snyder was over six feet tall and a noted bicycle rider as well as one of the early settlers around Lake McDonald. At the site of the present Lake McDonald

Lodge, he built the first hotel, which he sold to John Lewis in 1906. The Creek was sometimes called Goerge's Well. The Kootenai name for the mountain and lake was "Ear Fastened to Skin": *Ktapƚuqwat.*

SOFA MOUNTAIN sprawls over most of the southeastern section of Waterton Lakes Park. The mountain resembles a sofa. But "sofa" comes from the Arabic *suffah* meaning a cushion for a camel's saddle. It is possible that this Arabic root also appears in the term *Sufi*, for a kind of Muslim mysticism which includes Christian influences and a love of peace. George Gibbs gives the Kootenai name as *Kitlatla-anook.* Sofa Creek was once called Stoney Creek.

SOLDIER* MOUNTAIN is in the southeastern section of Glacier where the forest fires of 1910 made such havoc. The soldiers for whom the mountain is named were the "buffalo soldiers," the African-American troopers who fought the fire and saved this portion of the park from destruction. African-American troops were stationed at various times at Fort Shaw near Sun River, at Fort Assiniboine near Havre, and at Demersville. Many of them belonged to the Twenty-Fifth Infantry and had once been slaves. Others were cavalrymen. From their officers, who were almost always white men, they received many favorable commendations.

In the early days of national parks (before there was the National Park System of 1916), it was considered appropriate to use Army troops to patrol the protected areas. In the country around Glacier these troopers were almost always African-Americans. During the fires around Essex these infantrymen, under their two lieutenants, performed heroic acts against astonishing odds, for according to the officers' reports, local citizens deliberately started or re-set forest fires out of resentment against the new national park or because local lumber companies tried to get fallen timber for free. But when this game literally backfired and came near burning down the village of Essex, the good citizens appealed in desperation for the troopers to save them. Logan was superintendent at the time and has his name all over the place, whereas the troops and their officers who did the job are uncommemorated except by this simple name Soldier Mountain and perhaps by Shaffer Creek.

The Kootenai is Good Nose: *Ksu·kun.*

SOLOMON'S BOWL: This is one of the Morning Glory Lakes on Morning Glory Creek. It is also known as "West Lake," "North Star Lake," and "Jonah's or Jonas Bowl." The reason for these Biblical names is not clear. But Jonas (the Septuagint form of Jonah) was a chief of the Stoney Indians. The Stonies often came down into Glacier country from their home near Calgary.

SOUTH AMERICA: A snowfield on Mount Altyn, recognizable from Many Glacier Hotel early in the season.

SPERRY* GLACIER: Dr. Lyman B. Sperry, professor of geology and zoology at small colleges in Minnesota and Ohio, reached this glacier in 1886. The chalets here have made this glacier one of the most popular for tourists. Its Kootenai name is "Coyote's Son Ice" or "Wild Rhubarb Blossom Ice": *Misqułu'wum Akwiswitxu*. Coyote had a son (perhaps symbolized in the rhubarb) whom he tried to entertain by sliding down the ice. But the boy froze to death and Coyote wept bitterly.

SPLIT MOUNTAIN: Also called Separated Mountain and probably the Monroe Twins.

SPOT MOUNTAIN: A spot of snow lingers long and clear on its slope and may have occasioned the name. It also has the Blackfoot name of "Black Bear," *Sik-ohkyaiyo*, who led a raid into the Spanish lands in 1832 and may have been one indicted for the murder of Malcolm Clarke.

SPOTTED BEAR: The entry "Flathead Range" mentions Felix Droullette. He caught sight of a bear with a white belly. However, the account by Charles Shaw is more explicit: About 1861 two miners from California came to a Hudson's Bay post at Saleesh (near where Flathead River empties into the lake?) looking for a guide across the Divide. They secure the service of Félix Baptiste or Baptiste Zeroyal (maybe the same man), who leads them by way of Spotted Bear River across to Sun River. Near the mouth of the Spotted Bear (not then so named) they sight a black bear with a white belly.

SPOTTED EAGLE MINE and **MOUNTAIN:** The mountain rises off the southeast corner of Glacier near the headwaters of Badger Creek in an area sacred to vision questers. This name has been applied to a mining claim in Glacier Country but is also borne by a family among the South Piegans, by a famous warrior of the Nez Perce, and in the name of the Sioux who are known as the "People of the Spotted Eagle." Is there a thread that unites all these recipients of the name "Spotted Eagle"? I do not know. But it is worth noting that the eagle is featured also in European mythology, for example, as the Bird of Jove, as the lightning-bearer, and in the Bible where it is paired off with the serpent. (See *Proverbs* 30:19.) The eagle is also paired off in the Aztec tradition, pictured on the national flag of Mexico, and the Plains and Northwest Coast tribes emphasize the Thunder Bird. Among the Sioux the eagle is the messenger of the *Wakan Tanka*, the Great Spirit, and is known as *Wambli Galeshka*. The warrior of the Nez Perce named "Spotted Eagle," *Tipyalana Temanihn*, represented the "treaty Nez Perce," those who sided with the missionaries and the U.S. government as opposed to the "non-treaties" who followed Chief Joseph. Another Nez Perce chief (in this case of the "non-treaties") was "Eagle from the Light or the Rising Sun," perhaps again a reference to the eagle as messenger from the Great Spirit.

The story of the origin of the family name "Spotted Eagle" goes back to Washington Irving's *The Adventures of Captain Bonneville*, Prince Maximilian's *Travels in the Interior of North America*, Lieutenant Bradley's *Land of the Blackfeet*, and other old accounts of the fur trade. It must have been a favorite yarn of the frontier but involves a mystery never solved.

A Mexican "trapper" or free trader named Loreto came up from near Santa Fe, perhaps with Isidoro Sandoval or Pablo or both. There is some reason to think he was in Jim Bridger's brigade even during an approach to the Sierra Nevada, and a companion in the Rocky Mountain Fur Company with Marcelino Baca. He ransomed a girl of the

Blackfoot Confederacy named *Sinopáki* (Kitfox Woman) who was held captive by the Crows. With her and their baby boy he attended the trappers' rendezvous of 1832 and then moved north with Bridger's outfit when they encountered the war party of Eagle Ribs (described in the entry under that name). In the tense moments that ensued, the war party formed one line and the trappers another, and each side sent a delegate into the no-man's-land between them to smoke a pipe of peace. Among the Blackfeet warriors Sinopaki recognized her long-missed brother and rushed over to embrace him or serve as interpreter.) But Bridger hid his rifle as he rode forward as if to shake hands. When the rifle went off, the pandemonium drove Bridger back to his own lines with Blackfeet arrows in his buttocks. Sinopaki's horse broke away, perhaps reared and unseated her and ran back to the trappers' lines. Her tiny baby in a cradleboard was strapped to her empty saddle. Loreto seized his little son and raced across the no-man's-land to restore him to his mother's breast. In spite of the admiration for this brave act, Sinopaki was not allowed to return to her husband.

During the year that followed for lonely Loreto, he may have lived with the Nez Perces and acquired the name Spotted Eagle. But he was present in 1833 at the trappers' rendezvous on Green River, with such famous figures of western history as Captain Bonneville, Sir William Drummond Stewart, Manuel Alvarez and Baptiste, son of Sacajawea. Then Loreto resigned from Rocky Mountain Fur and joined American Fur at the Piegan post on the Marias River (Loma, Montana). There he served as an informant to Prince Maximilian and an assistant to Alex Culbertson. Whether he had rejoined his wife and son is a disputed point, but within a few years he is said to have been shot by a horse-raider. Evidently, that was the story Culbertson gave to Lieutenant Bradley.

Descendents claim that he went to live with the Nez Perces but if so, was it before or after his employment at the Piegan post? His name Spotted Eagle has now been passed on to his descendents and to the mountain peak. The mountain was probably named for Loreto's son, *Pitaw-kihzipimi* or *Kihzipi-Pita(w)*, who became a noted medicine man and conjurer who attracted the admiration of Walter McClintock and is well accounted for in McClintock's books.

Two mysteries remain in the story of Loreto. Where did he get the name Spotted Eagle? And did he die as some say or did he recover? Recent evidence indicates that a skilled medic, Jean-Baptiste Moncravie, was on his way up to the Piegan post from Fort Union just about the time Loreto was wounded. If Moncravie saved his life, Loreto may then have gone to the Nez Perces who would have given him the name Spotted Eagle. But if that is true, what relation, if any, did he have with the well-recorded Nez Perce warrior of that name?

The Nez Perce warrior Spotted Eagle or *Tipyalana Temanihn* belonged to the "treaty Nez Perces," that is, those who complied with Governor Stevens as well as the Presbyterian missionaries. They were the Upper Nez Perces as distinguished from the Lower or "non-treaty" Nez Perces led by White Bird, Looking Glass, and Joseph. The theory that Loreto survived among the Nez Perces adds that that he became an Army scout. This would align or identify him with Spotted Eagle and Lt. John Mullan in support of the U.S. Army. However, the same account also states that Loreto refused to oppose Joseph and so apparently gave up scouting to follow Joseph into Montana and then go back to visit the Piegans once again. I cannot recommend one version or the other. The story is like a novel in which *you* determine the ending.

SPRAGUE* CREEK: The earlier name was Jacksonville, probably for Jacksonville, Illinois, where some tourists hailed from. The creek was also called Frost's River, after trapper John Frost. It may be that the Sprague for whom the creek was named was J. E. Sprague, friend of Tom Jefferson and contractor for Snyder's hotel (1895), but perhaps for D. D. Sprague, civil engineer and official of the Great Northern, or he may even be the Sprague who was a member of the posse that conducted Quantrell Jim Cummings from Old Agency to Demersville. (But see *Who Was Who.*)

SPRUCE* CREEK is an old name for Howe Creek. There is also a stream by this name in the northwestern corner of Glacier. (See SAGE.)

SQUARE LAKE and **PEAK**: Descriptive. The Kootenai name is "Sitting Porcupine," perhaps also descriptive: *Kanqamik Niłksaq Akwukłi'it.*

SQUAW* MOUNTAIN: This peak has recently been re-named. (See DANCING LADY.)

STANTON* MOUNTAIN, GLACIER, and **CREEK**: These features were probably named for Mrs. Lottie Stanton, who is said to have been popular with railroaders in construction days. Evidence of her popularity emerges from the various geographical points that bear her name: a creek, lake, and glacier along the railroad and Stanton Mountain north of Lake McDonald. A confusing mix of names occurs just south of Glacier where Stanton Creek drains Stanton Lake on Mount Grant under Grant Glacier while Stanton Glacier lies on Great Northern Mountain, and Mount Stanton is away off beyond Lake McDonald.

Lottie and her husband, Bad Rock Stanton, ran a livery stable in Demersville. In 1891 Lottie was with a party of five people visiting the guide Geduhn, when a couple of them decided to climb the present Mount Stanton. But when they got to the top, they found Lottie already there ahead of them. She knew a direct route. So the mountain was dubbed Lottie Stanton Mountain.

There is, however, a rival story: Ernest Christensen named the peak for a Lady Stanton, evidently an English aristocrat who visited the area with a Canadian party, before the park was established. So maybe both stories are true. Maybe neither of them. And the one about the lady aristocrat could tie in with the story about Sir John MacDonald. (See McDONALD.)

Schultz lists a Nez Perce name for Mount Stanton – or just possibly for the complex of Mounts Stanton and Vaught as they appear together in some views – say from Highway Two, and certainly from the foot of Lake McDonald. Who assigned the Nez Perce name Schultz does not say, but it is the name of Chief Joseph himself, one of the greatest figures in the history of the Pacific Northwest. He was called to national attention by Helen Hunt Jackson. Schultz gives his name as it was commonly written and translated: "Thunder Traveling Over the Mountains." However, Allen Slickpoo maintains that the name should be transcribed this way: *Hinmatoyalatk'ikt*, and that its true meaning is Thunder Emerging. (What the thunder rolls up from is not indicated, but it may be from the water.) Just why Joseph should have a Kootenai name too, I do not know, but here it is: *Ksusałkikqtiłik Numa Akwukłi'it*, and it is said that such was the name Joseph acquired in his vision quest. Having led the epic-making exodus with Looking Glass and White Bird, he was defeated and perhaps tricked into surrender in 1877 at the foot of the Bear Paw Mountains. He promised to "fight no more forever." The ever-benign U.S. Government saw to that by keeping him a virtual prisoner for the rest of his days. But at the surrender White Bird and Joseph's own daughter Sarah escaped with a number of others across the border into Saskatchewan with great misery but some help from Métis and their French priest named Father Genin. They took refuge with Sitting Bull's band of Sioux, also escapees from the U.S.

Duncan McDonald was related to Joseph through his mother and somewhere in this area encountered some of his Nez Perce "relatives," probably refugees from White Bird's band in Saskatchewan trying to get back home to Idaho. Duncan was sent by the Deer Lodge newspaper to interview White Bird or his people, and he made a plea for them in the press. So it is possible that Chief Joseph's name is associated with Mount Stanton or Stanton-Vaught because of the lake called McDonald at their feet.

STARK PEAK and **POINT**: The name must be derived from the Stark mine on the mountain that belonged to the two Altyn miners Scott and Perley Stark.

STARR SCHOOL: A Blackfoot settlement just east of Glacier on Cut Bank Creek, it clusters around a school named for George Starr. He was a nephew to Michel Pablo who helped save the herd of buffalo on the Flathead Reservation. Of Mexican and Piegan ancestry, he bore the Blackfoot name of Kakatosi or Star and was active in the early history of Glacier and of the reserve as guide and interpreter, traditional dancer and tribal judge. He is said to have been one of the tribal group who went to San Francisco and perhaps Hawaii in 1915 for the Panama-Pacific Exposition. He also attended the commemoration for the Iron Horse in Baltimore in 1927 but died soon after his return home and left his one-room log house to the school district to establish Starr School. After about twenty years the people built another school from big logs they themselves dragged down from the mountains. Still later, they built a brick school, and always the school and the community were closely bonded. With consternation, the neighbors learned that 1995 was the last year for their school. (*Great Falls Tribune*, May 8, 1995.)

STARVATION* CREEK and **RIDGE**: The Kootenais include the ridge in the terrain covered by their name *Kintla*. The creek, which heads in British Columbia, is also called Dead Man's Creek. This may be the stream located by the U.S. Survey of 1861 at 114°21' and labeled *Kala'wu'k.*

STATUARY* MOUNTAIN was named by Evans for the pinnacles on its peak. That may explain the name of the vacation settlement Pinnacle on Highway 2. But the Kootenais had a better name: "Crazy Mountain" or *Ḳuktmanqa Akwukḷi'it.*

STIMSON*, MOUNT and **CREEK**: In 1891 George Bird Grinnell conferred on the peak now called Mount Logan the name of his hunting companion Henry Lewis Stimson of New York (1867–1950). Next year Stimson climbed Chief Mountain with an Indian guide and Dr. Walter R. James, whose name Grinnell applied to the present Mount Stimson.

Eventually, Stimson became Secretary of War (1911–12, 1940–45), Governor General of the Philippines (1927–29), Secretary of State under Hoover (1929–33), and Secretary of War again under Franklin, Roosevelt, and Truman. Though certainly a man with a remarkable career and a definite place in the history of

Glacier, he has to share the responsibility for the internment of an estimated 120,000 Japanese Americans and the manufacture and dropping of atomic bombs on Hiroshima and Nagasaki.

Whether by design (perhaps illegal) or a mix-up of mapmakers, the name of Dr. James was switched to the peak on the east side of the park and the name Stimson transferred from the present Mount Logan to the former Mount James. Of all the instances of name switching and bungling this must be the prize case. As a result, there remains a bothersome question about the propriety of such a politically loaded name for a prominent feature in a national park that belongs to people of all political and ethnic persuasions.

For those who prefer a Native American name for Mount Stimson, one of the tallest majesties in Glacier and the tallest of all in the upper Flathead, it may be a consolation that there is a Kootenai name associated with the mountain: *Aqaɫku'tɫa*, often shortened to *Qaɫku'tɫa* and meaning "Flint Lodge." This can be a personal name and once belonged to a lady who lived to a grand old age and was taken under the protection of Chief Aeneas himself. Aeneas explored this portion of Glacier. (See MARIAS.) Many vision-questers must have been drawn to this mountain with its obvious display of the sacred basaltic band.

Around this mountain of many names curls Nyack Creek with its historic and prehistoric Indian trail which must have led many a vision quester to regard this peak as a sort of Zion. The earliest inhabitants of this country must have been aware of the peculiar weather condition around the top of this mountain. There are three peaks on Mount Stimson, and the highest of these peaks, Manito Point, has a naughty habit of appearing and vanishing in the clouds like something made of spirit instead of stone. I believe this situation has proved fatal to at least one hiker in recent years. Back-packers should be warned of this situation.

Though the Blackfeet have no known name for this peak, it does overlook the Divide and is visible far out on the prairie. Since it appears to send forth thunderstorms, it has been loosely referred to as the "aerie of the Thunder Eagle": *Kriszikúmi-Pítaw* or *Xiszikúmi-Pítaw*.

STONEY INDIAN* FLATS, LAKE, PASS, and **PEAKS:** This name was probably assigned by Kootenai Brown and later cut to "Indian Lake," etc. The Stoneys and the Sarcees are two small tribes near Calgary that played their roles in the Waterton-Glacier country but are usually overlooked, even more often than the Kootenais.

The Stoneys are a small branch of the Assiniboines. Vaught explains that after the buffalo were gone, the Stoneys began to hunt in the mountains more than ever. They would follow the ancient trail down the east side of the North Fork to McGee Meadows, at least until 1895, and may have crossed Huckleberry Mountain to McDonald Creek and the Middle Fork. George Treat, marshall of Great Falls, found Stoneys spearing fish at Lake McDonald in 1892, staying about a week and smoking their catch for the winter. Ahern met some during his exploration for the pass. In December of 1889 a large camp lingered around Demersville and enjoyed camping at Half Moon – to the consternation of white settlers. Their tribal name reflects the Cree term *asiniy* for stone or rock and may refer to the prehistoric custom of stone boiling. Like other Assiniboines, they belong to the Nakota branch of the Sioux. In Waterton Lake Park there is a site called Stoney Indian Flats, as well as Indian Springs.

Chief Dave Crowchild of the Sarcees was the man to do something about the neglect of public concern for his people and the Stoneys. A world-traveler with the Moral Re-Armament movement in Canada, he had traveled to Brazil, Switzerland, Japan, and elsewhere, and in 1960 gathered a Native group led by himself and his wife, the Stoney chief Walking Buffalo and the Kootenai chief Joseph David. Walking Buffalo or Tatanka Mani was then close to ninety years old. In early March this group caught a flight to Hawaii, Fiji, and New Zealand. For welcoming ceremonies they appeared in native attire. At Auckland, they met the Maoris at the airport with an exchange performance of traditional dances. New Zealand was so fascinating to them that they spent six weeks traveling 3,262 miles through that country. (They must have had to do a lot of zigzagging since the length of the country is hardly a third of that mileage.) In Australia too they exchanged dances with the aborigines of Queensland, where there are also various Pacific Islanders in residence. South Africa was less hospitable because the country was in a racial turmoil. So they turned north through Africa to Italy and Switzerland and then westward to home. (See also SARCEE.)

STRAWBERRY MOUNTAIN: This elongated mountain outside park boundaries looms over Belton/West Glacier as guardian of the west entrance to Glacier. Its name seems to have been applied by mistake, while its other name, "Boxcar," is more descriptive. The mountain used to be called "Rainwater" for a family from Wisconsin that once lived near its base, whereas Strawberry is only a little butte squatting snugly between Rainwater and Desert Mountain. This little mountain does indeed resemble a strawberry. It is nicknamed in tongues as diverse as Anglo and Aztec: "Dew Drop," "Chocolate Drop," "Emory

Point," and "Belton Point." An old Blackfoot war trail is said to go around its base. Desert Mountain is supposed to have been named for a landslide or avalanche that stripped off vegetation.

STREET* CREEK and **MOUNTAIN:** This creek is in Glacier while the mountain is in Waterton, where it also bears the name Mount Boswell. Jack Street was a Northwest Mountie who with fellow Mountie Achille Rouleau was a frequent guest of Kootenai Brown at Waterton Lakes and on trips through the mountains. Jack was killed by an avalanche on the side of the mountain that now bears his name.

STRIPED ELK* LAKE: Probably named for a Blackfoot chief or warrior.

STUMP LAKE: An alternate name for Ladyhead Lake. No explanation is known for either name.

SUE* LAKE has also been called "Summit Lake," "Iceberg Lake," and even "the Fountain of the Gods" – which the credulous are assured is an Indian name! Schultz, with his anti-church bias, propagated the notion that the Indians had many gods, but even he never proposed a name such as this.

SULLIVAN MEADOW was named for a local family.

SUMMIT* CREEK, MOUNTAIN, and **STATION:** "Summit" is a plausible name for a creek and a station but redundant for a mountain, even though this one looms over the Continental Divide at Marias Pass in a massive pyramid. The Blackfoot name is *Mokakínsi-istaki* or just *Mokakékin* (the Backbone). And "the Backbone" is a general term for the Rockies or the Divide. About the 1930s this sharp peak was called "Vega Tip" – a reference to cigars?

SUNRIFT GORGE was named by Superintendent Kraebel in 1926. Formerly, it had been known as Jeannette Gorge.

SURPRISE* PASS: No reason for this name is on record, but it sounds like something Evans would think of. Dr. Frank Oastler was one of the first persons known to have crossed this pass, although Dan Doody had a cabin near here.

SWEETGRASS BUTTES are not located in either Glacier or Waterton but punctuate the eastern horizon in clear view and just south of the border. They are "island mountains." But they are so closely bound up with the history and tradition of Waterton/Glacier that we can hardly overlook them. According to tribal lore, Napi made the Sweet-

197

grass Buttes by tearing them out of Chief Mountain to show the Great Spirit how clever or powerful he was. Their old French name is *les Trois Buttes*, and the three highest peaks are Gold Butte, West Butte, and East Butte (Mount Royal), remnants of volcanism. Their name in Blackfoot is *Katoyísix*, an animate plural for sweet pines. The term *katoyís*, however, has a variety of meanings: blood clot, perfume, and balsam. McClintock uses *katoya* to translate balsam fir, sweet pine or *abies lasiocarpa*. He adds that it is used as incense, perfume, hair oil and poultices for fevers and chest colds. The Blackfoot name for sweetgrass, however, is *sipazimo(i)*, which McClintock identifies as Vanilla Grass or *Sevastana odorata*, also used for incense, perfume and shampoo. In this case, the English name of the buttes must be a misnomer. Curiously enough, the word *katoyís* is also the name of a hero, the Blood Boy or monster-slayer.

The Sweetgrass Buttes are famous in Montana history as one of the favorite hunting grounds of the tribes, rich in game of all sorts but especially buffalo. Near here there was a breeding area, and the buffalos lingered late in great numbers while they were disappearing elsewhere, filling the Indians with false hopes. They attracted hunters from far and wide, even Métis from Pembina with their Red River carts to be loaded up with meat and hides. But the end of the buffalo did come and hope faded into disillusion.

Later Spanish Basques came to this region to pasture their sheep and built their typical *atalayas* or observation towers.

When an Indian discovered gold in the Sweetgrass Buttes (1884), whites began to move in regardless of Indian rights on their own reservation. Some of the "best people" staked claims or bought them up. Finally Congress sent out the Northwest Commission to "buy" Indian lands and in February of 1887, Chiefs White Calf, Three Suns, and many other disillusioned Blackfeet "sold" this portion of their reserve to the commissioners. Describing this sad event years later to anthropologist John Ewers, the tribal elders referred to it as the time "when we sold the Sweetgrass Buttes."

SWIFTCURRENT* CREEK, FALLS, LAKE, GLACIER, MOUNTAIN, PASS, RIDGE, and **MINING DISTRICT**: Grinnell promoted this name about 1885, translating the Indian term which in Blackfoot is *íxikuoyiyé tahtai* (swift-flowing stream) and probably used for both the Bow and Saskatchewan. And the Saskatchewan, of which this stream in Glacier is a tributary, has a name derived from the Cree, *kisiskátsiwan*, with the same meaning. It is hard to see how the name Swiftcurrent can be logically applied to a lake.

The Indian names for this lake are said to be "Jealous Woman's (Women's) Lake" and "Beaver Woman's Lake." Both Schultz and Adolf Hungry Wolf tell the story about the name "Jealous Woman's," though somewhat differently. One version: The young Kootenai Big Knife had twin sisters for wives, Beaver and Weasel, both of whom he loved. But Weasel was jealous of Beaver, and try as Big Knife did to treat them evenhandedly, her jealousy grew out of bounds. One day Big Knife found two otters at play in the Swiftcurrent River and tried to shoot them both to get two otter skins. He did get one, but the other escaped. So Big Knife gave the one hide to Beaver and promised Weasel to get hers the next day. Not good enough. Weasel challenged Beaver to swim the lake till one of them died. It was Weasel who died, and Beaver and Big Knife who were left to weep. The name Beaver Woman has been transferred to a lake in Martha's Basin, while the name Jealous Woman has been moved to Bullhead Lake.

For a time Swiftcurrent Lake and Falls were named for a lumberman, McDermott. Perhaps he was the mine claimant Frank P. McDermott. The names McDermott, Grinnell, and Apikuni are all said to have been applied in this area about 1887 by Lieutenant J. H. Beacom of Fort Shaw, who died a colonel in Mexico in 1916. The Pass used to be called Horsethief Pass, because allegedly it was used by the Indians to drive horses taken in raids.

Either Swiftcurrent Lake or Josephine was once called Lillian Lake. Besides the Swiftcurrent Glacier, there is also a North Swiftcurrent Glacier. Other more original names along the trail over the pass include "Nine Lakes Point," "Galen's Ladder" and the "Glory Trail Switchbacks." According to Vaught, the names "Swiftcurrent," "Duck Lake," "Flat Top Mountain," "Goat Mountain and Lake," and "Divide Mountain" were local popular names and so probably no one person can be singled out as the source of any of them.

The pass was used even in wintertime by Kootenais traveling to hunt buffalos on the prairies. Archaeological sites from "precontact times" have been located there by Reeves and Shortt. And it was also a favorite of prospectors. Grinnell found many signs of old Kaina campsites on Apikuni Flats, perhaps of hunters en route to or from Swiftcurrent Pass.

TAMARACK TRAIL is in Waterton Lakes Park. The tamarack is the larch tree, and the name is derived from Algonquin. But the precise derivation remains in some doubt. Perhaps the development of the word was influenced by two terms of Arabic origin, tamarisk and tamarind. In Arabic *tamr* means "date," so that "tamarind" *(tamrhind)* means "the date of India." Tamar is the name of two women in the Bible.

TAMARACK VALLEY is a small valley on Cosley Ridge in Glacier, one of the rare spots where the tamarack or larch grows on the east side of the Divide.

TEPEE* FLAT is on the Glacier side of the North Fork, opposite Tepee Creek. The name comes from the Souian roots *ti* (to dwell) plus *pi* (used for). A tipi is not just a tent but something of a Platonic wonder. It is both a home and a temple, is designed as a mandala and in form approximates the Golden Ratio (the ratio of the five black keys on the piano to the eight white keys).

TERRACE PARK is near the Little Matterhorn.

TETON COUNTY once included part of Glacier until Glacier County was formed. The word *teton* is colloquial French for "breast," sometimes applied to mountains. But it is also a Sioux word, the name of the largest and most westerly branch of the Dakota people. It means "prairie dwellers," *ti-tan-wan*. In popular usage these two separate origins have become fused and confused.

THEODORE ROOSEVELT* PASS is the route around the southern edge of Glacier followed by Highway 2 and the railroad. Portions of this route have other names as well: "Marias Pass," "John F. Stevens Canyon," etc. This is one of the two genuine presidential names in the International Peace Park. The other is Cleveland. Names that seem to refer to presidents of the U.S. but really do not are Grant, Lincoln, Jefferson, Wilson, Jackson, Harrison, Kennedy, Johnson, Ford, and Carter. The obelisk at Marias Pass commemorates the donation of the land by "Slippery Bill" Morrison of McCartyville in honor of Roosevelt. The question of whether Theodore Roosevelt ever set foot anywhere near Glacier National Park is a bit complicated. He was in Montana often and through the auspices of the Marquis de Mores was on hand in the early days of the Montana Stock Growers Association. Jack Reuter and Fred Herrig were old acquaintances of Roosevelt, Reuter as one of his cowboys in the Bad Lands and Herrig as a hunting companion. Roosevelt is said to have written both of them urging them to join his Rough Riders. Herrig joined up, but Reuter was out trapping in the North Fork and did not get the message until too late. Ace Powell claimed in his personal interview for the Park Service that Roosevelt wrote to Reuter about guiding him on a hunting trip, and Reuter responded with something like, "If you can't shoot any better than you can write, better stay home." (Roosevelt's biographer or hagiographer Hagedorn tells practically the same story but about a different hunting guide.) Anyhow, Ace Powell thought Roosevelt did not come here. Another old-timer Ben Hansen said that Roosevelt did come in 1910, crossed Brown's Pass with Reuter and started a forest fire! There is another oral report of Roosevelt at Saint Mary in 1910. He is known to have come on a hunting trip to the very northern part of Idaho, in the Selkirk or Purcell Mountains and perhaps to Kootenay Lake, British Columbia.

In his book *Ranch Life and the Hunting-Trail* Roosevelt tells us that in the fall of 1886 he went on a two-week hunting trip into the Coeur d'Alene Mountains of Montana between Heron and Horse Plains. He was specifically looking for mountain goat, or as he calls it "the white antelope-goat" (which may be more correct). Accompanying him was a Missourian turned mountaineer, "Bill" or A. W. Merrifield, Roosevelt's one-time foreman and many-times guide. When Merrifield quit his ranching days in the Bad Lands, he moved west to Montana and had a fine home – a mansion, in fact, on the western shores of Flathead lake near present-day Lakeside. (Flathead County Court House, Clerk and Recorder's office, Book 116, p. 148; deed to A. W. Merrifield et al., 8 June 1910.) It is still locally recalled that he entertained Roosevelt as his guest for a week or so during some such hunting trip as the one described in Roosevelt's book. The site of the Merrifield Place is still well known today, and I find one local resident who recalls seeing Roosevelt here during his own boyhood days when he was tagging along with his father.

Another hunting companion of Roosevelt's was Charles Conrad of Kalispell. They were drawn together, in spite of their differing politics, by their common concern with the cattle business. They apparently met at gatherings of the Montana Stock Growers. Roosevelt is said to have accompanied Conrad on one or more of his hunting trips into present Glacier National Park, and Roosevelt's room is still pointed out to tourists as the Antique Room of the Conrad Mansion in Kalispell.

Roosevelt's daughter, "Princess Alice" Roosevelt Longworth, visited Glacier, says Mrs. Chance Beebe in her interview for the Park Service. She may have had Joe Cosley for a guide, and certainly they would have made ideal sparring partners.

As president, Roosevelt once passed through Whitefish on the Great Northern with the Japanese diplomat Baron Okado and came out on the train platform at an unseemly hour in his nightshirt to address a few words to the on-lookers. (*Stump Town to Ski Town*, p. 50.) In August of 1934 Franklin Delano Roosevelt, Eleanor Roosevelt, and an assorted VIP party toured Glacier from west to east over Logan Pass and down into Two Medicine. The Blackfeet gave them each a name, and the park superintendent went into a state of ecstasy.

THOMPSON* CREEK and **MOUNT**: Who was Thompson? Well, there were mine claimants of this name, but there are two other strong contenders. There are reports of early maps bearing the name "Mount Thompson Seton" after the famous writer and naturalist Ernest Thompson Seton. Perhaps the name was shortened as the years went by. There is also the chance that the mountain was named for David Thompson, the explorer, geographer, and astronomer of the Canadian fur trade. In 1809 Thompson established a post at Thompson Falls, Montanan. In 1810 his companions in the area included Duncan McGillivray, La Gasse, and Le Blanc.

The Kootenai name for the creek: *KaqɫawxaɫA·ku Aknuxu'nuk* (Stabbed Inside Creek), and for the mountain *K iɫ isaq Akwukɫi'it* (Straight Legs Mountain).

THREE BEARS* LAKE: It sounds like a fairy tale but it is a Blackfoot personal name, *Niuóxk-oh-kyaiyo.*

THREE SUNS* MOUNTAIN: Named by Grinnell for a Piegan *Niuoxkatos,* who succeeded in the chieftainship in 1878 and whose alternate name was Big Nose. As a leader of the conservative wing, he was a rival to White Calf and probably before that, to Little Dog.

To the Kootenais the peak is "Red Sky": *Kanusil- miyit.* This is the name of a chief who was in office at some time previous to the treaty of 1855. He belonged to the portion of the tribe at Tobacco Plains on the Tobacco River or *Akánoho Akinmutuk* (Flying River, perhaps an allusion to the Flying Head). Red Sky is reported to have been killed by the Blackfeet about 1840.

In the northeast corner of Woodland Park in Kalispell, there is a grave now well kept with an elegant new gravestone set over an older one on which the markings are hardly decipherable. On the new stone the writing is clear: "In memory of the last of the Kootenai Indians of Flathead Valley. Buried here 1901: Cecilia Red Sky, 27, and her namesake, 4. Erected by Boy Scout Troop 33." This burial site must have been provided by Charles Conrad (1850–1902), founder of Kalispell and one-time proprietor of much of the land it occupies, and of course, the builder of the nearby Conrad Mansion.

THREETOPS* MOUNTAIN: Named by surveyor Evans, though the name has been assigned from time to time to various other mountains. The Kootenai name of this one is "Fox Mountain": *Nak̓yu Akwuk̓li'it.*

THUNDERBIRD* CREEK, FALLS, GLACIER, ISLAND, and MOUNTAIN: The thunderbird causes the thunder and lightning, especially in the lore of the tribes of the northern Plains and the Northwest Coast. Similar symbols appear around the world. In Greece, Rome and India thunder and the eagle are associated with Zeus or his equivalent, while in the Americas the thunderbird is related to the Feathered Serpent and to Quetzalcoatl. The eagle and the serpent show up together in the national flag of Mexico, in the Bible and in the thought of Nietzsche. Thunderbird totem poles are topped by the great bird spreading its wings and perhaps crouching on top of a grizzly that gently holds a little human in its paws. And all this in the circum-Pacific "hocker motif." The Plains Crees call the thunderbirds *ominikiwak* or *peyasewak.* The Blackfeet say *xiszikúmi-pita(w)* or as a few have it, *kriszikumi-pitaw).* The Dakotas entertain the concept of the Spotted Eagle, *wambli galeshka,* symbol of the Great Spirit.

The glacier now called Thunderbird also has been known as "Lone Wolf Ice." But Thunderbird Island has had that name for many years, and Dr. Ruhle claims it was the place where the Indians said they discovered a strange bird that their medicine man identified as the Thunderbird. Its eyes flashed lightning; its wings drummed thunder.

The island lies in Lower Saint Mary Lake and is no doubt the reason why the Kootenais called Saint Mary "Island Lake." On this island Schultz claims to have taken refuge from an angry Indian agent. Those were the days when the Saint Mary valley was Shangri-La between the U.S. and Canada. The ensuing winter was the terrible Starvation Time (1883). When Schultz called this famine to public attention, he was forced to flee from the government police and sought safety here with his Indian relatives. Since his wife's uncle Red Eagle was the owner of the Thunderbird Medicine, this incident may have been the occasion for the naming of Red Eagle Mountain, so prominent as viewed from this island. But one must always be a bit wary of stories in which the relator is the hero.

TINKHAM* MOUNTAIN: In 1853 Lieutenant A. W. Tinkham, with a Salish guide, made the first recorded crossing of Glacier, from Isaac Steven's camp on the west by way of Nyack Creek and probably Pitamakan Pass to Fort Benton in the east. There must have been countless crossings before this one on record. The mountain was once called Yellow Man and also Camel's Hump.

TRAPPER* CREEK, PASS, and **PEAK:** For the peak, see NUMA (which is the Kootenai word for "thunder"). Trapper Pass and Creek are now called Logan Pass and Creek, while Trapper Falls is now Bird Woman Falls. The Kootenai name for this pass was "Packs Pulled Over" because the cliff is so steep they had to haul up their baggage in packs by means of ropes, then slide them down the east side.

TRICK* FALLS, have now been renamed "Running Eagle Falls."

TRIPLE ARCHES: Three stone arches built under the road west of Logan Pass form a photogenic setting. Some claim that such work on "the Road" was done by stonemasons from Turkey, but confusion reigned in the Montana of the early twentieth century over the identity of ethnic groups.

TRIPLE DIVIDE* PASS and **PEAK:** Here the waters split three ways, to the Pacific, to the Atlantic, and to Hudson Bay, with a creek heading for each destination and named accordingly. The Blackfoot name is *Niuoxkai-itahtai* (three streams). François Matthes identified this spot, but it may have been identified years before in 1890 by G. E. Culver and Lieutenant Ahern.

There is another triple divide in Alberta where the waters go to the Pacific, the Arctic via the Athabasca River, and Hudson Bay via the Saskatchewan.

TROUT* LAKE: The Kootenai name is Spotted Lake, *Kalqaqmitqa Anuqnuk*, and the "spotted" may mean the trout since the Blackfoot name for trout is *sisokomi*, spotted fish. The map of 1846 shows the *Lac et Riviére à la Grosse Truite*, but it locates these waters about where Harrison Lake or Halfmoon or Great Bear Creek are located in reality.

TWIN BUTTES in Cut Bank valley may be identical with Amphitheater Mountain.

TWIN* FALLS are in the Two Medicine area.

TWIN* LAKES: There are three sets of these. One is between Reynolds and Fusillade, another among the North Lakes, and a third in Waterton Lakes Park.

TWO DOG* BAY and **FLATS** (which are anything but flat) are on Upper Saint Mary Lake. Two Dog was an old-timer whom Frank Harrison identified as Jack Harp. He pioneered locally in cross-country skiing. The Blackfoot form of his name is *Natoki-omita*. Emerson Brown's party from Texas (as reported by Veach) camped here with a trapper who may have been Jack Harp, but the date 1876 seems very early.

TWO GUNS MOUNTAIN is part of the cirque of Citadel, named after Two Guns White Calf, the son or adopted son of White Calf, the last dynastic chief of the south Piegans. Two Guns may have been one of the models for the profile on the "buffalo nickel."

TWO MEDICINE* CREEK, **LAKES**, **PASS**, **FALLS**, and **RIDGE**: The Blackfoot name is *Natoki-Okas(i)*. The root *oka* means "to sleep" and here refers to a dream or vision. One story claims that two medicine lodges for the Sun Dance were once erected on opposite sides of the creek. The site of these lodges may have been near the lake or else well down the river near the present site of Seville and the former railroad station Sun Dance. Two Medicine Ridge is also called Heavy Eyes, Sokapini, for Hugh Monroe's son Fran ois who in 1900 was mauled by grizzlies near here.

According to Chief Paul David of Tobacco Plains, young people of the Kootenais used to go to Two Medicine Lake for their vision quest. So the "dreadful river cave" of Two Medicine Creek, as Schultz calls it, must have been a vision quest site for Kootenais as well as Blackfeet. And in Chief Paul's account, the Kootenais came from far and wide, even from Lake Columbia in British Columbia, all the way to Two

Medicine. In their vision quest they were seeking a spiritual energy that they called *nupíka akokenok*, and therefore they named the Two Medicine River *Nupíka Akinmituk* (in the THREE SUNS entry, this word is spelled *akinmutuk*. I cannot say which is correct).

TWO OCEAN* GLACIER sheds into both the Pacific and the Gulf of Mexico, or at least it used to.

TWO SUNS MOUNTAIN is the southwestern arc of the cirque of Citadel. A head Kaina (Blood) chief of this name was, according to Schultz, the *Manístokos* in the days of the fur trade, perhaps also known as Bad Head or *Pakap Otokan* and therefore the father of Natawista, Seen Afar, and perhaps Calf Shirt. The term *manístokos* is now obsolete and sometimes defined as "Father of All Children" or "Everyone is his Child." (But I suspect it is an archaic form for "Mountain Chief.") Bad Head was also famous as the keeper of the Winter Count or calendar.

UNDERBULL MOUNTAIN: "The under(water) bull" or *stahz-stamik* of Blackfoot tradition may refer to some prehistoric mammal like the mammoth and mastodon, some of which still survived in America when the first humans arrived. And in the eastern part of what is now the U.S. some seem to have remained at the end of the Ice Age or about ten thousand years ago. Near Mexico City a spearhead was found embedded in a bone of such an animal.

UNNAMED MOUNTAIN: There are a number of unnamed mountains in the Waterton-Glacier complex. Several are in the northwestern portion of Glacier and especially in the Kintla Quadrangle (USGS Quadrangle, Kintla Peak, Montana.) There backcountry people sometimes call attention to them. Especially noticeable are two peaks, both 9,430 feet or 2874.3 meters in height according to the latest topographical map, one of these just south of Kintla Glacier, the other west of the same glacier. The first has a latitude of 48°55′29.6″ N and a longitude of 114°11′38.8″ W. The second peak is in latitude 48°55′52.2″ N and in longitude 114°13′14.8″ W. A third peak on the same map but unnamed is assigned the elevation of 9826 feet or 2995 meters/metres. These three stand in an arc around the southern edge of Kintla Glacier and Kintla Peak, so that we could designate them left to right X, Y, and Z. Or if you come from a country where you speak a Semitic language, you may want to read them right to left.

Some people would argue that it is better not to have all the mountains named. There is something artificial, even unnatural about naming mountains. Leave them in their virginal state as we should do with wilderness generally. When you put a name on something, you master it, so why not let the mountains go with God? I do see a point to this argument when I consider all the nonsense names listed in this book, names like Sue and Henry whom nobody knows, political names like Stimson, phony Indian names like Wahcheecheem, misspelled, mistranscribed, mistranslated to boot.

Another unnamed peak around 10,000 feet or 3,000 meters in elevation looms close to Mount Cleveland. Hikers and rangers have been alluding to it as Kiser Peak (in one spelling or the other: Kiser, Kyser, Kaiser). Historically, this was a name once attached to Mount Cleveland for reasons unknown. A professional photographer in Glacier was Fred Kiser, and Lee Kiser/Kyser has been mentioned in the entry LEE. However, the point referred to here seems to be a part of Mount Cleveland.

There is also some story that a peak near Waterton Lake has borne the name of "Seen (from) Afar," a famous Blood chief. I have not been able to identify such a mountain but have included a sketch of this interesting historical figure in the entry WATERTON NATIONAL PARK.

So it seems that there are more names floating around than there are mountains to put them on. On the other hand, there may be a mountain here or there that is waiting to be christened. So just in case someone still wants names, let me add that some years ago the superintendent of Glacier asked me to look for one or two Salish names for the park. The Salish tribal council sent me two recommendations: "Alexander No Horses" and "Victor Many Horses," whose thumbnail biographies are included in *Who Was Who in Glacierland*.

UZINA: This term is used for the Gros Ventres people. As a verb it means "to be paunchy" while the noun for "belly, guts" is *uzi*. I know of no reason to think these people are any more paunchy than the rest of us. (See ATSINA, GROS VENTRE.)

VALENTINE* CREEK: Frank Valentine was a packer who, with surveyor Sargent, crossed the formidable Ahern Pass in 1902. Son of William Valentine of New York, he seems to have been born in Iowa in 1880 and to have settled in Columbia Falls. Valentine Creek must be the "Copper Creek" where Louie Meyer began his prospecting career. The Valentine Logging Company had cabins, a dam, and a millpond in this region before the park era. (See COPPER, WHITE EAGLE.)

VAN ORSDALE'S FLUME: See NYACK.

VAN PELT'S MINE: John H. Van Pelt of Virginia and E. W. Reid had claims near Slide Lake (1905), which were named Virginia, Helena, Reid, and Good Enough.

VAUGHT*, MOUNT: The Kootenai name for this mountain is Big Old Man, *Kwiłqa Nuł' aqna.* L. O. Vaught was a summer resident at Lake McDonald and the first person known to write a history of the area. At least he started to write one and filled very many pages but got bogged down in preliminaries. But he must have collected some of his data first hand from persons living around him, and so I consider it wise to cite him from time to time – his facts as worthy of consideration, his opinions as oddities. The mountain was once named after his wife Helen or Helen Vaught since there is a Mount Helen elsewhere in Glacier. Henry Vaught, the first head ranger of Glacier, was not related.

VIGIL* PEAK: Evans gave this name because a single mountain goat kept vigil on his camp in this area. The Kootenai name of the peak is "Cut-his-throat," *Kqawaka'mik.*

VIMY PEAK and **RIDGE**, also called Observation Mountain, are in Waterton Lakes Park, except for a small portion of Vimy Ridge that stretches into Glacier. Formerly these features were known as "Vimy Mountain" and "Sheep Mountain." The name comes from Vimy Ridge in France, which was taken by Canadian forces in April, 1917.

VIRGINIA* CREEK and **FALLS**: These falls and Florence Falls may have been named for daughters of Senator Dixon. However, both of these names are also the names of mining claims. Schultz, indignant at the name Virginia, named the falls Crow Woman, after an Hidatsa (Minnetaree) captured by the Crows, then captured from the Crows by the Bloods and finally released. She was a longtime friend of Ipasha.

VULTURE* GLACIER and **PEAK:** no reason known for this name. However, there was a Kootenai chief of Tobacco Plains and of the band Akanahonek whose name was Dark Vulture. The name could well be the source of that name on the mountain and may also refer to the condor, which the Blackfeet called *ómahxapítaw*. This chief was succeeded by his son, but whether the name went with him is not certain.

WAHCHEECHEE* MOUNTAIN: This linguistic atrocity is supposed to be a Cree word for the sand hill crane, which was believed to carry smaller birds on its back and was regarded as the "Spirit of the Mountains." Zoologists, I believe, will not support this story. Dr. Ruhle may have picked it up from Frank Linderman, and the name Wahcheechee appears on a Forest Service topographical map. However, the Cree terms for "crane" are *otachahk* and *ochichak*, and for the "white crane" *wapichak*. Even these forms are misleading because according to the University of Alberta's Cree program the sound here represented by *ch* is *not* pronounced like *ch* in "church" but like *ts* in "cats."

So perhaps "wahcheechee" is not Cree at all but some other language? Let's try Chippewa, closely related to Cree. In Chippewa (Ojibwa) the term for "crane" is *ujejauk* and for "white crane" *waupijejauk*. None of this helps us decipher "wahcheechee." Dr. Ruhle claimed that the spelling "wahcheechee" resulted from a copy error.

The aberration "Wahcheechee" may be an attempt to write the name of a figure in Cree mythology, a "culture hero" similar to Napi in the Blackfoot tales. According to H. Christoph Wolfart, professor of linguistics at the University of Manitoba, the name should be written *Wisahkechahk*. (To make everybody happy, I would suggest *Wisahkezahk*.)

Another possibility is that someone assembled this term from the Chinese, in which all three syllables do occur with a large variety of meanings. But no matter how you look at it, "Wahcheechee" is hopeless as it stands now.

WAHOO CREEK is just south of Glacier. This word is said to be a Cree word for the elm tree, but as there are no elms here and the Cree words for the elm that I find in Cree dictionaries sound nothing like this, I leave this puzzle without solution.

WAHSEEJA* LAKE: This word is said to mean "white man" in Cree. But a standard Cree word for "white man" is *wapiskusuki* (white skin), while a U.S. American is *Kihzi-mahkoman* (Big Knife) and a British white man is *Akayasiw* (he who comes ashore). Aha, but if we scrounge some more and try other languages, we get Assiniboine (a Siouan language) *washeeju.* Does this help? (The moral is: Someone should do his/her homework.)

WALL LAKE lies just over the boundary in British Columbia. It is considered a rare gem nestled deep in the embrace of mighty cliffs. (See KISHINENA.)

WALTON* CREEK and **MOUNTAIN:** For Izaak Walton, the famous British author of *The Compleat Angler* (1593–1683). Walton Park was the home in England of Charles Waterton. (See below.) The Kootenai name for the creek and the mountain is "Beaver Foot": *Sina Akłik.*

WATERTON LAKES and **RIVER**: The lakes were once called the Kootenay Lakes, but the name "Waterton" was applied in 1858 by Thomas Blakiston for the English naturalist Charles Waterton. Earlier, the Upper Waterton Lake was labeled "Chief Mountain Lake" and then re-labeled "Mary's Lake" by Captain John Mullan. As if this were not chaos enough, along comes the U.S. Boundary Survey of 1861 with a name for Upper Waterton at 114 degrees: *A-kwote-kátl-nam Akawut-tla'nam.* A Blackfoot term for Waterton River means "where we fought the Kootenais." The lowest Waterton Lake is still called *Maskinonge.* That's Chippewa for "a big, ugly fish." Lower Waterton has also been called Knight's Lake.

An Indian trail to the Flathead Pass followed the west shore of Waterton Lake, and along this trail the west-side tribes like the Kootenai, Salish, Shoshoni, and probably Nez Perce sometimes made their way to or from the buffalo country. Over East Flattop, this trail brought wanderers from the Plains down into the Flathead valley and even to the Jesuit missions. But after the early smallpox epidemic, the Blackfeet grew stronger and forced other tribes south of Bow River or across the Continental Divide.

Charles Waterton Who was Charles Waterton? Though he never got close to me lakes and streams named after him in the national parks of Waterton (Alberta) and Glacier (Montana), this esteemed naturalist and pioneer conservationist was well known in England as the Shire of Walton Hall. He was born in Yorkshire in 1782 and he died there in 1865, but with many wanderings and fantastic adventures in between. Walton Hall was an old mansion built on a small island in a lake on an estate of many acres of once wild woodland. He turned this estate into one of the first bird sanctuaries or reserves in history.

Charles Waterton came of a family typical of the Catholic aristocracy of England during the Georgian Era when Catholicism was illegal. True, the discrimination against Catholics was no longer as severe as it had been in the age when "Romists" were publicly beheaded or degutted or both. In Waterton's era they were allowed elementary education but nothing at the higher level, were forbidden to enter the military (not such a great loss!), and of course were barred from all politics and could not attend mass or get married. Since many of the leading Catholics had plenty of money, they fled to New Zealand or got married on the Continent or kept privately sponsored chaplains at home. Young Charles began his formal education at age 10 from a little local Catholic school named Tudhoe. But one of the priests at Tudhoe resorted to the birch-rod until Charles bit him in the calf of the leg. Soon after that little Charles was transferred to the new Stonyhurst, where he acquired such an admiration for Jesuits that he wanted to become one. But he reasoned that he had to get married to propagate his brilliant family heritage.

He was a direct descendent of Sir (St.) Thomas More, whose head Henry VIII had sliced off, and also of saints and royal persons from Scotland, Germany, Russia, Savoy, France and Spain, the most famous Louis IX, King of France and his Spanish mother Blanca, and Edward I of England and his Spanish wife Eleanor, daughter of Spain's famous conquistador Fernando III.

Maybe it was for this Spanish heritage that his mother sent him and his younger brother to live with her two brothers in Spain. In 1802 away they sailed to Cadiz, where they managed to slip away from their guide but finally reached their uncles in Malaga. How delighted Charles was living at his uncle's country residence in the foothills where he could study the quails and the goldfinches, the red-legged partridges and even the flamingoes and monstrous vultures. And he gobbled up all he could learn of Cervantes and Don Quixote in the Spanish language to add to his own skill in poetry (especially the love poetry of Ovid). He wrote verses in both English and Latin. Once he was even able to visit Algeciras and Gibraltar and make scholarly observations on the apes of Gibraltar.

But alas, there were also mosquitoes. And the yellow fever, *el vomito negro*, rose up in Africa and by means of slave ships spread from Africa to the West Indies and from the West Indies to southern Europe, England, and the eastern United States. And it struck Malaga with a deadly blow that evidently did away with Charles' little brother and one of his uncles. Then came the terrible earthquake of 1804 which rocked Malaga to pieces. Charles managed to get aboard a ship that slipped out of port and passed the Rock of Gibraltar and at long last got back to England (maybe carrying the germs with it).

Charles felt like a bird himself since he was double-jointed and could put his foot on top of his head. Then up he could scale barefooted into trees and up walls to study birds' nests and just get into the life of birds themselves. Since his uncles had property in British Guiana, he crossed the ocean in 1804 to help care for it and spent many years wandering about South America, living mostly in Georgetown but thrashing through the jungles to Pernambuco, Brazil, and to Cayenne, French Guiana. He explored jungles with Indian guides, collecting specimens of fauna and birds and facing strange adventures – like riding on the back of a cayman. Among the friends he made in South America was a Scot named Edmonstone who had interesting daughters and one just born named Anne. The daughters were a half or quarter American Indian of the Arawak tribe, and Charles developed a firm friendship with the Edmonstone family.

On his four (?) returns home from South America, he would bring some exotic souvenirs, alive or otherwise. One of the living things was a wild cat – perhaps a margay or ocelot – that he could use at Walton Hall to hunt down the rats – though of course, not to hunt the birds. The rat was the one creature he permitted to be killed at Walton, and so he named the rats "Hanoverians" after the House of Hanover whose politics he did not appreciate.

About 1820 he made a trip or trips to Scotland where the Edmondstones now were living and the father himself was dying. One of his biographers suggests that perhaps he made an agreement with his old friend from the Guianas to take care of his three daughters after he died.

In 1824 he made a trip north from the Guianas into the United States, which he thought every educated Englishman should see, and was enraptured with Americans especially with "the fair Albanese" (no doubt a lady from Albany). From New York he journeyed into Canada by way of Niagara Falls. At Niagara Falls he became adventuresome and commemorated his experience by writing a few verses in the hotel register, a couple of which told how he longed to dance with "the fair Albanese" but could not because:

He sprained his foot, and hurt his toe,
On the rough road near Buffalo.
It quite distresses him to stagger a-
Long the sharp rocks of Niagara.
So there he's doomed to drink the measure
Of pain, in lieu of that of pleasure,
On Hope's delusive pinions borne
He came for wool and goes back shorn.

On he went to Montreal and Quebec, but he did not venture into the territory of the Hudson Bay Fur Company nor the tracks of the competitors XYZ, but it seems that he saw something of Ontario and a good deal of the province of Quebec, even the falls of Montmorency.

On his way south he paused at the West Indies. Everywhere he went he studied birds and often also reptiles. So by his pioneer bird and wildlife sanctuary at Walton, where no guns were allowed and nature must be preserved intact, he established a precedent in England.

He did a lot of traveling to continental Europe, especially to places like Rome and Aix-la-Chapelle (Aachen). At Rome he scaled the walls and probably the dome of St. Peter's as he did the trees of Walton but much to the disgust of the pope. There too he met William Makepeace Thackeray, the great English novelist. Thackeray was much impressed with him, his Catholic devotion and his charity to the poor. Another friend of Charles, and a confidential one as it seems, was the companion of Captain Cook, Sir Joseph Banks.

He also seems to have corresponded with Dickens, but I do not see any evidence that they ever met. He had met Darwin years ago in Edinburgh when Darwin was eager to learn something about taxidermy. Later on Charles whipped together a piece of taxidermy called the "Nondescript" which seemed to represent the "missing link" in Darwin's theory, part beast, part human. He named it after a tax collector who he felt had overcharged him.

When Anne grew to age 17, educated at a convent in Bruges, Belgium, under the supervision of Charles's aunt, he married her in Belgium in May 1829. Evidently it was a happy marriage but very brief because she died of childbirth in April 1830. Two of her sisters came to live with Charles at Walton Hall and helped take care of his baby son Edmund.

On one occasion Charles Darwin was invited to have supper with them. Darwin was amused if not altogether delighted with the two Jesuits who were also guests at the supper and with the two Indian sisters-in-law whom Darwin referred to in his private account as "Mulatresses." Although he rated Charles as an interesting person, he also regarded him as narrow-minded. But does Darwin's reference to the two sisters-in-law sound broad- minded?

Why Blakiston named Waterton Lakes after Charles is not clear. Perhaps a friendship between them goes unrecorded, or perhaps Blakiston was just eager to put onto maps the names of his colleagues in the natural history of the times. A mountain range at the border of Montana and British Columbia is named Galton, evidently after Darwin's cousin and fellow scientist. And Blakiston was also an ornithologist.

After the death of Charles' young wife Anne, he never again went to bed but slept on the floor with a blanket and an oak block for a pillow. He would rise in the middle of the night to pray in his chapel, or perhaps spend an hour at prayer around three or four A.M. and return to prayer when he got up and dressed. He often read Ovid in Latin and Cervantes in Spanish and (also in Spanish) something from a biography of the Jesuit San Francisco Xavier.

In 1865 Charles stumbled in his garden, fell and died from the fall soon afterwards. Quite an irony that the athletic climber of St. Peter's Basilica or the barefooted bird lover scrambling among the limbs of trees would die from a stumble in his own garden.

An Indian trail to the Flathead Pass followed the west shore of Waterton Lake, and along this trail, the west-side tribes like the Kootenai, Salish, Shoshoni, and probably Nez Perce sometimes made their way to or from the buffalo country. Over East Flattop, this trail brought wanderers from the Plains down into the Flathead valley and even to the Jesuit missions. But after the early smallpox epidemic, the Blackfeet grew stronger and forced other tribes south of Bow River or across the Continental Divide.

Literature of Waterton Park gives the legend of *Sahkúmapi*, The Boy, about the origin of Waterton Lake. Sahkumapi was a young warrior who was captured by seven evil ones and carried down into the under-world. There he met a lovely girl and while the evil ones slept the sleep of the wicked, Sahkumapi ran off with the young lady. This wily couple took with them a magic stick, a magic stone, and a magic basket of water. When the evil ones awoke and gave hot pursuit westward across the prairies, Sahkumapi threw down the stick. Up sprouted a great forest to impede the evil ones. When they started to catch up, Sahkumapi threw down the magic stone, and mountains literally soared up into the sky. Still the evil ones pursued. When Sahkumapi threw down the basket of water, what should appear but Waterton Lake, and the basket became a canoe in which the escapees made their final getaway.

A more corrupt version of this legend appeared in the *Lethbridge Herald*, and its allusions to an ass and to the devil as the Stoker (*Áwtazoki-w*) are obvious and for some readers titillating Euro-American contaminants: *Sahkúmapi-w* is a great young warrior but also as mischievous as Rambo, so the Stoker seeks him out for an alliance and takes Sahkumapi off to the land of devils. Alas, there's nothing there but serpents and one hungry ass which Sahkumapi is forbidden ever to feed. But Sahkumapi is capable of tricking the devil as well as anyone else and so he feeds the poor beast. Suddenly, the ass begins to talk like a woman and tells Sahkumapi that she has led a wicked life and is committed here to Devil Land in punishment. (Notice the Gnostic elements that enter an "Indian" legend as soon as a white man gets his tongue around it. Notice too that the Boy and the She-ass reverse the European story of Beauty and the Beast with overtones of our cruel story of Rimini and Francesca.) So this unlikely pair, the Boy and the Ass, gather together a stick, a stone, some moss, and a holy turnip. Then Sahkumapi jumps onto the ass and they speed away. The Stoker pursues. As he nearly overtakes them, Sahkumapi throws out the stick and the forests burst out of the ground entrapping the devil. When the Stoker almost catches up for the second time, Sahkumapi throws down the stone and up spring Sheep Mountain and Sofa Mountain. When the Stoker is about to get them the third time, Sahkumapi throws down the moss and a great swamp separates the pursued from the pursuer. Three times – that would be enough for a white man's legend because of our fixation on Three. But the sacred number to the American Indians is often four and since this is supposed to be an Indian story, we have to have four trials and four triumphs. The fourth crisis occurs at dawn when the Stoker is likely to find his prey asleep under Dead (or Sleeping?) Indian Mountain. All Sahkumapi has left to throw down is the turnip and that turns into the Waterton Lakes and leaves the poor Stoker on the opposite shore. Sahkumapi then goes home and turns into a good citizen. But he neglects the ass. She begs him to hit her over the head. He protests. She insists. When he finally obliges, she turns into a beautiful young bride just for Sahkumapi. Well, take it or leave it.

WATERTON LAKES NATIONAL PARK: Place names of Waterton differ in style from those of Glacier with more emphasis on Gaelic names, less on Indian names, while the French names derive more from World War I than from Canada's native French heritage. The scarcity of Indian names is attributed to the late arrival of the Blackfeet, Crees, and Stonies who pushed aside the Kootenais, but the trouble with this theory is that the "late arrival" of these tribes is probably a white man's legend. Of the many tiny lakes of Waterton, some like Peck and Knight are named for persons, others like Loon Lake and Deer Lake for fauna. Even the basins are named: Blue Grouse, Horseshoe, Oil.

But in the neighboring areas of Alberta Indian names are fairly numerous and more indicative of Waterton's history: Here are some not yet discussed in these pages: In Blackfoot, the name of towns *Ponoká* (Elk) and *Okotoks* (rocks), (*óhkotox-sko*: a rocky place). *Ponokái-sisahtai* or Elk River is used for the Bow, the Red Deer, and the Yellowstone in Montana. *Spitzi* (tall timber) is the name of the town High River; *nato-oh-xiskum* ("hot springs" or literally "holy thunder") is used for Banff or any other hot springs; *iszikum* (coulee) is the original name for the village Etzikom; *pahk-ohki* (bad water) is a station of the Central Pacific Railroad; *saami* (war bonnet) is the name of Medicine Hat, where a water monster is supposed to have appeared in the river. One Blackfoot name for Waterton Lakes is the same as that for St. Mary Lakes, *Paht-omahxikimi* (inside lakes); another is Kootenay Lake, *Kutenaiomahxikimi*, with sometimes the added explanation "where we fought the Kootenais." Calgary and Bow River are called both *Namahtai* from *námaii* (bow as a weapon) and *mohkínszis* meaning elbow. In Cree *mitóskwin* (elbow) is applied to both Calgary and the big bend of the Bow River; *muskiki* means "medicine"; *mahikan* (wolf) is the name of a mountain; Wetaskiwin should be *witaskiwinihk* (place to make peace); *Kananaskis* is said to mean "where rivers meet," but no language is designated and no proof offered.

Probably the most interesting of Cree names is that of Sounding Lake, reported as *ni-pi-kap-hit-i-kwek*, a good example of flawed transliteration. I suggest instead *nipi* (water) + *ka* (which) + *e-pitikwet* (thunders). So the word must mean Thundering Waters. It refers to a legend that an eagle rose up out of the waters with a serpent in its talons and amid an apparent clap of thunder. It reminds us of the Aztec story and the symbol on the flag of Mexico – and of course the Thunder Bird.

Kootenais called Upper Waterton Lake the Long Lake or *Kuók'inok*. After the international border was traced across it, they named it "Lake Cut in Two," *Kalásskinok*. The Middle Waterton Lake was named after Pebble Beach below the headquarters of Parcs Canada, "the Beach of Smooth Even Pebbles." Waterton River was called in Kootenai either "Tunaxa River" or "Darkened Eyebrows River," *A·qoqwatqálnam*. The Kootenai name for Bow River is *Láwo Akinmituk*, for Old Man River *A·kinkakelmi* or "racetrack" and for Pincher Creek *A·qoqáu Akinmituk* or "swamp".

Among its exotica, southern Alberta contains such place names as San Francisco Lake, named for (or by?) duck hunters who came up here from California, and Beauvais Lake and Provincial Park for Ren Beauvais who came in 1882 with a group of French settlers from Oregon to establish a ranch for fine horses.

The highest point on the eastern edge of the Rockies between Waterton and Banff National Parks is Tornado Mountain, 10,167 feet or 3099 metres in elevation and so called for the lightning and dark thunderclouds that gathered at its summit in 1915.

Southern Saskatchewan and the Alberta borderland also contain sites important to Blackfoot tradition: Cypress Hills – in the Blackfoot language Striped Earth or *Aiixkímiko (-koi)*—and the Great Sand Hills or *Omahkspaziko (-koi)*, "abode of the dead." And to the living it seems a notably dreary region.

While the names of Glacier National Park have made it possible to introduce persons historically important to the area, the names of Waterton do not so easily reveal its history. That is, not unless we do some digging. The main exceptions are the names of Blakiston and men in the boundary surveys.

Somewhat surprising is the way in which a man (always a man, never a woman) who has been politically correct and set foot somewhere in the vicinity of Glacier has his name smeared all over the map, Yet across the border an historically important figure and widely admired like George VI is barely noticed, even though he and his consort toured Canada in 1939 and visited the Kaina people. They at least remembered him.

To redress the balance just a bit, here are a few thumbnail sketches of persons unnamed on mountains but historically important to the Waterton region (more can be found in my *Who's Who*):

Constable Achille Rouleau (1857–1938) was one of the rare French Canadians in the ranks of the Mounties serving in western Canada. Born in Quebec and recruited in Ontario, he was noted for his cool, casual temperament and imperfect English. Assigned first to Fort Walsh in the Cypress Hills, most of his service appears to have revolved around Fort MacLeod, often coupled with Jack Street on patrols in and out of Waterton. Rouleau was a special favorite with the children of Kootenay Brown. He may have been in the honor guard for the Marquis of Lorne. His enlistment expired in 1885 near the climax of the Riel resistance when he retired to the area of Pincher Creek.

Henri Rivière (1867–1956) was born in France of French nobility and U.S. American ancestry. He ran off to sea "in the days of the square-riggers" and was a student at a French naval academy, but after a harsh discipline (flogging?), he fled to his relatives in the "Southern States" of the U.S., then to San Francisco, then to Butte, Montana, and a cowboy life around the Bow River, Alberta. His specialty was taming horses by*not* breaking them. He served as Game Guardian of Alberta 1911 to 1928. He also had movie roles in Hollywood. He was accompanying Jack Street when Street was killed by an avalanche. (See STREET.) His wife was Nellie Gladstone and they made their home at Pincher Creek, though Henri was in and out of Waterton much of the time.

Nellie Gladstone was the great-granddaughter of Scot William Gladstone from Montreal who pioneered in Alberta, and of Harriet Leblanc of French and Indian origin. The most noted member of the family has been "The Gentle Persuader," "the Indian Senator" James Gladstone. Currently, a young member of the family is gaining fame as a Blackfoot poet and singer. There is a Mount Gladstone just north of Waterton Park, 7,777 feet high, and a much higher one in New Zealand.

Samuel H. Middleton (c.1884–1964) was born at Burton-on-Trent, England and was educated at Nottingham University. The romantic call of the West lured him to Alberta as an Anglican missionary to the Peigans. Before long he was appointed to Saint Paul's School for the Bloods or Kaina and was ordained a priest. He received the Blackfoot name of Mountain Chief, *Ninàistako*. Married in 1911 to one of the teachers of the school, Kathleen Underwood, he had three children. In 1925 he transferred to the new Saint Paul's Residential School north of Cardston. He is the author of a book on the Blackfoot Confederacy that discusses the origin of the name for the Bloods, proposing that they should really be called the Many Chiefs or *Akàina* an archaic form of *akai + ina*. He also included data on the Blackfoot Syllabary, the Winter Count of Bad Head (*Pakap-Otohkan*), a sketch about Red Crow and an account of the adoption ceremony on the Viscount Alexander, Governor General of Canada, and his two sons. Most of all, however, he will be remembered as the major promoter of the Waterton-Glacier International Peace Park, now a World Heritage site.

Blue Lightning: in Cree *Sepihko-waskowtesiw:* the second wife of Kootenay Brown. One account says she was from Saskatchewan but was visiting with relatives at Babb when lonesome widower Brown paid five horses for her – a rather high price. But then he is supposed to have slyly got his competitors drunk, challenging them to a horse race and so winning back his five horses. Blue Lightning proved to be a good cook and an excellent housekeeper who polished her pots and pans until her guests could use them for mirrors.

And who were her guests? Probably Joe Cosley of course and the Mounties Street and Rouleau, Lord Latham, and Stavelyn Hill. She was a crack shot and accompanied Brown on his mountain treks, once over into the Flathead valley. When Brown died in 1916, she went to live with the Riviéres.

Seen Afar and often called Seen From Afar, was a son of the *Manistokos* and brother or half-brother of Natawista and Calf Robe the bully. But he was a peacemaker and so a counterpoint to his brother and possibly their father's successor as head chief of the Blood nation. His name sounds to me like *Pi-inakoym* and seems to refer to the fact that he was often seen in far places. However others translate his name to mean Seen From Afar and spell the Blackfoot form as *Pinukwiim* or *Peenquim* (Perhaps there is a dialectal shift in Blood-Piegan from *w* to *y*.) His more formal or sacred name was *Ap-onistai-sai-nakoyim* or White Calf Never Seen or Vanished, probably an allusion to the sacred white buffalo with plays on the terms for "seen" and "not seen' and the homonym for both "calf" and "holy" or *manito*. He was probably present at the Judith Council to sign the treaty of 1855. And he appears in a story by J. W. Schultz, "A bride for Morning Star."

I cannot vouch for the authenticity of this tale, allegedly told to Schultz by an old *engagé* from Saint Louis named Charles Rivois. In sum it goes this way: In 1856 Seen Afar leads a party on his third venture down into the Southwest, including Rivois, a Tewa named Far Pine, a beautiful girl named Lance Woman and her two rival suitors. Alex Culbertson cautions Rivois not to go, but Natawista says he should go to protect Lance Woman. At Taos they meet Kit Carson. But some Pawnee visitors kidnap Lance Woman. Seen Afar and his party pursue them across the Arkansas and the Platte to the Loup. There Lance Woman is about to be sacrificed alive to the Morning Star, but Seen Afar and his followers rescue her just in time (Hollywood style. The episode of the interrupted sacrifice may have been suggested by similar stories about Marcelino Baca and the Cattle Queen Libby Smith). Adolf Hungry Wolf tells more credible stories about Seen Afar. In sober truth, Seen Afar did wander into the Southwest and also up and down the Missouri River, perhaps as a messenger of intertribal peace. He died in the smallpox epidemic of 1870.

Alexander Staveley-Hill (1825–1905) from Staffordshire was one of the outstanding barristers of his time, deputy high steward of Oxford University and a conservative member of the House of Commons. To study the possibility of emigration to Canada, he went there in 1881 and bought a cattle ranch seventy miles south of Calgary, which he called New Oxley. He "wandered" about southern Alberta and into Montana and the Waterton-Glacier country 1881–4 accompanied by his friend Lord Latham. He wrote a book about these adventures with Latham called *From Home to Home*. To find more about Staveley-Hill, check "Hill" even though a town apparently named for him near Claresholm is called Stavely [*sic*].

WEASEL COLLAR* GLACIER: No information.

WEEPING WALL is made up of the rocks that shed water onto the Logan Pass road on the west side. Was the name suggested by the Wailing Wall in Jerusalem?

WEST FLATTOP* MOUNTAIN: See Flattop.

WEST GLACIER VILLAGE: See BELTON.

WEST LAKES is the name of an administrative district of Glacier National Park.

WHEELER LAKE should perhaps be called a pond. It was a favorite fishing spot for Senator Wheeler, but it must have been a trek in, up Logging Lake to Grace Lake. I suppose it was fed by the meltdown of ice in Vulture Glacier, and that would be a long way from the Wheeler cabin near the head of Lake MacDonald. It was there that Senator and Lulu Wheeler spent much of their summers, far from the controversy and the politics of Butte and Washington, D.C.

WHISKEY CREEK and **SPRING:** In the northwest corner of Glacier there used to be a few little settlements like Havreville. The mailman would pause here for a swig or two (so the story goes), and this practice did not improve the mail service.

WHITE CALF* MOUNTAIN: The Blackfoot term is *Ap-unista*. But the element -*unista* or -*onista* can mean either "calf" or "sacred" according to which of the two homonyms it comes from. Both Schultz and McClintock agree (for once!) that the original name of the chief was *Onistai-poka* (Wonderful or Manito Child), misinterpreted as White Calf. At any rate the man who had this disputed name was the last dynastic chief of the South Piegans. He was born about 1835 and signed the Judith treaty of 1855, perhaps influenced by Natawista. Noted for his bravery, he succeeded to the chieftainship in 1873, so it was he who had to lead his people during their years of decline and tragedy. Absent in Canada, he missed the massacre by Baker's men on the Marias but he understood it as a threat of genocide. In negotiation with white men he represented the compromising but reluctant faction, opposed by the right wing faction of Three Suns. When in 1880 he led his people to the last buffalo hunts around the Judith River, he was forced by the Army to return to a reservation devoid of wild game and wracked by famine. In 1887 he donated land on the Two Medicine River to the Jesuits for their Holy Family Mission. He died in Washington, D.C., in 1903.

WHITE EAGLE CREEK: The Blackfoot name for Valentine Creek is *Api-Pita*. Oddly enough, there is some reason to think that the word for "eagle," *pita(n)* is just a shortened form of an old Algonquin term for the bald eagle, "white tail." Presumably "White Eagle" was the name of a person, but Schultz does not mention anyone of this name, telling us only that some Stoney Indians encamped on this creek were attacked and driven out by the Crows. (See RED EAGLE.)

WHITE ELEPHANT LODE: This is one of the most interesting claims in Glacier, partly because the description is reasonably precise in contrast to the hazy notions of other claims. It was filed in 1899 by J. H. Sherburne, et al., and lay near the outlet of Iceberg Lake with another claim called the Copper King. Most claims in Glacier were never patented, and this one seems to be among them. Elephant names were popular among boomers: "Mastodon," "Mammoth," "Jumbo," "Elephant," and here and there in other parts of Montana there were other claims labeled "White Elephant." The irony may not have been intentional, but of course all claims in Glacier/Waterton Parks probably turned out to be white elephants. The names of mining claims suggest something about the claimants, especially their hopes and fears over the gamble they were taking. Examples, also from the east side of the Divide: "Maybe," "Mogul," "Seven Up." And if names like "Copper King" sing of fond hopes, fonder still are the hopes heralded by names that substitute silver for copper: "Silver King," "Silver Tip," "Silver Bow," "Silver Dollar," "Silver Star" – all on the east side too. And then there are the pious names, again on the east side, a list of saints: "Mary," "James," "Charles," "Paul," "Louis," "Lawrence," "Elmo".What seems surprising is the number of Indian names used at a time when racism was prevalent: "Sitting Bull," "Sun Dance," "Spotted Dog," "Spotted Horse," "Medicine Horse," "Mountain Chief," "Minnehaha," "Cherokee," "Chippewa Chief." However, a good many of the claimants of placers and lodes on the east side were members of some tribe. If you must have a name in Blackfoot for "white elephant," let me suggest *ap-inohxisi-w*, (long nose), the final *w* as a verbalizing suffix meaning something like "it is." I shall make no attempt to offer you the equivalent in Kootenai.

WHITE QUIVER* FALLS: This name is supposed to derive from the hero of a novel by Helen Fitzgerald Sanders, *The White Quiver*. However, it is also the real life name of a Piegan man who was remarkably clever at running off horses. He even got away with some that were impounded by the Northwest Mounted Police for a while. The falls used to be called prosaically, "Washboard Falls," and then perhaps poetically, "The Fountain of the Gods." This name is said to have been the creation of Joe Cosley.

WHITECROW* CREEK, GLACIER, LAKE, and **MOUNTAIN** were named by Dr. Ruhle. Whitecrow, a bird-like god(?), figures in an Indian story told by Eli Guardipee as the one who hid the buffalo. Napi tried to get them back. The historic event of the vanishing buffalo was linked with Red Old Man or *Mikapi*, whereas White Old Man brought them back. (This according to Schultz.) When the last buffalo hunts took place, around 1880 in the region of the Judith Basin, the white man was apparently thought to be playing the malignant role of Red Old Man. In fact, it was a desperate time. Indians gathered from far and wide, following the dwindling herds, so that traditional enemies converged on this last buffalo range. Schultz was present for this last round-up, and Joe Kipp, Ipasha and Crow Woman, Eli Guardipee, Charles Rose or Otahkomi, Running Rabbit, White Calf, Crowfoot, Spotted Eagle, yes, even Sitting Bull, the Cree leader Big Bear, and rebel visionary Louis Riel. Several salvaged buffalo were acquired by Michel Pablo at this time, fulfilling the role of the White Old Man who saves the buffalo.

But all in all, the population of these last buffalo camps in the Judith country was an explosive mixture to say the least. Many Métis or Red River people came down from Canada, probably with their famous squeaky Red River carts, and among them Louis Riel. The concept of the Almighty Voice really belonged to Riel. Big Bear was moved to join Riel, but Crowfoot saw it all as the vanity of vanities. Yet it was Crowfoot who astounded everyone by his courage in keeping the peace at this last desperate buffalo hunt. When some Crees tried to steal Crowfoot's horse by night, he simply rode out to them alone and invited them as friends into his tipi. So startling was this act of reconciliation that it worked. But in the end, all hope vanished with the buffalo. Everyone had to turn homeward to starve on their sterile reservations, some of them driven by Army troops, some staggering along on foot, sick and hungry. Many never made it. Such was the whimper with which the Indian world came to an end.

WHITEFISH MOUNTAIN and **RANGE:** The term for "whitefish" is given in Kootenai as *matit*. Though evidently a misinterpretation, the name Whitefish was attached to Otokomi Mountain. Later it was erased from the Rising Sun area of Glacier altogether. But it was retained as the name of the ranges to the west of Glacier, as well as for the lake and the railroad town at the southern foot of these mountains.

WILBUR CREEK and **MOUNT**: The peak was named by Grinnell in 1885 for E. R. Wilbur. Unfortunately, such a name has no relevance for us today. Who was E. R. Wilbur? If he has surviving relatives the name may mean something to them. The Pinnacle Wall is connected to this peak and jauntily sports its "diorite band" sandwiched into Siyeh limestone. Schultz's list names this mountain for *Isokwi-awótan* (Heavy Shield), who opposed the Kootenai outlaw Cut Nose. The Blackfoot name for the creek is Mink, *suyikaiiyi*. Mount Wilbur was first climbed by Norman Clyde in 1923.

WILD* CREEK has also been known as Johnson Creek. But who was Johnson?

WILD GOOSE ISLAND is the little gem in Upper Saint Mary Lake, said to be named for Canadian geese that nest there. The Blackfoot name *Natosapi* is composed of *nato(s)-* (holy) + *-api* (person, elder). It may have been applied by Schultz on tour with the Barings in 1886.

WILSON* RANGE stands on the international line in the northeastern part of Glacier and the southeastern corner of Waterton. Wilson Range, Sofa Mountain, and Vimy Ridge terminate the lengthy Lewis Range at its northern end.

The *Lethbridge Herald* attributes the name of the range to an engineer, G. W. Wilson. While this is a possible source of the name, it seems more likely that it honors Sir Charles William Wilson (1836–1905). He was secretary to the British Boundary Commission of 1858–1862, and his record of this adventure was published (1970) under the title *Mapping the Frontier*.

In the entry AKAMINA we have already noticed what an interesting person Lieutenant Wilson was, but the way to appreciate him is to read his delightful journal. He was not only a writer but also and artist and made pictures of the expedition. Perhaps it was the recreational breaks in Victoria or San Francisco that kept him in good humor, and his description of the dances led by Sir James and Lady Douglas will put the reader in a good humor also. Sir Charles (only "Lieutenant" at the time of the survey) had an uncle and godfather in Philadelphia where he sponsored the Academy of Natural Science.

Sir Charles was born in Liverpool, began his education there and continued it at Bonn University to join the royal engineers. He was appointed in February of 1858 to be the secretary of the commission to "delimitate" [*sic*] the boundary between the U.S. and British North America. With Commissioner J. S. Hawkins (eventually to become both Sir and General), Sir Charles traveled by way of Panama to Esquimalt, arriving there 12 July. The achievement of marking the forty-ninth parallel from the San Juan Islands to Akamina is described in the *Dictionary of National Biography Supplement* as a venture through "primeval forests, over mountains 7,000 feet high, and in a climate of extreme temperatures, almost uninhabited and unknown." (Actually the mountains reached much greater height than 7,000 feet, e.g. Mount Baker). The account adds that the temperature fell to thirty degrees below zero (presumably Fahrenheit) at night "in the hardest winter known."

This was just the beginning of Sir Charles' career, and took off sharply when he volunteered to survey Jerusalem. Beginning in 1864, he made surveys that proved the Dead Sea in March was 1292 feet below the level of the Mediterranean and six feet more in summer. After a respite, he was sent to Palestine and made a "reconnaissance" between Beirut and Hebron. After surveying in Scotland and the British midlands and getting married in 1867 to Olivia Duffin, he was sent to survey in the Sinai Peninsula. After surveying in Ireland, in 1878 he was in Serbia and in 1879 became British military consul-general in Anatolia. He did a lot of travel and study in Turkey and in 1882 was assigned to Egypt and two years later to join the expedition to relieve the forces under "Chinese" Gordon up the Nile in Khartoum. When the expedition arrived two days late to save Gordon and his followers from the general massacre, he was forced to defend himself in the shock wave of national frustration. However, he weathered the storm well enough to be awarded the rank of Major General. In the meantime he and Olivia had four sons and a daughter.

In 1899 and 1903 he was back in Palestine engaged in the questions over the sites of Golgotha and the Holy Sepulcher, assuming a more or less "traditional" side of the disputes.

WINDMAKER* LAKE used to be called Oyster Shell Lake, perhaps a name of Kootenai origin. Windmaker is a figure in Blackfoot folklore, sometimes represented as the Medicine Elk, a huge elk that dwells in the waters. So far as I know, no one has claimed to have shot it.

WINDY CREEK is also called "Emanon Creek." "Emanon" is backwards for "noname."

WINNAKEE (Winakee, etc.): A campground and former rafting facility near West Glacier. It seems that this term is derived from an Algonquin expression meaning "dirty (muddy) ground."

WINONA LAKE and **RIDGE**: The ridge is just west of Glacier, but the lake lies inside park boundaries and was labeled "Mud Lake" until recently when the name Winona was restored to it. While one opinion asserts that the term *winona* is a Chippewa verb meaning "to breast feed," another opinion regards it as a Santee Sioux word referring to the first-born child if that child is female. It may be both. It was the name of a village of the Mdewakanton Sioux which eventually became a white man's town under the same name in Winona County, Minnesota. From there it has spread to at least a dozen other states. The name is also attributed to a sister of Teton Sioux Chief Sitting Bull who bore a premature baby.

It is also the name of the mother of Nanabozho (Manabozho: note the Algonquian shift *m* to *n*). Longfellow spells it Wenonah for the mother of his Hiawatha. In this story Winona is the daughter of "the daughter of the moon, Nokomis," and in Cree *nokom* does mean "my grandmother." But poor Winona falls in love with the wicked West Wind, gives him male quadruplets, and when he abandons her, she dies the death of the bereft. This, of course, makes the West Wind the original dead-beat dad. Sometimes legends are uncomfortably realistic. The oldest of the quadruplets is Nanabozho (Hiawatha in Longfellow's poem), who is brought up by his grandmother Nokomis. His favorite brother is sadly assigned to care for the dead. The third brother goes north to become the Great White Hare. (No, no, not the Great Spirit.) (See MICHE WABUN.) The fourth brother is no good like his father and becomes the antagonist to Nanabozho.

In Montana Winona is a claim name. In the early 1880s the English Earl, Lord Latham, his friend Alexander Stavely-Hill and their party made an expedition across the Divide from Kootenai Brown's post at Waterton to the Tobacco and Flathead valleys. They could have passed near this area and conferred the name of Stavely Hill's "pretty little sorrel mare" (Winona) on this lake.

WOLF GUN* MOUNTAIN: Wolf Gun was the name of a Kootenai man. (See LONEMAN, LOGGING.)

WOLFTAIL MOUNTAIN: Grinnell gave this name to the mountain, but "Wolf Tail" is the Kootenai name for the North Fork of the Flathead River. Evans called the mountain "Little Bear," and Schultz says that Little Bear was the Kootenai name: *Kławłanana*.

This is a rare instance in which we have a double source for a Kootenai name, that is, some degree of confirmation. See HEAVY RUNNER for the Piegan chief "Wolf Tail." See NORTH FORK for the Kootenai name.

WOODRUFF'S FALLS: See NYACK.

WURDEMAN* LAKE: J. V. Wurdeman was a member of the U.S. Boundary Survey of 1861. This lake is one of the North Lakes. Its Blackfoot name is that of a Piegan warrior, *Pixi-awaná* (Bird Rattle).

WYNN* MOUNTAIN: For Frank B. Wynn, a scientist who was killed during a climb on Mount Siyeh in 1927. Wynn is a spur of Siyeh, and Grinnell had named this spur "Point Mountain." Then it took on the name of the mining town Altyn. But at last in 1927 the mapmakers transferred "Altyn" and called this spur "Wynn."

X: a name for mining claims!

XIXTAKI: This is a simplification of the term for "beaver" in Blackfoot, literally, "wood-biter." It occurs in many names in Glacier, but it's such a tongue twister that even native speakers have been known to have trouble with it. The correct form is *xis'xtaki(w)*, composed of *xi-* (wood, stick) + *sixtaki* (to bite) with the *i* of the latter stem elided.

YARROW CREEK in Waterton Park is named for the yarrow that grows on a creek in Scotland.

YELLOW* MOUNTAIN is notable for its yellowish color and for the evidence it offers of the Lewis Overthrust. In 1885 or 1886 it was named Robertson Mountain for Lt. Samuel Robertson who came over to Saint Mary from Fort Assiniboine and made a map showing Chief Mountain, Mount Jean (West Butte of the Sweetgrass Buttes), Appekunny Mountain (now Apikuni), Joe's Creek (Kennedy Creek?), Bessie Creek (now unknown), Helen's Lake (Duck Lake), Crowfoot Mountain (at the head of Divide Creek, now Kakitos?), Red Crow Mountain (now Kupunkamint or Curly Bear), and Florence and Virginia Falls. The map is dated 1887. Chiefs Red Crow of the Bloods and Crowfoot of the North Blackfoot were then still alive.

YELLOW FISH MOUNTAIN: See OTOKOMI, ROSE, WHITEFISH.

YELLOW WOLF MOUNTAIN: Yellow Wolf (or Yellow Coyote), *Otah-ápisi*, was the brother of Black Eagle and the uncle of Schultz's wife Natahki (by one account). After Black Eagle's death, Yellow Wolf married his brother's wife Pataki (Carrier Woman) and so took over the role of grandfather to Schultz's son Hart.

YOUNG MAN MOUNTAIN: This is a Kootenai name applied originally to what is now the Camel's Hump, but the name "Young Man" has now been transferred to this mountain nearby.

ZEPHER: The name of two claims south of Glacier in the Felix district. As with other mining claims in the park the fortune it promised proved ephemeral.

ZOO CAVE: A cave with mammal remains but no known human remains, but its name derives from the evidence that it has been the den of a carnivore. This is one of three caves discovered fairly recently near each other, and 217 meters of it have been mapped. It occurs in what is called Altyn limestone, but this name is not accurate since it is formed mostly of dolomite, the oldest known sedimentary rock in Glacier.

BIBLIOGRAPHY

Aldington, Richard. *The Strange Life of Charles Waterton, 1782-1865.* Evans Bros., London,1949

Anderson, Anne. *Plains Cree Dictionary in the "Y" Dialect.* Edmonton, 1971.

Archives of Arlington National Cemetery.

Archives of Flathead County, Kalispell, Montana.

Archives of Teton County, Choteau, Montana.

Archives of the U.S. Military Academy, West Point.

Baker, Marcus. *Survey of the Northwestern Boundary of the United States, 1857–1861.* Department of the Interior, Bulletin of the U.S. Geological Survey, No. 174, Washington, D.C., 1900.

Barry, John Neilson. "Spaniards in Early Oregon." *Washington Historical Quarterly* 23:1932, 25–34.

Bell. *Old Fort Benton, Montana.* Ye Galeeon Press: Fairfield, Washington, 1975.

Blackfeet Heritage Program. *Blackfeet Heritage: 1907–1908.* Allotment census. Browning, Montana, n.d.

Blakiston, Thomas. See Palliser, John.

Boas, Franz. *Kutenai Tales.* Washington, D.C.: Bureau of American Ethnology, Bulletin No. 59, 1918.

Boller, Henry A. *Among the Indians.* Milo M. Quaiffe, ed. University of Nebraska Press, 1972.

Bracken, Joseph, S.J. *The Divine Matrix: Creativity as Link Between East and West.* Orbis Books, Maryknoll, New York, 1995.

Buchholtz, C. W. *Man in Glacier.* Glacier Natural History Association, 1976.

– – –. "William R. Logan and Glacier National Park." Manuscript. University of Montana, 1968.

Calf Robe, Ben, with Adolf & Beverly Hungry Wolf. *Silsiká: a Blackfoot Legacy.* Good Medicine Books, Invermere, British Columbia, 1979.

Campbell, Marius R. *The Glacier National Park.* Washington, D.C.: U.S. Geological Survey Bulletin No. 600, 1914. *Canadian Encyclopedia.* Canadian Permanent Committee on Geological Names. *Gazeteer of Canada: Alberta Repertoire Geographic deu Canada.* 2nd Alberta bilingual edition. Ottawa, Ontario, 1974. *Catholic Encyclopedia.*

Catlin, George. *The North American Indians.* 2 volumes. John Grant: Edinburgh, 1926.

Cheney, Roberta Carkeek. *Names on the Face of Montana.* Missoula, Montana: University of Montana, 1971.

Clark, Ella E. *Indian Legends from the Northern Rockies.* Norman, Oklahoma: University of Oklahoma Press, 1968.

– – – and Margot Edmonds. *Sacajawea of the Lewis and Clark Expedition.* University of Oklahoma Press, 1968.

Clarke-Turvey, Joyce. "Clarke History." Manuscript.

Coburn, Walt. *Pioneer Cattleman in Montana.* Norman, Oklahoma: University of Oklahoma Press, 1968.

Coues, Elliot, ed. *History of the Expedition under the Command of Lewis and Clark.* 3 volumes. Dover, New York: 1965.

– – – , ed. *New Light on the Early History of the Greater Northwest: The Manuscript Journals of Alexander Henry and of David Thompson, 1799–1814.* 2 volumes. Minneapolis: Ross and Haines, 1965.

Daly, Reginald Aldeworth. *Geology of the North American Cordillera of the Forty-Ninth Parallel.* Part I. Department of Mines, Geological Survey, Memoir No. 38. Ottawa: Government Printing Bureau, 1912.

De Santo, Jerry S. "The Legendary Joe Cosley." *Montana, the Magazine of Western History.* Winter 1980.

De Smet, Pierre-Jean, S.J. *Life, Letters and Travels of Father Pierre-Jean De Smet, 1801–1873.* 4 volumes. Edited by Hiram Martin Chittenden and Alfred Talbot Richardson. New York: Kraus reprint (wit the original 4 volumes printed in two).

De Voto, Bernard. *Across the Wide Missouri.* Houghton Mifflin, 1947.

Dempsey, Hugh A. *Crowfoot.* Norman, Oklahoma: University of Oklahoma Press, 1972.

– – – . "Indian Names for Alberta Communities." Calgary: Glenbow-Alberta Institute, 1969. *Dictionary of National Biography*

Diettert, Gerald A. *Grinnell's Glacier: George Bird Grinnell and Glacier National Park.* Mountain Press, Missoula, Montana, 1992.

Duvall, Allen J, co-author with Clark Wissler, q.v.

Dyke, Paul. "Lone Wolf Returns to That Long-Ago Time." *Montana, the Magazine of Western History.* Winter 1972.

Edington, Brian W. *Charles Waterton.* The Lutherworth Press, Cambridge, 1996

Ege, Robert J. *Strike Them Hard: Incident on the Marias, January 23, 1870.* Bellevue, Nebraska: The Old Army Press, 1970.

Elmore, Francis. Notes, manuscript. Glacier Park Archives, the Museum.

Elrod, Morton J. *Elrod's Guide and Book of Information on Glacier National Park.* Missoula, Montana: 1924. *Encyclopaedia Britanica* Engelter, Mable and Betty Schafer. *Stump Town to Ski Town: the Story of Whitefish, Montana.*

Ewers, John C. *The Blackfeet, Raiders on the Northwestern Plains.* Norman, Oklahoma: University of Oklahoma Press, 1958.

– – – . "Iroquois Indians in the Far West." *Montana, the Magazine of Western History.* Spring 1963.

– – – . "Richard Sanderville, Blackfoot Indian Interpreter. Blackfoot, ca. 1873-1951." *American Indian Intellectuals,* edited by Margot Liberty, Smithsonian Institution, 1976.

Flandrau, Grace. *The Story of Marias Pass.* Great Northern Railway, 1935.

Foley, Michael F. *An Historical Analysis of the Administration of the Blackfeet Indian Reservation by the United States, 1855–1950's.* Manuscript. Indian Claims Commission, Docket No. 279-d, n.d.

Frayley, John. "The Bootleg Lady of Glacier Park." (On Josephine and Dan Doody.) True West, Sept. 1990.

Fuller, R. Buckminster with Jerome Agel and Quentin Fiore. *I Seem to Be a Verb.* Bantam Books, 1970.

Garcia, Andrew. *Tough Trip Through Paradise, 1878-1879.* Edited by Bennet H. Stein. Boston: Houghton Mifflin, 1967.

Geographic Board of Canada, Department of the Interior. *Place-Names of Alberta.* Ottawa, 1928. *Great Falls* (Montana) *Tribune.* 14 June 1898; 5 August 1958.

Grinnell, George Bird. *Blackfoot Lodge Tales.* Scribners, 1892, 1920.

– – –. "Some Indian Stream Names."

– – –. "To the Walled-In Lakes."

– – –. "A White Blackfoot." *We Seized Our Rifles.* Edited by Eugene Lee Silliman. Missoula, Montana: Mountain Press, 1982.

– – –, and Theodore Roosevelt, eds. *Hunting in Many Lands.* Washington, D.C.: Boone and Crocket Club.

– – –, and Charles Sheldon, eds. *Hunting and Conservation.* Washington, D.C.: Boone and Crockett Club, 1925.

Guardipee, Eli. "Interview by Park Naturalist with Eli Guardipee." Glacier National Park Headquarters library.

Hafen, LeRoy R., ed. *The Mountain Men and the Fur trade of the Far West.* 10 volumes. Glendale, California: The Arthur H. Clark Co., 1965. *Helena* (Montana) *Weekly Independent.* 20 September 1988.

Hagedorn, Hermann. *Roosevelt in the Bad Lands.* Boston: Houghton Mifflin, 1921.

Hanna, Warren L. *James Willard Schultz.*

– – –. *Montana's Many-Splendored Glacierland.* Seattle: Superior Publishing Co., 1976.

– – –. "The Naming of St. Mary Lakes." *Montana Magazine of the Northern Rockies.* Summer 1976.

– – –. *Stars Over Montana: Men Who Made Glacier National Park History.* Glacier Natural History Association, 1988.

Harrington, Leona. *History of Apgar.* Manscript, c. 1950.

Harrod, Harold L. *Mission Among the Blackfeet.* Norman, Oklahoma: University of Oklahoma Press, 1971.

Haught, John F. *The Cosmic Adventure.* 1984.

Havard, V., M.D. "The French Half-breeds of the Northwest." *Smithsonian Annual Report,* 1890.

Hill, Alexander Staveley. *From Home to Home.* 1885 (reprint 1966).

Hodge, Frederick Webb, et al. *Handbook of the American Indians North of Mexico.* 2 volumes. Washington, D.C.: Bureau of American Ethnology, Bulletin No. 30. 2 volumes. Reprinted by Pageant, 1959.

Holterman, Jack. *Mountains All Aglow.* Glacier Natural History Association, 1991. (A series of monographs with lists of sources, some of which are related to details of this present work: "Andrew Garcia"; "Bad Guys in Glacier Park"; "Baring Brothers"; "Blakiston"; "Blue Blood," (royalty in Glacier Park); "Blue Lightning" (on the wives of Kootenay Brown); "Captain Fournier"; "Charlie's Friends" (on Charlie Russell); "Chippewa-Crees in Glacier Country"; "Hugh Monroe"; "Kuntza" (on "Coonsa"); "Lady MacBeth Was a Gentlewoman" (on Senator and Mrs. Wheeler); "Little Dog"; "Loreto"; "Mary, Mary, Quite Contrary" (on Mary Roberts Rinehart), "The Saga of McDonald"; "On to Akamina!"; "Pablo of the Buffalo" (on the acquisition of the buffalo herd at Moiese, Montana); "The Paper in the Bottle" (on the Cannons and the naming of Mount Cannon); "Rancher to Ranger" (on Horace Brewster), "Sally Carasco and the Launch for Saint Mary"; "Sandoval"; "The Smugglers"; "Thibodo" (an early explorer of Waterton/Glacier Country); "The Twenty-fifth Infantry in Glacier Park Country"; "Vision Quest"; "West Pointers Explore Glacier National Park" (included are John Mullan, Woodruff, Van Orsdale, Robertson, Beacom, and sometimes Ahern. The monograph on Ahern is printed separately as well). These monographs are all available in the local libraries. The latest monograph is "Charles Waterton," 2003.

– – –. *Place Names of Glacier/Waterton National Parks*. Glacier Natural History Association, 1985. (The first edition of this present book.)

– – –. *Who Was Who in Glacier Land*, Paper Chase, 2001

Holtz, M. E., and Katherine I. Bemis. *Glacier National Park: Its Trails and Treasures*. New York: George Doran Co., 1917.

Hungry Wolf, Adolf. *Good Medicine in Glacier National Park*. Healdsburg, California and Golden, British Columbia, 1971.

Hunter, Emily and Betty Karpinsky. *Plains Cree Glossary*. University of Alberta, Edmonton, 1994.

– – – & – – – with Jean Mulder. *Introductory Cree, Parts I and II*. University of Alberta, Edmonton, 1994.

Jessett, Thomas E. *Chief Spokan Garry, 1811–1872*. T. S. Denison & Co., 1960.

Johns, Sam, compiler. *The Pioneers*. Ten volumes plus index. Manuscript, 1943. (Available at the Kaispell branch of Flathead County Library, it contains many miscellaneous items of local historical interest.)

Johnson, Olga Weydemeyer. *Flathead and Kootenay*. Glendale, Calfornia: The Arthur H. Clark Co., 1969.

Johnston, Basil. *Ojibway Heritage*. New York: Columbia University Press, 1976.

Kidder, John. "Montana Miracle: It Saved the Buffalo." *Montana, the Magazine of Western History*. Spring 1965.

Larpenteur, Charles. *Forty Years a Fur Trader on the Upper Missouri*.

Laut, Agnes C. *Enchanted Trails of Glacier National Park*. New York: Robert M. McBride, 1926. *Lethbridge Herald*, 3 April 1931.

Linderman, Frank Bird. *Kootenai Why Stories*. New York: Scribners, 1926.

– – –. *Montana Adventure: The Recollections of Frank B. Linderman*. Edited by Harold G. Merriam. Lincoln, Nebraska: University of Nebraska Press, 1968.

Long Lance, Buffalo Child (real name Sylvester Long). *Long Lance*. New York: Cosmopolitan Book Corp., New York, 1929.

MacDonald, Graham A. *Where the Mountains Meet the Praries*. Parcs Canada, 1992. (A History of Waterton Lakes National Park.)

Malouf, Carling, and Paul C. Phillips. *Flathead, Kutenai, and Upper Pend d'Oreille* [sic] *Genealogies*. Missoula, Montana: 1952.

Maximilian, Prince of Wied-Neuwied. *Travels in the Interior of North America: 1832–1834*. 4 volumes. Thwaites Edition. Reprinted by AMS Press, New York, 1966.

McClintock, Walter. *Old Indian Trails*. Boston: Houghton Mifflin, 1923.

– – –. *The Old North Trail*. London: Macmillan, 1910.

McDonnell, Anne. Notes in *Contributions*. Vol. 10. Montana Historical Society, Helena.

Mengarini, Gregory, S.J. *Recollections of the Flathead Mission*. Edited by Gloria Ricci Lothrop. Glendale, California: The Arthur H. Clark Co., 1977.

Middleton, S. H. *Kootenai Brown: Adventurer, Pioneer, Plainsman, Park Warden and Waterton Lakes National Park*. Lethbridge, Alberta: 1954.

Miller, Wick R. *Newe Natekwinappeh: Shoshoni Stories and Dictionary*. University of Utah Anthropological Papers, No. 94. June 1972.

Montana Historical Society. *Contributions*. Volumes 1, 3, 10. Helena, Montana.

Morgan, Lewis Henry. *The Indian Journals, 1859-62*. Edited by Leslie A. White. Ann Arbor, Michigan: University of Michigan Press, 1959.

Nankivell, John H. *History of the Twenty-Fifty Regiment, United States Infantry, 1869–1926.* New York: Negro Universities Press, 1927.

National Archives, Washington, D.C. *Census Reports for the Blackfeet and Salish/Kootenai Reservations.* Records of the Adjutant General's Office, 1780–1917. Record Group 94. *National Geographic Magazine:* 2 & 3 1908; April 1995. *The Northwestern Montana Territorial Centennial Program Book.* Kalispell, Montana, 1964.

O'Neil, Carle. *Two Men of Demersville.* 1990.

O'Meara, Walter. *Daughters of the Country: The Women of the Fur Traders and Mountain Men.* New York: Harcourt Brace, 1968.

Palliser, John, Thomas W. Blakiston, et al. *Exploration – British North America: Papers, 1859.* 2 volumes. Reprint. New York: Greenwood Press, 1969.

Pinchot, Gifford. "George Patrick Ahern." Obituary. *Assembly,* January, 1943.

Pringle, Heather. *Waterton Lakes National Park.* Parcs Canada, 1986.

Pumpelly, Raphael. *My Reminiscences.* 2 volumes. Holt, 1918.

Rakestraw, Lawrence. "Forestry Missionary" (on Ahern). *Montana, the Magazine of Western History,* Autumn 1959.

Rinehart, Mary Roberts. *Tenting Tonight.* Boston: Houghton Mifflin, 1918.

– – –. *Through Glacier Park.* Boston: Houghton Mifflin, 1916.

The (Fort Benton, Montana) *River Press.* 19 February 1890.

Robinson, Donald H. *Through the Years in Glacier National Park.* Edited by Maynard C. Bowers. Glacier National History Association, 1960.

Rodney, William. *Kootenai Brown.* Sidney, British Columbia: Gray's Publications, 1969.

Ronan, Mary Margaret. *Frontier Woman: The Story of Mary Ronan.* University of Montana, 1973.

Roosevelt, Theodore: See Grinnell, George Bird.

Ross, Clyde P. *Geology of Glacier National Park and the Flathead Region, Northwestern Montana.* Geological Survey Professional Papers, No. 296. Washington, D.C.: 1959.

Ruhle George C. *Roads and Trails of the Waterton-Glacier National Parks.* Glacier National History Association, 1972.

– – –. Comments in *Glacier Nature Notes* 3:5 (May 1930).

– – –. *Place Names.* Manuscript printed in the Columbia Falls, Montana *Hungry Horse News,* 1975.

Russell, Andy. "The Quality of Endurance." Lethbridge, Alberta *Herald,* 24 March 1972.

Sabo, Louis L. "When Wagon Trails Were Dim: George Bird Grinnell, 'Father of Glacier Park.'" Manuscript.

Sanders, Helen Fitzgerald. *The White Quiver.* New York: Duffield, 1913.

Schaeffer, Claude E. Manuscript notes in the Glenbow Museum & Archives, Calgary.

– – –. *Montana, the Magazine of (Western) History,* April 1952.

Schemm, Mildred Walker. "The Major's Lady: Natawista." *Montana, the Magazine of Western History,* January 1952.

Schultz, Hart Merriam. See Dyke.

Schultz, James Wilard. *My Life As An Indian.* Boston: Houghton Mifflin, 1906.

– – –. *Blackfeet Tales of Glacier National Park.* Boston: Houghton Mifflin, 1916.

– – –. *Friends of My Life As An Indian.* Boston: Houghton Mifflin. 1923.

– – –. *Signposts of Adventure.* Boston: Houghton Mifflin, 1926.

– – –. *Blackfeet and Buffalo*. Edited by Keith C. Steele. Norman, Oklahoma: University of Oklahoma Press, 1962.

Shaw, Charlie S. *The Flathead Story*. USDA Forest Service, 1967.

Shea, Marie Coffe. *Early Flathead and Tobacco Plains*. 1977.

Slickpoo, Allan P. Sr. and Deward E. Walker Jr. *Noon Neemepoo*. Nez Perce Tribe of Idaho, 1973.

Smith, Donald B. *Long Lance: The True Story of an Imposter*. Nebraska, 1983.

Sunder, John E. *The Fur Trade on the Upper Missouri, 1840–1865*. Norman, Oklahoma: University of Oklahoma Press, 1965.

Thrapp, Dan L. *Encyclopedia of Frontier Biography*. Three volumes with a supplement. University of Nebraska Press with the Arthur H. Clark Company, Spokane, Washington, 1988.

Tims, J. W. (Rev.) *Grammar and Dictionary of the Blackfoot Language in the Dominion of Canada*. London: n.d. (c. 1889).

Turney-High, Harry Holbert. *The Flathead Indians of Montana*. Menasha, Wisconsin: American Anthropological Association, 1937.

– – –. *Ethnography of the Kutenai*. American Anthropological Association, 1941. Reprinted by Kraus Reprint Co., New York, 1969.

Uhlenbeck, C. C. *A Concise Blackfoot Grammar*. Amsterdam, Netherlands: 1938.

– – –, and R. H. Van Gulik. *An English-Blackfoot Vocabulary Based On Material From the Southern Piegans*. Amsterdam, Netherlands: 1930. AMS reprint 1979.

Vaught, L. O. *History of Glacier National Park*. An incomplete manuscript in the Glacier Park Library with other documents in the park Archives. *Washington* (D.C.) *Star*. 14 May 1942.

Waterton, Charles. *Wanderings in South America*. Oxford University Press, London, 1973

Watkins, E. A., et al.: *Dictionary of the Cree Language*. Toronto: 1938. *Weekly Missoulian*. Missoula, Montana 19 September 1888.

Weide, Bruce. *Trail of the Great Bear*. Falcon Press, Missoula, Montana, 1992.

Whetstone, Daniel W. *Frontier Editor*. New York: Hastings House, 1956.

White, Thain. *Kootenai Place Names of the Flathead Lake Region in Northwest Montana*.

Willard, John. *Adventure Trails in Montana*. Helena, Montana: 1964.

Williams, M. B. *Waterton Lakes National Park*. Ottawa: Department of the Interior, n.d.

Wilson, Charles William. *Mapping the Frontier: Charles Wilson's Diary of the Survey of the 49th Parallel, 1858–1862, while Secretary of the British Boundary Commission*. Edited by George F. G. Stanley. Seattle: Washington University Press, 1970.

Wissler, Clark. "The Social Life of the Blackfoot Indians." Vol. 7, Part 1 (pp. 44–5), Anthropological Papers. American Museum of Natural History, 1911.

Work Projects Administration. *Montana: A State Guide Book*. Hastings, New York. 1939–49.

World Heritage Committee, United Nations Educational, Scientific, and Cultural Organization (UNESCO). *The World Heritage List 2002*. <http://whc.unesco.org/nwhc/pages/doc/mainf3.htm>. Last checked 2 July 2003. Also see <http://whc.unesco.org/>.

Yenne, Bill (William J.). *Switchback*. WY Books, Kaispell and San Francisco, 1983.